:dition

aw

Turner

HODDER
EDUCATION
PART OF HACHETTE LIVRE UK

Orders: please contact Bookpoint Ltd, 130 Milton Park, Abingdon, Oxon OX14 4SB. Telephone: (44) 01235 827720. Fax: (4) 01235 400454. Lines are open from 9.00-5.00, Monday to Saturday, with a 24 hour message answering service. You can also order through our website www.hoddereducation.co.uk

If you have any comments to make about this, or any of our other titles, please send them to educationenquiries@hodder.co.uk

British Library Cataloguing in Publication Data
A catalogue record for this title is available from the British Library

ISBN: 978 0 340 94160 7

First Edition Published   2003
This Edition Published   2007
Impression number   10 9 8 7 6 5 4 3 2
Year   2011 2010 2009 2008

Cover photo from © James W. Porter/Corbis
Typeset by Phoenix Photosetting, Chatham, Kent.
Printed in India for Hodder Education, part of Hachette Livre UK,
338 Euston Road, London NW1 3BH by Replika Press

Contents

Preface

This book is primarily aimed at students on A Level Law courses, but there is no reason why it should not be used by any first-time student of tort.

It is a companion to the very successful textbooks *The English Legal System* by Jacqueline Martin and *Criminal Law* by Diana Roe and also to my own book, *Contract Law*.

Since tort is essentially a common law area, much of the book is devoted to cases and case notes, and these are separated out in the text for easy reference.

Since the book is also intended to be a practical learning resource, rather than a prose-heavy text, each section of the book contains activities of different types. These include self-assessment questions, some of which are mere comprehension, while others are designed to be more thought provoking. A variety of other activities such as quick quizzes, multiple choice tests, case tests, etc. are also included to encourage maximum interaction.

From September 2006 OCR A Level Law has moved to a four-module specification, with first teaching of the new A2 from September 2007. The new option papers at A2 include a new model of assessment: the 'dilemma board', with objective questioning. In the exam this will take the form of a factual scenario followed by four propositions, with candidates having to use pure legal reasoning to support or reject these propositions. I have often used dilemma boards with students in a more diagrammatic form. Examples of dilemma boards for practice are produced here for most chapters of the book and the appropriate answers are given in an appendix at the back of the book.

Each section of the book also contains a Key Fact chart, summarising the most important points contained in the section, which can also act as a revision aid. Wherever they would meaningfully add to the text and aid learning I have also included diagrams or flow charts.

Many chapters also contain sections entitled 'Points for Discussion' or 'Comment'. These occur where there are controversial points that are often the subject of essay titles in examinations.

Finally, a number of chapters also contain a brief explanation of how to attempt either an essay or a problem question on the area.

The final chapter provides insight into how to deal with the synoptic element of both OCR and AQA specifications.

I hope that you will gain as much enjoyment in reading about the law of torts, and answering the various questions in the book, as I have had in writing it, and that you gain much enjoyment and interest from your study of the law.

The law is stated as I believe it to be on 31st March 2007.

Acknowledgements

Example questions have been reproduced with the kind permission of AQA (p. 241).

Material has been quoted from the following titles:

Baker, D. (1996) *Baker: Tort*. London: Sweet & Maxwell (6th edn) on pp. 176, 178; Jones, M. (2002) *Textbook on Torts*. Oxford: Oxford University Press on p. 2; Rogers, W. V. H. (1994) *The Law of Tort*. London: Sweet & Maxwell (2nd edn) on p. 126; Rogers, W. V. H. (ed.) (2002) *Winfield & Jolowicz on Tort*. London: Sweet & Maxwell (16th edn) on pp. 2, 125, 178.

List of Figures

Table of Cases

Table of Statutes and Other Instruments

EU Legislation

Directives

Treaties and Conventions

Chapter 1

The Origin and Character of Tortious Liability

1.1 The origins, functions and purposes of the law of torts

1.1.1 The origins of tort

The law of torts, like the law of contract, has its origins in the early common law of the Middle Ages. It is similarly based on obligations. In the case of contract law, these obligations are set by the parties in advance of the contract. In the case of tort, the obligations are set by law.

The word 'tort' comes from the French word meaning 'wrong'. So, a tort is a wrong, and since we are concerned in tort with remedying wrongs rather than punishing them, it is a civil wrong. In the modern law the emphasis in tort has developed very much towards a law of interrelated duties. As a result, the law of negligence has achieved increasing importance, and has developed numerous individual aspects.

However, the historical background was very different. The law of torts developed initially, through the early writ system, as a response to specific circumstances, and to provide remedies for the damage done in commonly recurring situations. Where a person had suffered loss or damage of a particular kind, the early courts would design a new writ, an original writ, to suit the circumstances. This helps explain the very disparate range of interests to which the law of torts applies. It also helps to explain why it is correct, really, to refer to the 'law of torts' rather than 'tort law', and why there is no single, coherent pattern of liability for all interests covered by the law of torts.

The early law, then, developed remedies of two main types:

- An action for trespass – this was a means of providing a remedy for interference that was both direct and intentional, the common examples being interference with land, with property, and with the person himself.
- An action on the case – this was originally a means of remedying indirect interference or damage caused carelessly. (But, in effect, it contains the origins of the law of negligence.)

As a result, individual torts gradually developed with different ingredients required to prove liability. Sometimes these overlapped, but more often, together with the shortcomings of the writ system itself, they could mean that a potential claimant was left without a remedy because his factual circumstances did not fit the specific requirements of a tort.

1.1.2 The functions and purpose of the law of torts

Winfield has said that:

'Tortious liability arises from the breach of a duty primarily fixed by law: such duty is towards persons generally and its breach is redressed by an action for unliquidated damages.'

Michael Jones puts it more simply:

'The law of torts is primarily concerned with providing a remedy to persons who have been harmed by the conduct of others.'

The standard model for liability in tort in the modern day would be that the defendant's act (or omission) has, through the defendant's fault, caused damage to the claimant of a type which is recognised as attracting liability.

There are two precise aims of the law of torts that also, to a degree, point towards the main two remedies available, damages and injunctions.

- Compensation – the main outcome of a successful tort action is to compensate the victim of the wrong to the extent of the damage suffered.
- Deterrence – the most satisfactory way of dealing with any wrong is to ensure that it does not happen again or, even better, to prevent it occurring at all.

A third possibility that exists in other jurisdictions, but not to any great extent here, is to punish. The most usual way of doing this is through the awarding of exemplary or punitive damages. In America, for instance, a jury in a personal injury action can award punitive damages reflecting their dissatisfaction with the wrong.

Compensation

As will be seen in the final section of the book, the purpose of tort damages is, as far as is possible for money to do so, to put the injured party in the position he or she would have been in had the tort not happened.

The simple question here is whether the system does, in fact, adequately compensate the victims of the wrongs. A number of points must be considered in this respect:

- For a start, only those who can show fault are able to bring a successful action.
- The tort system is incredibly expensive to run. The Pearson Committee, in 1978, identified that the cost of operating the system amounted to 85% of the money paid out to successful claimants. This is why, right up to the present Woolf reforms, there have been moves to try and reduce the costs of civil justice.
- Claiming through the tort system is also subject to delays. Again, the Pearson Committee found that an average time for resolution of personal injury claims was three-and-a-half years. This was one of the reasons for originally changing the jurisdiction of the High Court and County Court in the Courts and Legal Services Act 1990.
- Very often a claimant will be forced to settle for less than he or she actually claimed for and therefore is not fully compensated for the wrong suffered.
- Worst of all is the maxim, 'never sue a man of straw'. In other words, a claimant can go without compensation at all where the tortfeasor is of insufficient means to justify suing in the first place.

Deterrence

Within the tort system most deterrent effects will operate, generally, on a market level rather than specifically against individuals. In many instances it is corporations or other large bodies that are responsible for committing torts, but even where torts are committed by private individuals damages awarded will usually be paid from a claim for insurance.

The obvious example of this is where a person's negligence causes a car crash. The third party element of their motor insurance will be claimed against to pay for the damage to the other car and to compensate any injuries caused to other parties to the accident.

The driver at fault will lose his/her no claims bonus and their insurance premiums will increase in amount, so this is the deterrent effect: in order to avoid high insurance premiums the driver must drive safely and carefully and avoid causing accidents. The same principle operates at a higher level, with a company's public liability or employers' liability insurance.

Of course, deterrence can operate on other levels. Where professionals are sued successfully,

not only are their insurance premiums at risk of increasing, but their reputations can be damaged, sometimes irreparably. High awards of damages in defamation actions may not harm the publishers as much as the reputation it can give them for inaccuracy and falsehood.

Overall, then, the principle of deterrence in tort is based on the aims of reducing both the frequency and costs of wrongdoing.

Comparisons with other methods of compensation

Many of the problems associated with seeking compensation through the tort system, identified above, were considered in detail by the Pearson Commission in 1978, which was set up following the 'thalidomide scandal'. Children were born with severe deformity to limbs after their mothers were prescribed a drug during pregnancy. The children had no proper action available to them since, at the time the drug had its disastrous effect on them, they were not yet born.

The Commission was required to assess the appropriate means of compensating death and personal injury:

- in the course of employment
- in road traffic accidents
- through the manufacture, supply or use of goods or services
- on premises belonging to or occupied by another
- otherwise caused by the act or omission of another, where compensation is recoverable only on proof of fault or under the rules of strict liability.

The Commission did not recommend the abolition of the tort system in the case of personal injury and fatal accident. It did, nevertheless, accept all of the criticisms referred to above. To counter these it recommended the introduction of a partial system of 'no-fault' liability through a strengthening of the social security system in the case of road traffic accidents and industrial injuries, as well as some extension of strict liability in the case of product liability.

There is a precedent for a no-fault scheme of compensating personal injuries. Such a scheme was set up in New Zealand in 1972. Under this comprehensive scheme, claimants suffering a personal injury would make their claim through a state body, the Accident Compensation Commission. Benefits are payable on a weekly basis, with up to 80% of earnings and lump sum payments in the case of some permanent disabilities. However, these are inevitably lower than could be gained through the tort system. The principal opposition to introducing this type of compensation in the UK seems to be the cost to public funds, and it is unlikely that the UK would introduce such a scheme in the future.

There are, of course, some alternatives to the tort system already in place:

1. Social welfare and social security
Public responsibility for the victims of personal injury is demonstrated in a number of ways through contributory and non-contributory benefits, and through health and welfare support. Medical treatment is available through the National Health Service without having to make immediate payment. A wide range of benefits is available for those suffering personal injury and permanent disability, although in all cases benefit rates are set only at subsistence levels. The victim of a tort still has the option to use the tort system to gain higher levels of compensation.

2. Private insurance
Many victims of torts have private insurance that they are able to claim on. This may be standard life insurance in the case of fatal accidents. There are also accident insurance policies now available, as well as insurance for permanent disabilities

making it impossible for the person affected to continue employment.

3. Criminal Injuries Compensation Authority
Where the act causing the injury has also been prosecuted as a crime, then it is also possible to make a claim from this publicly funded scheme. Awards under the scheme are generally set at very low levels, however.

4. Occupational schemes
Many people enjoy extended wages during sickness and absence through injury in their contracts of employment. In the case of injuries sustained at work, there are often compensatory payments available from employers. Occupational pension schemes often allow for early retirement on health grounds. Finally, many workers who are members of trade unions receive payments from benevolent funds during periods of absence from work through illness and injury.

1.2 The character of the law of torts

1.2.1 The interests protected by the law of torts

These are of four main types (the first two here being closely linked):

- Personal security – this concerns the safety of the individual and may include:
  - trespass to the person
  - possibly defamation
  - negligence (particularly medical negligence)
  - possibly trespass to land or trespass to goods
  - other interesting developments in personal injury, such as claims for psychiatric damage
  - possibly concepts such as privacy, although this is a fairly ill-defined right and not well developed.

- Reputation – this is clearly a specialist extension of personal security. It is interesting because it can conflict with the right to freedom of expression. Obvious examples are defamation, malicious falsehood and, to an extent, deceit.
- Property – this is obviously concerned with the property rights of the individual, whether real (land) or personal (all other). It can include all torts involving land, e.g. nuisance, trespass to land, *Rylands v Fletcher*, trespass to goods, and it may also include negligence.
- Economic interests – tort is much more concerned with remedying physical damage and personal injury than economic loss, so this type of action is much more controversial and problematic. However, there are significant elements of recoverable economic loss, such as the tort of negligent misstatement, and special damages, but the law of torts is less willing to allow recovery for a pure economic loss, e.g. loss of profits, which is much more readily associated with contract law.

1.2.2 The types of harm

Some torts are actionable *per se,* that is without needing proof of any damage. The torts based on trespass are good examples of this, as is libel.

However, tort is usually about compensating the victims of wrongs.

Sometimes, however, even though damage has been caused, it is of a type that does not give rise to liability. Here the expression *damnum sine injuria* would apply. A good example of such a situation would be legitimate business competition, while actions to procure a breach of contract would be tortious.

Another significant expression is *injuria sine damno*. This involves a legal wrong without any harm necessarily being done. An example is again trespass to land.

It is also common to talk of strict liability in

tort, as well as in crime. In crime it indicates that there is no requirement for criminal intent, *mens rea*. In tort it refers to there being no requirement to prove fault. Liability under both the Animals Act 1971 and the Consumer Protection Act 1987 is strict. It was traditionally said that *Rylands v Fletcher* is a tort of strict liability. However, the requirement in *Cambridge Water Co v Eastern Counties Leather plc* (1994) that damage should be foreseeable seems to make this less than true.

1.2.3 The parties to an action in tort

Straightforwardly, as elsewhere in civil law, in the law of torts a claimant will sue a defendant.

The picture can become more complex where there is more than one defendant. If the loss or damage is the responsibility of more than one defendant and they are both at fault, then their liability may be:

- independent
- joint
- several.

Independent liability is when two or more defendants are liable for different torts. Each individual tortfeasor is then independently liable for the damage (s)he has caused.

An example of independent liability would be as follows: Chris is walking away from a football match and is punched by Lee, a fan of the away team (assault). When he is driving home from the ground another motorist, Jason, pulls out of a side road without looking and collides with Chris's car (negligence).

Joint liability is when two or more tortfeasors engage in the same tortious act, often, but not always, with a common purpose. Even though both are liable, often only one is sued, e.g. where vicarious liability applies; though sometimes, for example in medical negligence, both parties are joined.

An example of joint liability would be as

follows: Chris injures his spine when a fellow employee and known practical joker, Gordon, pulls his chair from under him (battery). Chris's employers, Dodgy College, are well aware of Gordon's practical jokes and have failed to discipline him in the past (vicarious liability).

Several liability is when two or more defendants act independently but cause the same damage. The claimant has the choice of which tortfeaser to sue, but will usually choose the one that is better placed to pay damages.

An example of several liability would be as follows: Chris is driving home from hospital when two motorists, Hayley and Tracy, both pull out of side roads without looking, damaging his car and causing him severe whiplash injuries.

1.3 Fault liability and its alternatives

1.3.1 The mental element in tort

Generally, the law of torts has developed as a system based on fault liability. This obviously refers to the culpability of the defendant in a comparable way to the mental element in crime.

In tort, any mental element to be found is one of three types:

- malice
- intention
- negligence.

Malice

Generally, the motive of the wrongdoer is irrelevant in determining liability.

Bradford Corporation v Pickles (1895)

In order to force the claimant council into buying his land, the defendant extracted water from his land which had the effect of draining the claimant's reservoir. Even though the defendant acted with clear malice, the claimant's action failed. He was acting legitimately according to his own property rights.

There are, however, exceptions to the general rule when malice is significant to proving the tort:

- In certain torts it is an essential ingredient of the tort, e.g. malicious falsehood.
- In certain torts it can affect liability, e.g. in nuisance, where malice by the defendant could be an indication of an unreasonable use of land, or where malice on the part of the claimant could defeat his claim.

Similarly, a good motive can have an impact on the tort, as in the defence of necessity.

Intention

Here, three loose groupings are possible:

- Torts deriving from writs of trespass – the common feature in all is the requirement of direct intentional harm, so it is the intention to cause harm that is critical, not the degree of harm caused, e.g. trespass to the person, to land and to goods.
- Torts where fraudulent behaviour is an essential element – the defendant is liable because he knows his statement to be untrue or he acted recklessly, not caring whether it was true or not, e.g. malicious falsehood, deceit.
- Torts based on conspiracy – here the claimant can always show that the prime purpose of the agreement was to harm him, e.g. any of the so-called economic torts, such as conspiracy to procure a breach of contract, which was common at one time in actions against trade unions.

Negligence

Negligence is obviously a major tort in its own right, but it is also indicative of an objective standard of behaviour that is set by law.

It is falling below an appropriate standard that is measured objectively, resulting in liability for the failure to take care. So, in this sense it can also be seen as a state of mind.

The consequence of applying negligence as a test of liability is that victims who are unable to show fault on the part of the defendant (his failing to take appropriate care) go uncompensated. The point being that the process of investigating the facts necessary to prove fault may be costly and ultimately prohibitive.

1.3.2 Fault liability

Proving fault is a major requirement in most torts, particularly those based on principles of negligence. In fact, fault is only not an issue in those torts that are actionable *per se*, i.e. without having to prove damage.

There is perfect logic in having to prove that someone was 'at fault' for the damage caused. It is no more than to say that they are responsible because they failed to match up to the standard that was required of them, or failed to do something that they were duty bound to do.

However, fault also has many unfair aspects. Proving fault can often be very difficult for the claimant, and this is the reasoning behind the development of the doctrine *res ipsa loquitur,* where the burden of proof is effectively reversed.

Fault liability is unfair to claimants because of the difficulty of finding proof and evidence. One consequence is that victims of events that have happened in the public eye may be unfairly advantaged over an ordinary claimant.

The requirement of fault can also be unfair on defendants because liability is not based on their degree of culpability, but on the effect of their acts or omissions on the claimant.

It is also unfair on society generally because it creates classes of victims who can be compensated and classes that cannot. In the case of the former, the defendant will be made financially responsible for the claimant's injuries/damage/loss, whereas in all other cases a potential claimant may have to be supported by public means. Unsuccessful medical negligence claims would be an obvious example of this.

The fault principle is often justified on the basis that it punishes wrongdoers and also has deterrent value. It is hard to see how either is really accurate. Most damages these days are paid out of insurance. A tortfeaser's prime concern will often only be the effect on his no claims bonus. Where defendants are corporations or public bodies it is hard to see where there is either punishment or deterrent. The rail disasters of recent times are an example of that, and have been the reason why there have been calls for a more effective criminal offence of 'corporate killing'.

In any case, the administration of the tort system by the judges is heavily influenced by policy considerations, the Hillsborough disaster litigation being a classic example. So, often application of the fault principle is only arbitrary.

The Pearson Report in 1978 advocated a no-fault scheme on the lines of the New Zealand model. This was never acted upon, and although there have been two no-fault medical negligence Private Members' Bills since, neither was accepted.

1.4 Tort compared with other areas of law

1.4.1 Tort and contract law

Sometimes both the law of contract and the law of torts are seen as a general law of 'obligations'. Certainly both branches of the law compensate victims for the harm done to them. Both branches of the law are also ultimately based on duties owed by one party to another.

The traditional distinction between the two is the character of the duty owed. In the case of torts, specific duties are imposed by law and apply to everyone. In contract law, the duties are imposed by the parties themselves and only operate to the extent agreed upon before the contract was formed. Similarly, in the case of tort the duty is usually owed generally to all persons likely to be affected by the tort. In contract law, on the other hand, the duty is only to the other party to the contract.

Nevertheless, the distinction is not always so clear, and there are many complications and overlaps. In the law of contract many duties are now imposed on parties by statute and, as a result of European law, irrespective of the actual wishes of the parties to the contract. This has been particularly the case in the area of consumer contracts. In the law of torts, in those situations where the law does allow recovery for a pure economic loss, the distinction between the two again is blurred somewhat.

There can be overlap, too, in areas such as product liability, where there can be a claim for negligence and also for breach of implied statutory conditions under the contract. In such circumstances a choice is sometimes made whether to sue a manufacturer in tort or a supplier under contract law.

Similar complications have arisen in the field of medicine. Normally we would expect legal actions to be brought in medical negligence in tort. However, where a patient has taken advantage of private medicine the rules of contract law can be invoked. If they are, they may have a more satisfactory answer, if for instance the contractual duty is higher than the duty in tort.

Difficulties can also arise because of the doctrine of privity in contract law and the exceptions to it, although legislation has removed some of the hardships here. However, the absence of a contractual relationship again may not prevent an action being brought for a breach of a duty in tort, if such a duty exists.

1.4.2 Tort and criminal law

Many torts and crimes have their origins in the same basic principles of law. Actions for assault and battery are obvious examples.

On this basis there are many overlaps, and dual liability is often possible, e.g. a motorist could be charged for a Road Traffic Act offence but also successfully sued by the other road user to whom he caused damage.

There are, however, also clear distinctions between tort and crime. The most immediately obvious is the involvement of the state in the prosecution of crime.

Another clear difference is the outcome. In crimes, if the state is successful in prosecuting its case the result will be punishment of some form. In a civil action, in tort the successful claimant is, of course, seeking a remedy.

Besides this, the standard of proof, the terminology and the procedures involved all differ considerably.

1.5 The effect of human rights legislation on the law of torts

The Human Rights Act 1998 (which came into force in 2000) has incorporated into English law the European Convention on Human Rights. The Act is limited in its scope. It incorporates Articles 2 to 12 into English law, as well as Articles 14 and 16, but there are other significant Articles, as well as the protocols, that are omitted. The Act allows courts the means to make declarations of incompatibility on new legislation and also, to a degree, to control the activities of public bodies. The Act also requires that all primary and secondary legislation should be interpreted so as to be compatible with provisions of the Convention. In certain areas of tort law judges were aiming at compatibility with Convention Articles even before the passing of the Act. Defamation is an obvious example.

Despite its limitations, it is possible for the Act to have some impact on many aspects of the law of torts. This is because so many Convention Articles are appropriate to the law of torts:

- **Article 2 – the right to life.** This is obviously of relevance to trespass to the person, but is particularly appropriate to medical torts, as recent cases such as *Pretty v UK* show. In the case, Diane Pretty's argument that the right to life had a corresponding right to end life and therefore to assisted suicide was rejected, as was her claim that the same decision of the English courts was a breach of Article 3.
- **Article 3 – freedom from torture, inhuman or degrading treatment.** Again, this has relevance to trespass to the person, and defences like lawful chastisement of a child have had to be rethought.
- **Article 4 – freedom from slavery.** Again, trespass to the person is appropriate here, and there are also consequences for the employment relationship.
- **Article 5 – the right to liberty apart from lawful arrest.** Again, this is particularly appropriate to trespass to the person. It has implications for the interpretation of mental health legislation, and also for the exercise of police powers under legislation such as the Police and Criminal Evidence Act 1984. It has been the subject of action with cases such as *Osman v UK* (1999), and is also controversial in that the Government, in passing the Human

Rights Act, chose to derogate from Article 5(3) the right of a person detained to be brought promptly before the court in order to maintain the effectiveness of the Prevention of Terrorism Act 1989.
- **Article 6 – the right to a fair trial and proper procedural safeguards.** This is one area that already causes controversy. It is significant that the Government, in passing the Act, chose not to incorporate Article 13, the right to an effective remedy. The right under Article 6 has already proved significant in negligence actions in cases such as *Barrett v London Borough of Enfield* (1999) where the possible immunity from legal action enjoyed by certain public bodies) was at issue.
- **Article 8 – the right to respect for private and family life, home and correspondence.** This Article can have an impact on the law of defamation and, indeed, trespass and nuisance. There have never been specific privacy laws in English law, to the annoyance of many public figures, although it is questionable how much impact it could have on, for example, the use of telephoto lens cameras by the paparazzi. The implementation of rights of privacy would, in any case, have to be balanced against the right to freedom of expression given in Article 10.
- **Article 9 – freedom of thought, conscience and religion.** Again, this has clear implications for the law of defamation and impacts also on unlawful arrest.
- **Article 10 – freedom of expression.** This is of obvious relevance to defamation. One of the major controversies in modern society is the activities of the media and the extent to which they are free to expose public figures. There is also a clear problem in balancing the freedom of speech under Article 10 with the potential right to privacy in Article 8.

Activity

Self-assessment questions

1. In what ways is it more accurate to refer to 'a law of torts' than to tort law?

2. What are the two main remedies used in the law of torts?

3. What are the two major purposes of the law of torts, and which is the easier to achieve?

4. In what ways can the tort system act as a deterrent?

5. How effective is the tort system of compensation by comparison with the other methods available?

6. What are the main interests protected by the law of torts?

7. What is the difference between *damnum sine injuria* and *injuria sine damno?*

8. In what ways are joint liability and several liability distinguished?

9. In what ways would 'intention' be essential as an element of a tort?

10. What is the effect of a bad motive in tort?

11. What part can 'malice' play in tort?

12. Why was Pearson critical of fault liability?

13. What possible alternatives are there to fault liability?

14. In what ways is tort closer to contract law than to crime?

15. What is the major difference between contract and tort?

16. What similarities exist between tort and crime?

17. Why is damages a very artificial remedy in the case of tort law?

18. What are the possible effects of human rights legislation on the administration of the law of torts?

Chapter 2

Negligence: Duty of Care

2.1 The origins of negligence and the neighbour principle

The origins of negligence lie in other torts in a process known as an action on the case, a method of proving tort through showing negligence or carelessness. The modern tort of negligence begins with Lord Atkin's groundbreaking judgment in *Donoghue v Stevenson*. A new approach was necessary in the case because no other action was available.

The judgment is important not just for the decision itself, or for identifying negligence as a separate tort in its own right, but also for devising the appropriate tests for determining whether negligence has actually occurred.

Donoghue v Stevenson (1932)

The claimant claimed to suffer shock and gastroenteritis after drinking ginger beer from an opaque bottle out of which a decomposing snail had fallen when the dregs were poured. A friend had bought her the drink, so she could not sue in contract. She claimed £500 from the manufacturer for his negligence and was successful. Lord Atkin's judgment contained five critical elements:

- Lack of privity of contract did not prevent the claimant from claiming.
- Negligence was accepted as a separate tort in its own right.

- Negligence would be proved by satisfying a three-part test:
  - the existence of a duty of care owed to the claimant by the defendant
  - a breach of that duty by falling below the appropriate standard of care
  - damage caused by the defendant's breach of duty that was not too remote a consequence of the breach.
- The method of determining the existence of a duty of care – the so-called 'neighbour principle'. As Lord Atkin put it:

  'You must take reasonable care to avoid acts or omissions which you can reasonably foresee would be likely to injure your neighbour. Who, then, in law, is my neighbour? … persons who are so closely and directly affected by my act that I ought reasonably to have them in my contemplation as being affected so when I am directing my mind to the acts or omissions in question'.

- A manufacturer would owe a duty of care towards consumers or users of his/her products not to cause them harm.

So, from the 'neighbour principle' of Lord Atkin the tort of negligence is identified as being based on foreseeability of harm. The case gives us one clear example of a relationship where possible harm is foreseeable and a duty of care then exists – the duty of a manufacturer to the consumers or users of his or her products.

2.2 Proximity and policy – the test in *Anns*

Over many years the tort of negligence developed incrementally, case by case, with a duty of care being established in numerous relationships. Lawyers were able to use the neighbour principle to argue for the extension of negligence into areas previously not covered by the tort, where damage was a foreseeable consequence of the defendant's acts or omissions.

At a much later stage, the test was simplified. The new test did not depend on a duty of care being determined in a given case according to how the case fitted in with past law. Under the new test, a duty would be imposed because of the proximity of the relationship between the two parties unless there were policy reasons for not doing so. This, of course, means legal proximity (the extent to which the deeds of one can affect the other), not proximity based on physical closeness.

Anns v Merton London Borough Council (1978)

The local authority had failed to ensure that building work complied with the plans, and as a result the building had inadequate foundations. The claimant, a tenant who had leased the property after it had changed hands many times, claimed that the damage to the property threatened health and safety and sued successfully. The decision was clearly arrived at on policy grounds. Lord Wilberforce, in framing the two-part test, suggested the appropriate method of determining whether or not the defendant owed a duty of care in a given case. First, it should be established that there is sufficient proximity between defendant and claimant for damage to be a foreseeable possibility of any careless act or omission. If this was established then it was only for the court to decide whether or not there were any policy considerations that might either limit the scope of the duty or remove it altogether.

Lord Wilberforce's two-part test led to some significant developments in the law of negligence in the 1980s, particularly in relation to economic loss and nervous shock (see later, for instance *Junior Books v Veitchi* (1983) in section 6.3.2). However, these developments were not always considered appropriate and the two-part test caused distress among many judges.

In a series of cases in the 1990s criticism of the two-part test was expressed.

Lord Keith, in *Governors of the Peabody Donation Fund v Sir Lindsay Parkinson & Co. Ltd* (1985), suggested that whether or not it was just and fair to impose a duty was a more appropriate test than mere policy considerations.

Lord Oliver, in *Leigh and Sillivan Ltd v Aliakmon Shipping Co. Ltd* (The Aliakmon) (1985) considered that the test should not be considered as giving the court a free hand to determine what limits to set in each case.

In *Yuen Kun-yeu v Attorney General of Hong Kong* (1988) Lord Keith also argued that the test had been '*. . . elevated to a degree of importance greater than its merits . . .*', which he also felt was probably not Lord Wilberforce's intention.

These judgments all show a more cautious approach in determining the existence of a duty of care. As a result of this, the two-part test was later discarded and the case of *Anns* also overruled.

Murphy v Brentwood District Council (1991)

A house had been built on a concrete raft laid on a landfill site. The council had been asked to inspect and had approved the design of the raft. The raft was actually inadequate and cracks later appeared when the house subsided. The claimant sold the house for £35,000 less than its value in good condition would have been, and sued the council for negligence in approving the raft. The House of Lords held that the council was not liable on the basis that the council could not owe a greater duty of care to the claimant than the builder. In doing so, the court also overruled *Anns* and the two-part test, preferring instead a new three-part test suggested by Lords Keith, Oliver and Bridge in *Caparo v Dickman* (1990).

2.3 The modern three-part test from *Caparo*

In *Caparo v Dickman* the House of Lords had in fact shown some dissatisfaction with the two-part test and preferred a return to the more traditional incremental approach by reference to past cases. The test was able to change in *Murphy* because they had identified an incremental approach with three stages.

Caparo v Dickman (1990)

Shareholders in a company bought more shares and then made a successful take-over bid for the company after studying the audited accounts prepared by the defendants. They later regretted the move and sued the auditors, claiming that they had relied on accounts which had shown a sizeable surplus rather than the deficit that was in fact the case. The House of Lords decided that the auditors owed no duty of care since company accounts are not prepared for the purposes of people taking over a company and cannot then be relied on by them for such purposes. The court also considered a three-stage test in imposing liability appropriate:

- first, it should be considered whether the consequences of the defendant's behaviour were reasonably foreseeable
- secondly, the court should consider whether there is a sufficient relationship of proximity between the parties for a duty to be imposed
- lastly, the court should ask the question whether or not it is fair, just and reasonable in all the circumstances to impose a duty of care.

Reasonable foresight

The basic requirement of foresight is simply that the defendant must have foreseen the risk of harm to the claimant at the time he or she is alleged to have been negligent.

This is slightly confusing given the fact that a claimant must then go on and satisfy the remoteness of damage test. It is also confusing because foreseeability of harm is also a necessary ingredient of proximity. However, although the two are quite closely linked they are still distinct concepts.

Foresight is always critical, of course, in determining whether or not there is a duty of care owed. It should also be remembered that there is no general, all-embracing duty of care. The existence of the duty depends on the individual circumstances.

Topp v London Country Bus (South West) Ltd (1993)

A bus company did not owe a duty of care when leaving a bus unattended which joy riders stole, injuring the claimant.

It is, of course, possible that attitudes to what is considered reasonably foreseeable can change, as can be seen from comparing the next two cases.

Gunn v Wallsend Slipway & Engineering Co. Ltd (1989)

There was held to be no duty of care to a woman who contracted mesothelioma from inhaling asbestos dust from her husband's overalls. At the time the risk was felt to be unforeseeable.

However, a contrary line has since been adopted. This will very often depend on the availability of technical information at a given point in time.

Margereson v J W Roberts Ltd (1996)

Here, the danger of children playing near an asbestos factory inhaling dust and contracting related illnesses was said to be foreseeable, even though the events in question were in 1933.

Proximity

Proximity was a major part of both the neighbour principle and Lord Wilberforce's two-part test, and is still a major factor in identifying the existence of a duty of care.

John Munroe (Acrylics) Ltd v London Fire and Civil Defence Authority (1997)

Here there was held to be insufficient proximity between a fire brigade and individual owners of property for a duty to respond to calls to be imposed.

Determining whether there is proximity also inevitably seems to be influenced by policy considerations.

Hill v Chief Constable of West Yorkshire [1988]

There was insufficient proximity between the police and the public for a duty to be imposed to protect individual members of the public from specific crimes. So, relatives of victims of the Yorkshire Ripper had no claim against the police for any careless or ineffective handling of the case. The argument that the Ripper's thirteenth victim would not have died but for the negligence of the police investigation was therefore rejected.

The distinction between foreseeability and proximity can be shown when examining the area of liability for nervous shock. Where physical damage is caused by the defendant's negligence it is not difficult to establish proximity. There is quite clearly physical as well as legal proximity. However, where the damage is nervous shock and the claimant is a secondary victim, physical proximity may be much more tenuous. The foreseeability of harm may not be problematic. Nevertheless, the claimant in this situation then needs to go on to establish the relationship with the primary victim, the closeness in time and space and the witnessing of the event or its immediate aftermath with his own unaided senses in order to establish liability.

Fairness and reasonableness

This requirement is, in reality, identifying that there must be a limit to liability and no duty will be imposed unless it is just in all the circumstances.

Hemmens v Wilson Browne (1994)

A man had instructed his solicitors to settle a sum of money on a third party. The deed was then negligently drafted so that the gift was unenforceable. There was no duty owed by the solicitors to the third party in question when it was in the power of the man to remedy the situation by instructing the drafting of another document but he had changed his mind and refused to do so.

However, it may be that the requirement that it is just and reasonable to impose a duty is little different in practice to the policy considerations of former times, particularly in respect of duties allegedly owed by public bodies.

Ephraim v Newham London Borough Council (1993)

Here, the court felt that it would not be fair to impose a duty of care on the defendant council to ensure the existence of a fire escape in landlord accommodation. They had advised the claimant on availability of flats and the claimant was then injured in a fire. The flat was without a fire escape.

There are clearly overlaps between all three parts of the new three-part test. The circumstances in which the courts will accept that it is just and reasonable to impose a duty are inevitably intertwined with the foreseeability of harm and the proximity of the parties. Besides this, there appears to be very little difference between the fair and reasonable requirement and pure policy considerations. It is questionable, therefore, whether the courts have merely replaced one uncertain test as to whether a duty exists with another equally uncertain test.

2.4 Points for discussion

Policy has always been a major consideration in determining liability in negligence.

As Winfield puts it:

'the court must decide not simply whether there is or is not a duty, but whether there should or should not be one'.

2.4.1 Policy factors considered by judges

A great number of factors may be considered by judges in deciding whether or not to impose a duty of care on a defendant in a particular case.

- Loss allocation – inevitably, judges are more likely to impose a duty on a party who is able to stand the loss, so the role of insurance is clearly a major determining factor.
- Practical considerations – the courts, for instance, may be willing to impose vicarious liability on companies that can then plan effective policies for the future avoidance of liability.
- Moral considerations – for instance, the public might be more prepared to accept a 'good Samaritan' law than would the judges.
- Protection of professionals – Lord Denning in particular expressed concern here that professionals should not be prevented from working by restrictive rulings.
- Constitutional considerations – the judges are not keen to be seen as law makers, which they acknowledge is Parliament's role.
- The 'floodgates' argument – judges are reluctant to impose liability where to do so might encourage large numbers of claims on the same issue. This does not appear to be a morally justifiable position and it has particularly hampered the development of liability for nervous shock.
- The beneficial effects of imposing a duty for future conduct – in *Smolden v Whitworth and Nolan* (1997) the court imposed a duty on a rugby referee who failed to control a scrum properly.

2.4.2 Policy and the refusal to impose a duty

Judges have often, in the past, identified policy reasons as the justification for refusing to impose liability in certain situations, and there are many examples.

a) Liability of lawyers for court work

> ### Rondel v Worsley (1969)
>
> The claimant argued that he had only lost his case in court because of the negligent presentation of the case by the barrister. The court refused to impose a duty because fear of a negligence action might prevent the barrister from effectively carrying out his duties in court, and in any case could lead to cases being re-opened, thus ending certainty in litigation.

The judges have, however, subsequently removed this immunity because there are now better ways of avoiding abuse of process.

> ### Hall v Simons (2000)
>
> The appeals involved three separate claims against solicitors for negligent handling of proceedings. The solicitors all claimed immunity from a negligence action in respect of advocacy. The Court of Appeal held that none of the claims were covered by the immunity. The House of Lords, in a court of seven judges with three dissenting, decided that there was no longer any need for immunity in civil proceedings as collateral attacks like these would normally be struck out as an abuse of process, so there was no longer any justification.

b) Immunity of judges

It was declared in *Sirros v Moore* (1975) that a judge would not be liable for any negligence done in the performance of judicial office. However, with inferior judges it is possible that there is liability for acts done in excess of jurisdiction.

c) Liability of the police to the public

As we have already seen in *Hill v Chief Constable of West Yorkshire* (1988), one argument here is that there is an alternative means of compensating through a claim to the Criminal Injuries Compensation Authority.

However, this is not always the case, and in certain circumstances the courts are prepared to impose a specific duty on bodies such as the police.

> ### Reeves v Commissioner of the Metropolitan Police (1999)
>
> Police were holding a prisoner who was a known suicide risk. When the prisoner did commit suicide the court rejected the police defence of *novus actus interveniens*. The suicide was the very risk that the police should have been guarding against.

The sort of blanket immunity from negligence actions enjoyed by the police has in any case led to the issue being challenged in a human rights context.

> ### Osman v United Kingdom (1999)
>
> Osman was killed by one of his teachers who formed an unnatural attachment to the boy. The teacher was convicted and later detained in a mental hospital. In a civil action for negligence against the police, the court rejected the claim on the basis of the immunity in *Hill*. A subsequent application to the European Court of Human Rights identified that this contravened Article 6. While the court appreciated that the rule was in place to ensure the effectiveness of the police, it had not been balanced with the rights of the public.

However, the courts are still reluctant to accept that a duty is owed by the police to witnesses and victims of crime.

Brooks v Commissioner of Police for the Metropolis (2005)

Brooks, the friend of murdered teenager Stephen Lawrence, claimed that he was badly treated by the police in their investigation of the crime, both as a witness and as a fellow victim. The House of Lords refused to accept that the police owed him a duty of care. To impose such a duty would prevent the police from concentrating on their primary functions and would lead to a defensive approach to tackling crime.

d) Liability of public authorities

Many recent cases concern the duty owed by public authorities, very often for failures to act rather than negligent acts. Very often judges will refuse to impose a duty because of lack of proximity.

K v Secretary of State for the Home Department (2002)

A Kenyan citizen was imprisoned for offences and a deportation order was issued. The Home Secretary then ordered his release and the Kenyan later raped the claimant. Although it was foreseeable that the man would commit further crimes, the court would not accept that the Home Secretary owed a duty to the claimant as there was insufficient proximity.

Alternatively the courts will not impose a duty where alternative remedies are available.

Matthews v Ministry of Defence (2003)

The claimant suffered injuries from exposure to asbestos fibres while serving in the Navy between 1955 and 1968. The Navy was immune from tort actions under the Crown Proceedings Act 1947. An alternative compensation system was created in 1987. The House of Lords held that there was no duty in negligence.

e) Specific types of claim

The courts have also been reluctant to allow claims in certain circumstances that they feel would otherwise offend a superior principle, e.g. the action for 'wrongful life' is denied because of the 'sanctity of life'.

McKay v Essex Area Health Authority (1982)

A pregnant woman was not advised that she had contracted German measles and that her child would thus be born severely disabled. The claim was obviously made so that the parents would have the means to support such a severely disabled child. The court would not impose a duty on a doctor to advise of the need for an abortion in such circumstances because that would interfere with the idea of the sanctity of life, and policy would not allow that.

They have been similarly reluctant to accept the existence of a duty of care in situations where there is traditionally no obvious legal protection in English law, e.g. privacy.

Kaye v Robertson (1991)

A famous TV actor suffered severe head injuries in an accident and was in intensive care. A newspaper then sent a photographer to the hospital to take a flash photograph. While the Court of Appeal did allow an injunction to prevent publication of the photograph, they were unable to find that there was any actionable battery or libel, and there was no duty that could give rise to an action in negligence. There was no right of privacy.

2.4.3 Policy and the three-part test

One of the major concerns expressed about Lord Wilberforce's test from *Anns* was that it put too much power in the hands of judges to decide cases on policy issues alone.

While the test may have been flawed, it is almost inevitable that policy considerations will still have a part to play in determining liability. The major difference is that under *Anns* this was openly done, whereas now there is the danger that it might be done much more secretly. Policy was clearly a consideration in the decision in *Hill*, even while that very aspect of the test in *Anns* was subject to wider criticism.

Policy has been an issue, then, in determining the duty of care owed by public regulatory bodies.

Philcox v Civil Aviation Authority (1995)

The Authority here was held not to owe a duty of care to the owner of an aircraft to ensure that he properly maintained that aircraft. Any duty arising out of the Authority's supervisory role was owed to the public.

It has also been a determining factor in the development of the immunity of actions enjoyed by professionals, and lawyers in particular.

Kelley v Corston (1997)

There was no duty of care owed by a barrister for negligent advice to settle prior to a court hearing on ancillary relief in divorce proceedings.

Policy also seems to have operated in protection of the public services.

Capital & Counties plc v Hampshire County Council (1997)

A fire officer ordered sprinklers to be turned off and this then led to more extensive damage. While the employers were liable because of having caused extra damage, the court identified that there was in general no duty owed by a fire brigade for the negligent handling of a fire.

It is clear that, even though a particular duty might exist, judges are reluctant to extend a public duty too far to avoid making public bodies responsible.

Clunnis v Camden and Islington Health Authority (1998)

The defendant Health Authority had an obvious duty of care to treat and to provide after care on discharge from hospital for the claimant, who had a long history of mental illness. The Court of Appeal would not accept that this duty extended so that the defendants would be liable when the man stabbed another man to death and was convicted of manslaughter.

This seems to be particularly so in the case of breaches of statutory duties by public bodies, where otherwise the possible deterrent effects of tort could be fully used.

Phelps v London Borough of Hillingdon (2000)

Because of breaches of statutory duties under the 1944 and 1981 Education Acts by educational psychiatrists, children were not diagnosed as having learning difficulties. Nevertheless, the House of Lords decided that there was no intention in either Act that there should be a civil action for damages for such breaches. Lord Slynn said:

'although the duties were intended to benefit a particular group, mainly children with special educational needs, the 1981 Act is essentially providing a general structure ... The general nature of the duties imposed on local authorities in the context of a national system of education ... the remedies available by way of appeal and judicial review indicate that Parliament did not intend to create a statutory remedy by way of damages.'

While policy appears to have been a major factor in developing immunity for public bodies, it now appears that this immunity may be under threat because of the human rights implications.

X v Bedfordshire County Council (1995)

This was a series of appeals for striking out actions against public authorities. One line involved child abuse where the local authority failed to act after the children were referred to them. The argument was that the children suffered long-term damage that could have been avoided had the council acted promptly. The other group involved a failure to provide special needs facilities. In the case of the child abuse negligence it was held that it would not be just or reasonable to impose a duty, since it would cut across the council's other statutory obligations, and remove resources that could otherwise be used for child protection. The justification given by the judges in the House of Lords was that the statute that the council were allegedly in breach of was for the benefit of the public generally, not only individuals.

The case was later taken to the European Court of Human Rights (under a different name) and a different answer given.

Z and others v United Kingdom (2001)

The European Court of Human Rights accepted that the children had been subjected to inhuman and degrading treatment contrary to Article 3, but also that they had been refused an effective remedy contrary to Article 13. This result may mean that English courts will be forced to rethink the blanket immunity from liability that they have in the past been prepared to offer public bodies.

Activity   **Problem Solving**

In the following situation, state which types of loss are recoverable from the manufacturer under the principle in *Donoghue v Stevenson*.

Sacha bought a new toaster last week and at the second time of using the toaster it burst into flames. When she bought it, the toaster was in a sealed package, and on both occasions that she has used it she has followed the manufacturer's instructions precisely. Sacha is not in any way to blame for the damage that has resulted.

- The toaster was completely destroyed and Sacha wants a replacement.

- The decorating in the kitchen has suffered smoke damage, and a cupboard behind the toaster was burnt so badly that it needs replacing.

- Sacha's arm was badly burnt when she tried to put out the fire.

Activity

Self-assessment questions

1. Why is *Donoghue v Stevenson* such an important case?

2. Exactly who or what in the law of negligence is a 'neighbour'?

3. What are the three main ingredients that must be proved for a successful claim of negligence?

4. In what ways was the test in *Anns* such a radical change from before?

5. Why did the House of Lords discard this test in *Murphy*?

6. Is the new test actually any better?

7. What factors does a court now take into account in determining whether or not to impose a duty of care?

8. What is the role of policy in establishing a duty of care?

Key Facts

- Negligence requires the existence of a duty of care, which is breached by the defendant and causes damage to the claimant that is not too remote a consequence of the breach – Lord Atkin in *Donoghue v Stevenson*.
- The existence of a duty is established by reference to Lord Atkin's 'neighbour principle' – neighbours are those people who are so closely affected by our deeds that we should take care to avoid harming them.
- A development of the test was Lord Wilberforce's two-part test from *Anns v Merton London Borough Council* – first, see if there is sufficient proximity between claimant and defendant to impose a duty; second, decide whether policy reasons will prevent a duty being imposed.
- This test was overruled in *Murphy v Brentwood District Council*.
- A new three-part test for establishing a duty from *Caparo v Dickman* is now used – is there proximity, is the damage foreseeable, is it just and reasonable to impose a duty?
- Policy has always played a part in deciding whether to impose a duty, e.g. immunity of barristers from negligence actions for work done in court – *Rondel v Worsley*.
- The 'floodgates' argument, for example, has been a regular justification for not imposing a duty of care.
- A dislike for deciding cases purely on policy grounds was one of the reasons for overruling *Anns*.
- Now policy may still be a factor, only a more hidden one – *Hill v Chief Constable of West Yorkshire*.

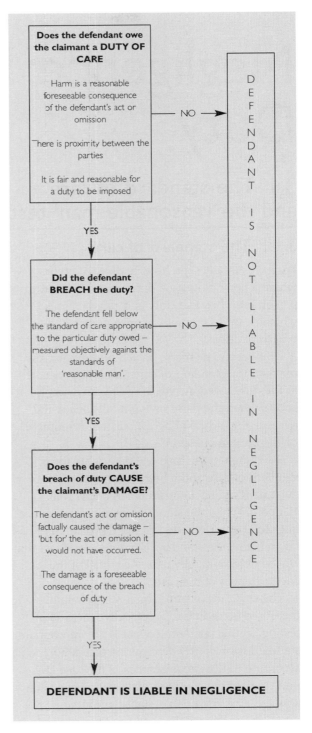

Figure 1 *Flow chart illustrating the essential elements for proof of negligence*

Chapter 3

Negligence: Breach of Duty

3.1 The standard of care and the 'reasonable man' test

3.1.1 The standard of care

We have already seen how negligence occurs where a person owing a duty of care to another person breaches that duty and causes damage which is not too remote a consequence of the breach of duty.

This second element, breach of duty, actually refers to the standard of care that is appropriate to the duty owed. A breach of the duty simply occurs when the party owing it falls below the particular standard of behaviour that is required by the duty in question.

The judge in the case will determine the standard of care and whether or not the defendant's behaviour has fallen below that standard. While the standard in any situation is a question of law, whether or not the defendant has fallen below the standard is a question of fact that will be determined by reference to all of the circumstances of the case.

The standard of care required is generally measured according to an objective method of testing. In this way, while what is the appropriate standard is obviously determined factually, according to the circumstances of the case, it is nevertheless the standard that would have been adopted by a 'reasonable man' confronted by the same circumstances that will be taken as the measure by which the defendant's actions will be judged.

3.1.2 The 'reasonable man' test

The objective standard measured according to the standards of the 'reasonable man' was first identified in *Blyth v Proprietors of the Birmingham Waterworks* (1856).

> ### *Blyth v Proprietors of the Birmingham Waterworks (1856)*
>
> A water main was laid in which there was a 'fire plug'. This was a wooden plug in the main that would allow water to flow through a cast iron tube up to the street when necessary. A severe frost loosened the plug and water flooded the claimant's house, the cast iron tube being blocked with ice. The frost was beyond normal expectation. There was nothing that the defendants could have reasonably done to prevent the damage and there was no liability. Alderson B explained that
>
> *'Negligence is the omission to do something which a reasonable man, guided upon those considerations which ordinarily regulate human affairs, would do, or doing something which a prudent and reasonable man would not do.'*

The test, on the face of it, seems simple enough. The question is, who is the reasonable man by whose standards we are supposed to judge our behaviour?

Judges have, over time, attempted to define the character of the reasonable man in order that the objective standard can be more closely understood. In *Hall v Brooklands Auto-Racing Club* (1933) Greer LJ defined the reasonable man in the following terms:

'The person concerned is sometimes described as "the man on the street", or as the "man on the Clapham Omnibus", or, as I recently read in an American author, the "man who takes the magazines at home and in the evening pushes the lawnmower in his shirt sleeves".'

The precise characteristics associated with the reasonable man have also been considered.

Glasgow Corporation v Muir (1943)

Here, small children were scalded when a tea urn was dropped. The urn was being carried through a narrow passage where the children were buying ice creams when the corporation allowed a church picnic to come inside on a rainy day. MacMillan LJ concluded that,

'The standard of foresight of the reasonable man is an impersonal test. It eliminates the personal equation and is independent of the idiosyncrasies of the particular person whose conduct is in question. Some persons are, by nature, unduly timorous and imagine every path beset by lions; others, of more robust temperament, fail to foresee or nonchalantly disregard even the most obvious dangers. The reasonable man is presumed to be free from both over-apprehension and from over-confidence.'

In fact, the breach of duty is another way of saying that the defendant is at fault and is therefore liable for the damage caused. The issue of whether liability should always be based on fault or whether there should be a no-fault liability system is a controversial question and one that we will return to.

Certainly in practice, who or what is the reasonable man, and what constitutes an objective standard, are concepts determined by the judges in a case. Judges, in reaching a decision, will also base their judgment on either policy or expediency as the need arises.

Policy considerations that can influence a judge include:

- Who can best stand the loss – clearly, a claimant needs to claim from a party who can afford to pay. The key rule in deciding whether or not to bring a case is 'Never sue a man of straw' (a person of no means).
- Whether or not the defendant is insured – in most circumstances in the modern day it will be an insurance company rather than the actual defendant who will pay the compensation. This would be the case, for instance, in the case of motorists, employers, professional bodies, manufacturers, etc.
- The extent to which the decision will prevent similar behaviour in the future – the tort system is mainly about compensating for loss and damage suffered, but it should also have a deterrent element.
- Whether or not the decision would 'open the floodgates' to further cases.
- Whether or not particular types of actions should be discouraged – for instance, against the police or administrators of the law.
- Whether or not there are alternative means of gaining a remedy.

3.2 Determining the standard of care

Through the cases judges have developed a number of rules concerning those things that should be taken into account in determining the standard by which the defendant's behaviour should be measured.

3.2.1 Foreseeability of risk

There is no obligation on the defendant to guard against risks other than those that are within his/her reasonable contemplation. It would be unfair to make a defendant responsible for the unforeseeable.

> ### Roe v Minister of Health (1954)
>
> A patient became paralysed after being injected with nupercaine, a spinal anaesthetic. This had been stored inside glass ampoules, themselves stored in a sterilising fluid, phenol. Evidence at the trial showed that the phenol solution had entered the anaesthetic through hairline cracks in the ampoules, contaminating it and causing the paralysis. There was no liability because such an event had not previously occurred and was unforeseeable as a result.

Nevertheless, if the defendant is aware of the possibility of harm (s)he must guard against it, and it will be a breach of the duty of care to fail to.

> ### Walker v Northumberland County Council (1995)
>
> Here, a senior social worker had suffered a nervous breakdown. His employers knew that he might suffer another breakdown when he returned to work if the pressures of his work were too severe and stressful. They took insufficient steps to reduce the pressures of his workload and, when he was again made ll, they were in breach of their duty to take reasonable steps to avoid psychiatric injury, knowing of his state of health.

3.2.2 The magnitude of the risk

We must all guard against the risk of doing harm. This is only reasonable. The degree of caution that we must exercise will be dictated by the likelihood of the risk. The magnitude of the risk then can be balanced against the precautions that must be taken in order to avoid it.

> ### Bolton v Stone (1951)
>
> Miss Stone was standing outside a cricket ground and was hit by a cricket ball that had been hit out of the ground. She was actually 100 yards from where the batsman had struck the ball. The batsman was 78 yards from a 17 foot high fence over which the ball had travelled. This was quite incredible and it was shown that balls had only been struck out of the ground six times in 28 years. There was no negligence. The cricket ground had done everything reasonably possible to avoid risks of people being hit.

The defendant, though, must take into account any factors that might increase the risk of harm occurring.

> ### Haley v London Electricity Board (1965)
>
> Here, a hole was being dug along a pavement and a hammer was left propped up on the pavement to warn passers by of the presence of the hole. A blind man was passing and his stick failed to touch the hammer and he tripped and fell which left him deaf. It was held that there was a sufficiently large proportion of blind people in the community for precautions to be taken that would protect them also, and the cost would be very low. The defendants were liable for negligence.

In industry this now means making risk assessments in both general and specific circumstances.

Davis v Stena Line (2005)

A passenger on a ferry fell overboard in bad weather conditions. There was a high risk of such accidents and this was well known to the company, although it had failed to train the crew adequately for such accidents. The captain of the ferry tried a risky rescue up the side of the boat and the man died, although a passing ship which had spotted the man could have launched a fast rescue boat to save him if the captain had agreed. The court accepted that the captain's rescue attempt had little chance of success and it was negligent of the captain not to consider the better alternative. The company was negligent for failing to train the crew properly.

3.2.3 The extent of the possible harm (the 'thin skull' rule)

The court will not only be concerned with the likelihood that harm will occur, but the risk that the harm will be great if it does occur. In this sense the defendant must 'take the claimant how he finds him', the so-called 'thin skull' rule.

Paris v Stepney Borough Council (1951)

The claimant here was a mechanic who was already blind in one eye. He was then blinded in the other eye in an accident at work when his employers had failed to supply him with safety goggles that they were legally required to do. They were then liable to the defendant to the extent of causing his total blindness rather than merely for the loss of the sight in the one eye. The claimant's partial sight meant that the duty towards him was necessarily greater than normal.

The same principle can apply even though the foreseeable harm is psychological rather than physical.

Walker v Northumberland County Council (1995)

An area social services officer had particularly onerous and stressful responsibilities and suffered a nervous breakdown. He returned to work after three months on the understanding that there would be a lighter workload and less pressure. He was nevertheless expected to clear up the backlog and suffered a further breakdown leading to eventual dismissal on ill health. The employers were held to have breached their duty to protect his psychological well being and health.

It is also possible for the characteristic in question to be to do with something other than the claimant's health or physical characteristics.

Mattocks v Mann (1993)

Here, the claimant was able to recover the cost of hiring a replacement vehicle used during a delay caused by the insurers' negligent failure to pay for repairs to her vehicle. She was unable to pay for the repair costs herself, and it was foreseeable that she would hope that the insurers would meet those costs.

3.2.4 The social utility of the activity

A defendant can sometimes escape liability in a case because it is possible to show that there was a justification for taking the risk in question. This might be so, for instance, where the defendant acts to avoid a potentially worse event.

Watt v Hertfordshire County Council (1954)

A woman was trapped in a car crash. The fire station summoned to the incident had a special heavy jack for using in such circumstances. It would normally be taken to the scene properly secured in its own vehicle, but the vehicle was elsewhere. The jack was taken unsecured in another vehicle because of the emergency and when the driver was forced to brake sharply the jack moved, injuring a fireman. There was no negligence because the situation was an emergency and justified the risk.

However, this will not mean that the taking of any risk at all can be justified. Only the precise circumstances can justify the taking of the risk.

Griffin v Mersey Regional Ambulance (1998)

There was liability when an ambulance drove through a red light and crashed. However, the other motorist was held to be 60% contributorily negligent.

3.2.5 The practicability of precautions

The reasonable man only has to do what is reasonable in order to avoid risks of harm. This means that there is no obligation to go to extraordinary lengths, particularly if the risk is slight.

Latimer v AEC Ltd (1953)

A factory became flooded after a torrential rainstorm. The water mixed with oil and grease on the floor, making the surface very slippery and dangerous. When the water subsided, sawdust was spread over the floors in order to make them secure. There was not enough to cover the whole floor and Latimer slipped on an uncovered patch and was injured. The House of Lords held that everything reasonable had been done in the circumstances and, balancing out the possible risks, it was unreasonable to expect the factory to be closed. There was no negligence.

Generally, though, where the defendant has sufficient control of circumstances to be able to avoid the harm, he or she would be obliged to act. This is particularly so where the welfare of the claimant is entrusted to the defendant.

Bradford-Smart v West Sussex County Council (2002)

The Court of Appeal accepted that a school would be in breach of its duty of care to its pupils if it failed to take steps that were within its power to put a stop to bullying. The court accepted that this could apply even to incidents that arose off the school premises, although in general it was accepted that only rare exceptions would give rise to a breach of duty, and that the present case was not such an occasion.

3.2.6 Common practice

A negligent activity cannot be excused merely because it is common practice. Nevertheless, the fact that something is generally practised may be strong evidence that it is not negligent, otherwise it would not normally be carried out.

This, of course, is not an absolute principle and it will not necessarily be negligent merely to fail to follow common practice.

> ## Brown v Rolls-Royce Ltd (1960)
> An employee contracted dermatitis. The employers provided adequate washing facilities but they did not provide a barrier cream that was commonly used in the industry. They were not negligent in not providing the barrier cream because it could not be shown in the case that using the cream was guaranteed to prevent the condition.

> ## Mullin v Richards (1998)
> Here, two 15-year-old schoolgirls were 'fencing' with plastic rulers. One ruler broke and one of the girls was injured in the eye. The Court of Appeal held that since such games were commonplace and would normally not lead to injury then the injury was unforeseeable to girls of that age and there was no negligence.

3.3 The standard of care and different classes of defendant

The standard of care is measured objectively, but the courts have often looked at whether the standard may differ according to the type of person who owes the duty.

3.3.1 Children

Traditionally, there was little case law involving the standard of care owed by children. Case law from other jurisdictions indicated that a child was not expected to have the same skill or understanding as an adult and therefore the standard of care owed was that appropriate to the age of the child in question.

> ## McHale v Watson (1966)
> A 12-year-old boy injured a girl in the eye when he threw a steel rod at a post. There was held to be no negligence.

This seems to be more of a subjective than an objective test, but the English courts have tended to follow it.

However, the judges have been willing on occasions to make awards of contributory negligence against child claimants.

> ## Armstrong v Cottrell (1993)
> The judge in this case was prepared to reduce damages for a 12-year-old by a third because he felt that children of that age should know the Highway Code.

This can even be to a high level of reduction with quite young children.

> ## Morales v Eccleston (1991)
> Damages were reduced by 75% when an 11-year-old ran into the road to recover his football and was knocked down.

3.3.2 The disabled

Where a person is sick or suffering from a disability it is likely that the standard of care owed is what would be appropriate in the case of the reasonable man suffering the same illness or disability. It is inevitable that the same degree of care will not be expected as would be for a person in normal health.

A person suffering from a disability of the mind may be liable for the torts (s)he commits if sufficiently aware of the quality of the act.

> ## Morris v Marsden (1952)
>
> Here, the defendant was a schizophrenic who attacked a claimant and was thus accused of battery. It was held that persons suffering from a mental illness could be liable for intentional torts even if unaware that their actions were wrong, provided they knew the quality of the act they committed.

3.3.3 Motorists

In general, the same standard of care is expected of all motorists regardless of their age or experience, and even of learner drivers.

> ## Nettleship v Weston (1971)
>
> A learner driver on her third lesson crashed into a lamppost, injuring the person teaching her to drive. The Court of Appeal found that she was liable despite being a learner driver. As Lord Denning put it,
>
> *'The learner driver may be doing his best, but his incompetent best is not enough. He must drive in as good a manner as a driver of skill, experience and care'.*

Lord Denning identified in the case that this is probably to do with the fact that motorists are obliged to carry compulsory insurance and therefore the degree of risk associated with the particular class of driver can be reflected in the insurance premium they are expected to pay.

The principle might even extend to a motorist who becomes physically incapable of controlling the vehicle because of a physical impairment.

> ## Roberts v Ramsbottom (1980)
>
> A driver crashed into a stationary vehicle after suffering a cerebral haemorrhage (a stroke). He continued to drive after the seizure and the court felt that he was negligent for doing so. The court accepted that a defendant would have a defence if his actions were entirely beyond his control, but that here the driver should have stopped driving immediately.

However, a motorist will not be liable if (s)he is unaware of the disabling condition that causes the loss of control.

> ## Mansfield v Weetabix Ltd (1997)
>
> Here, it was held that the driver could not have reasonably known of the infirmity that led to his loss of control and the subsequent accident, so there was no fault. The last case was said to be wrongly decided on this point, but was still correct in that the driver continued to drive when he should have known that he was unfit to do so.

3.3.4 People engaged in sport

The standard of care appropriate to participants in sport is the ordinary standard of reasonable care. The level of care required will depend on the circumstances of the case, including whether the player is a professional or an amateur.

> ## Condon v Basi (1985)
>
> Here, the ordinary standard of reasonable care was applied when a footballer was injured in a dangerous and unacceptable tackle during an amateur football match. Sir John Donaldson suggested in the case that a much higher degree of care would be expected of a professional footballer.

Professional players are assumed to be more knowledgeable of the potential risks and consequences of injury and are thus more likely to be found in breach of their duty of care to fellow professionals.

McCord v Swansea City AFC Ltd and another (1997)

Here, a tackle by a player of the defendant football club ended the claimant's career. While the judge was not prepared to consider the tackle as reckless, it was a serious mistake of judgment that amounted to a breach of his duty of care to fellow players.

However, the level of care required is always taken in the context of the individual circumstances because of the inherent risk of injury of which each player is aware.

Pitcher v Huddersfield Town Football Club Ltd (2001)

The claimant suffered a knee injury after a rash tackle, ending his career. The judge did not accept that the defendant player had fallen below an appropriate standard. He had mistimed his tackle, but such errors of judgment were commonplace in the sport.

While participants in sport are inevitably aware of the risks of engaging in sporting activities, particularly contact sports of any kind, they are nevertheless to be protected from unnecessary harm by the officials in the game. In this way a referee in a sporting contest owes a duty of care to the players.

Smolden v Whitworth (1997)

In a colts rugby match, i.e. one involving young and inexperienced players, the referee had been approached by the coaches about repeated collapsing of the scrum by players on the other side. He failed to control the scrums properly and eventually one player was seriously injured, leading to paralysis, when the scrum collapsed. The Court of Appeal agreed that the referee had fallen below the standard of care that he owed to the players. They were, however, eager to emphasise that the judgment was appropriate to the colts but not to the senior game, where the players would be more experienced.

A spectator at a sporting contest is generally said to consent to the risks associated with being present at the sport. A person engaged in the sport, then, will not be liable in negligence to a spectator for any injuries or damage caused in the normal course of the sport, unless the sportsman has shown a blatant and reckless disregard for the safety of the spectator.

Wooldridge v Sumner (1963)

A photographer stood behind a line of shrubs marking the perimeter of the arena at the National Horse Show at White City Stadium. The defendant tried to take a corner too fast on his horse, with the result that the horse plunged through the shrubs and injured the claimant. The Court of Appeal held that the defendant was not liable for negligence, but had merely made an error of judgment in how fast he should be going at the time.

The duty of care owed to a disabled participant in sporting events will be greater than that owed to an able bodied sportsman, simply because the disability will require a greater degree of care.

> ## *Morrell v Owen (1993)*
>
> Here, athletics coaches were held to be in breach of their duty of care to a paraplegic archer. The disabled athlete was hit on the head by a discus and suffered brain damage as a result.

3.3.5 People lacking specialist skills

If a person carries out a task requiring a specialist skill (s)he will be judged according to the standard of a person reasonably competent in the exercise of that skill. However, this does not mean that an amateur will be expected to show the same degree of skill as would a professional.

> ## *Wells v Cooper (1958)*
>
> A tradesman delivering fish was injured when a door handle fitted by the householder came off in his hand. The Court of Appeal held that the appropriate standard of care was that of a reasonably competent carpenter. The claimant's complaint was that the handle was fixed to the door with three-quarters of an inch screws that he claimed were inadequate. Since these were the screws that a carpenter would have used there could be no negligence.

Nevertheless, a person not possessing specialist skills will not be expected to exercise the same standard of care as a skilled person unless that standard is appropriate to the circumstances.

> ## *Phillips v Whiteley (1938)*
>
> A jeweller pierced ears in a whitewashed room using sterilised equipment. When the claimant contracted a blood disorder the jeweller was not negligent. He had taken all reasonable steps in the circumstances to avoid the risk of harm and could not be fixed with the same standard of care as a surgeon performing an operation. The appropriate standard of care was the degree of care that should be taken by a jeweller carrying out the procedure, not that which would be appropriate to a surgeon.

3.3.6 People using equipment

In general, where people use equipment they are taken to know how to use it properly, unless it is very specialist equipment requiring specialist skill. So, where a person suffers injury, loss or damage while using the equipment there is no requirement by the other party to check that they are able to use it properly, and so no breach.

> ## *Makepeace v Evans (2000)*
>
> The claimant was a decorator hired by the first defendant sub-contractors, who in turn were hired by the second defendant main contractors. The claimant used a scaffolding tower provided by the second defendants. Their site agent did not enquire whether the claimant was competent to use it. When the claimant was injured on it his action against the second defendants failed. It was a standard piece of equipment in the trade, and they were entitled to assume that he was able to use it, or seek advice. The court held that to say otherwise would be to 'extend the nursemaid school of negligence too far'.

Activity   *Quick Quiz*

Consider how it will be decided whether there has been a breach of a duty of care in the following situations.

● Jamie is an 11-year-old boy who has caused a crash by running out in front of cars while playing 'chicken'.

● Tom has been injured when stones from a quarry hit him on his head after blasting. He was walking on a pavement a mile away from the quarry. The quarry face is shielded by a high hill, and no previous explosions from the quarry have ever caused this to happen before.

● Tan, an acupuncturist, has been treating Rachel for pains in her shoulders. Tan has followed normal methods precisely, but Rachel has suffered a rare infection.

● During a forest fire, Tristram used explosives to blow up his neighbour, Ali's trees in order to prevent the fire from spreading to his own farm and also to the nearby village of Trumpton.

3.4 The standard of care of experts and professionals

3.4.1 The *Bolam* test

Professionals do not conform to the usual rules on the breach of duty in negligence and therefore are more appropriately considered as a special category on their own.

The standard of care appropriate to professionals is not judged according to the 'reasonable man' test, so his/her actions are not compared with those of the 'man on the Clapham omnibus'.

On the contrary, a person exercising specialist skills is to be judged by comparison with his/her peers, other people exercising the same skill. The standard test is found in a case alleging medical negligence, but it is equally appropriate to all professionals.

Bolam v Friern Hospital Management Committee (1957)

Mr Bolam suffered from depression and entered hospital to undergo electro-convulsive therapy. The practice, as the name suggests, causes possibly quite severe muscular spasms. The doctor giving the treatment failed to provide either relaxant drugs or any means of restraint during the treatment. The claimant suffered a fractured pelvis, and the question for the court was whether there was negligence in the practice of providing neither restraint nor relaxants. The court received evidence that a number of different practitioners carrying out the type of treatment took different views on the use of restraints or relaxant drugs. McNair J established the standard of care appropriate to professionals, concluding that:

'.. *where you get a situation which involves the use of some special skill or competence, then the test as to whether there has been negligence or not is not the test of the man on the top of a Clapham omnibus, because he has not got this skill.*'

· The actual test was: '*the standard of the ordinary skilled man exercising and professing to have that special skill.*' Since there were doctors who would have carried out the therapy in the same manner, the doctor here had acted in accordance with a competent body of medical opinion and there could be no negligence.

3.4.2 Applying the test

The test, not surprisingly, has caused controversy. Nevertheless, the House of Lords has subsequently approved it in relation to various aspects of medical treatment and responsibility. It has, for instance, been accepted as appropriate in determining the level of information a doctor should give when obtaining consent from a patient.

Sidaway v Governors of the Bethlem Royal and Maudsley Hospitals (1985)

Mrs Sidaway had suffered persistent pain in her right arm and shoulder and had, on the advice of her surgeon, consented to a spinal operation to relieve the pain. On obtaining consent, the doctor had accurately informed her that there was a less than 1% risk of something going wrong. What Mrs Sidaway claimed the doctor had not told her was the potentially catastrophic consequences if something did go wrong. In the event, while the operation was carried out without negligence, the damage did occur and she was left paralysed. She sued on the grounds that the surgeon had been negligent in failing properly to warn of the possible extent of the damage. The House of Lords held that the degree of information given by the doctor conformed to '*a practice accepted as proper by a responsible body of neuro-surgical opinion …*', so that there was no negligence. They also rejected the idea that there should be a doctrine of 'informed consent' as there is in other jurisdictions, because this would make operation of the *Bolam* test impossible.

The House of Lords in *Chester v Afshar* (2004) accepted that there must be circumstances in which doctors do owe a duty to warn of risks, otherwise they would have a discretion not to warn of risks at all (see 4.2).

The rule has also been accepted and held to apply to diagnosis of illness.

Maynard v West Midlands Regional Health Authority (1985)

Here, consultants operated before the results of certain tests they had ordered became available. They both considered that the patient had pulmonary tuberculosis, but also felt that she might have Hodgkin's disease, and decided to operate immediately without benefit of the information from the tests. She claimed that the operation damaged her vocal cords unnecessarily. There was no negligence because they had followed a practice approved by a responsible body of medical opinion, even if conflicting practices were possible at the time. Lord Scarman stated that:

'*There is seldom any one answer exclusive of all others to problems of professional judgment. A court may prefer one body of opinion to the other; but that is no basis for a conclusion of negligence*'.

This is understandable since a misdiagnosis could lead to the wrong treatment being carried out.

Ryan v East London and City HA (2001)

A child suffered a permanent spinal disability after an operation that had been carried out because of a misdiagnosis of a spinal tumour. There was a breach of duty because without the negligent diagnosis the child would have received the correct treatment and not suffered the disability.

On this basis doctors are also bound to take proper account of technical information in reaching a diagnosis.

Hunt v NHS Litigation Authority (2002)

Here, the doctor failed to realise the full implications of a cardiotocograph, gave a mother in labour drugs to speed up her labour, and left her in the care of midwives, attending periodically. In fact, the doctor should have noticed that the baby had an irregular heartbeat and that something was wrong. The baby suffered brain damage when it was born with the cord tight around its neck. The doctor should have carried out a forceps delivery at a much earlier stage if she had reacted correctly to the information from the tests.

It is also accepted that the test applies to medical treatment, so that all aspects of medicine fall within the scope of the rule.

Whitehouse v Jordan (1981)

A senior registrar had carried out a forceps delivery of a baby. The baby had become wedged and suffered asphyxia and brain damage. The allegation was that the doctor had used the forceps with too much force and that was the cause of the damage. In fact, the mother gave evidence that she had been lifted off the bed when the forceps were applied to the baby's head. In the House of Lords, Lord Edmund-Davies rejected the view put forward by Lord Denning in the Court of Appeal that an error of clinical judgment should not necessarily be the same as negligence. He considered that:

'… while some errors may be completely consistent with the due exercise of professional skill, other acts or omissions … may be so glaringly below proper standards as to make a finding of negligence inevitable.'

Nevertheless, he confirmed that the *Bolam* test was the appropriate test by which to measure standards of professional activity.

The rule that the appropriate standard of care in relation to professionals is measured against the standard held by a reasonable, competent body of professional opinion is not a rule exclusive to doctors. It can be applied to professionals generally. A person professing to exercise a particular professional skill will be expected to act in accordance with the standards accepted by a competent body of opinion expert in that skill.

Luxmoore-May v Messenger May and Baverstock (1990)

Auctioneers sold paintings at auction for £840. Some months later the paintings were resold for £88,000. It was alleged that the auctioneers were negligent in failing to recognise that the paintings were the work of a famous artist. The Court of Appeal held that the auctioneers should be judged according to the standards of a competent body of opinion skilled in the profession of the auctioneers. In the event they were not negligent because it was shown that there could be divergence of opinion on the origins of the paintings.

The standard is that appropriate to the professional exercising and professing to possess the skill in question. It is not, therefore, possible to argue that the standard is reduced because the defendant lacks experience. So, the junior doctor must exercise the same degree of skill as the experienced doctor.

Wilsher v Essex Area Health Authority (1988)

A baby was born prematurely and with an oxygen deficiency. A junior doctor then administered excess oxygen by mistake. The junior doctor inserted a catheter in an artery rather than a vein and a registrar failed to spot the mistake. The baby was later found to be nearly blind. A possible cause of the blindness was the excess oxygen. The House of Lords rejected the Health Authority's argument that the standard of care expected should be reduced because it was a junior doctor. Accepting such an argument would then mean that the care a patient was entitled to would depend on the experience of the doctor who treated them. This was unacceptable and negligence was held to have occurred in the case, although the Authority were not liable on causation.

The *Bolam* test will, in any case, apply even though the defendant lacks the appropriate professional qualifications and is not applying the same reasoning that a professional would apply.

Adams and another v Rhymney Valley District Council (2000) CA

The defendant council fitted double-glazed windows in the claimant's council flat. The windows had removable keys and the council did not fit smoke alarms in the flat. The keys were not kept in the windows. During a fire one of the claimants was badly injured breaking the windows trying to get out, and three of the claimant's children died in the fire. The trial judge rejected the claim on the basis that the council had exercised the skill of a competent window designer in fitting windows with removable keys. The Court of Appeal dismissed the appeal and rejected the argument that *Bolam* had been wrongly applied. Even though the council had not consulted police or fire brigade, they had not produced a negligent design for the windows.

The standard expected of the professional is that of a competent body of professional opinion, not of professional opinion generally. So, it is possible for the practice of the professional in question to be accepted in fact by only a minority of professionals.

Defreitas v O'Brien and Connolly (1995)

A doctor specialising in spinal surgery considered that an intricate exploratory operation was necessary. The argument that there was negligence because, as it was shown, only 11 out of over 1,000 surgeons who regularly performed the operation would have operated in the case was rejected. The Court of Appeal held that the number involved could be seen as a competent body of medical opinion in the circumstances.

Common practice among a profession is often cited as indicating that the practice is acceptable and not negligent. There are, of course, some practices that can be seen as negligent regardless of whether they are commonly carried out or not.

Re Herald of Free Enterprise (1987)

It was argued that it was standard practice for the bow doors of roll-on roll-off ferries to be left open on leaving ports. It was still, however, seen as being a dangerous practice and negligent on the part of the master of the ferry.

One final aspect of the standard of care expected of professionals is that they should keep reasonably abreast of changes and developments in their profession. They would not, however, be expected to be immediately aware of all new ideas.

Crawford v Board of Governors of Charing Cross Hospital (1983)

Here, a patient suffered brachial palsy following an operation. It was argued that this was due to the position of his arm during a blood transfusion, and that the anaesthetist should have been aware of the risk because of a recent article in *The Lancet*, a journal for doctors. The court rejected the argument. There was no negligence because the reasonable doctor cannot be expected to keep up with every new development.

This might include even unorthodox or unusual practices.

Shakoor v Situ (t/a Eternal Health Co) (2001)

The claimant, who suffered from a skin condition, went to a Chinese herbalist who prescribed a remedy. The claimant later died of acute liver failure that was found to be a rare and unpredictable reaction to the remedy. The claimant's widow brought proceedings, alleging negligence in prescribing the remedy, or alternatively, in failing to provide warning of the risks. The court held that it was necessary to consider the standard of care of a practitioner of alternative medicine. It was implied that (1) he was presenting himself as competent to practise within the system of law and medicine under which his standard of care would be judged; (2) he knew, rather than believed, that the remedy was not harmful; and (3) if a patient reacted adversely to the remedy and, as a result, sought orthodox medical help then this would be discussed in an orthodox medical journal. In the instant case, the actions of the herbalist were consistent with the standard of care appropriate to traditional Chinese herbal medicine in accordance with established requirements. So there was no breach of duty.

However, it is important that where guidelines are issued by government or by the professional bodies governing the professions that indicate best practice, then professionals should act according to those guidelines.

Thomson v James and Others (1996)

A GP failed to follow government guidelines in advising parents on vaccinations for rubella, measles and mumps. A child was not vaccinated following the advice of the GP and contracted first measles and later meningitis, and was brain damaged as a result. The doctor was negligent in failing to issue proper advice.

3.4.3 Criticism of the *Bolam* test

Although the test is the appropriate method of determining whether a professional has fallen below an appropriate standard of care and is, therefore, negligent in a given case, it has not been without its critics. Indeed, there are numerous problems with the rule.

- The test allows professionals to set their own standard in negligence actions – in the case of people other than professionals the standard is an objective one, measured against the 'reasonable man'. In this case, the court will decide what the appropriate standard is. In the case of professionals, however, the standard is measured subjectively, according to what other professionals, brought to court as expert witnesses, say it is.
- As such, it protects professionals to a greater degree than is the case for anyone else – it is sufficient for a professional to bring to court a fellow professional to say that he would have done the same in the circumstances for the allegation of negligence to fail.
- Practices that are only marginal may be accepted as a result – the danger is that the test can legitimise practices that are highly experimental without real credibility, or at the least practices that few other responsible practitioners would carry out.

- There is a danger that professionals will close ranks, and even if this is not the case, the criticism will certainly be made and this can have the obvious effect of undermining confidence in the profession.
- It is impossible to say what a reasonable, competent body of professional opinion is – in some cases this can just amount to a question of numbers. The judges in any case are in effect leaving the definition to be made by those accused of the negligence.

There have, in fact, been a number of cases where doubt has been cast on how appropriate the test is, and where judges have preferred to take a more objective view.

Lybert v Warrington Health Authority (1996)

Evidence was introduced to show that a warning given by a gynaecologist concerning the possibility of a sterilisation operation failing conformed to established practice. Nevertheless, the Court of Appeal was prepared to declare that the warning was inadequate and therefore negligent.

Most recently, the House of Lords has suggested that it is for the court in each individual case to determine what is the standard of care appropriate to the professional against whom the negligence is alleged, and not for professional opinion.

Bolitho v City and Hackney Health Authority (1997)

A two-year-old boy was in hospital being treated for croup. His airways became blocked and, despite being summoned on more than one occasion by nursing staff, a doctor failed to attend. The boy suffered a cardiac arrest and brain damage as a result. This could have been avoided if a doctor had intubated and cleared the obstruction. The hospital admitted that the doctor was negligent in failing to attend. Nevertheless, they claimed that they were not liable because the doctor stated that even if she had attended she would not have intubated and so the cardiac arrest and brain damage would in any case have occurred. Evidence was introduced to show that there were at the time two schools of thought as to whether or not to intubate in such circumstances. The case is ultimately one of causation and whether the *Bolam* test applies at at that point, but the House of Lords rejected the view that because certain medical opinion accepted the practice of the doctor in question that they were bound to accept it because of *Bolam*. Lord Browne-Wilkinson suggested that:

'if, in a rare case, it can be demonstrated that the professional opinion is not capable of withstanding logical analysis, the judge is entitled to hold that the body of opinion is not reasonable or responsible.'

Activity   *Problem Solving*

Consider how the courts would determine whether there was a breach in the following situations:

1. Harold is a gynaecologist who, when called by midwives because of a difficult birth, nevertheless persuades the midwives to continue. The baby dies during delivery. Certain doctors suggest that only a caesarian section delivery was appropriate in the case, but Harold states that, even if he had attended, he would not have carried out a caesarian, and other doctors say that they would have acted similarly

2. During a forceps delivery of Martha's baby Harold, an inexperienced doctor who has never performed a forceps delivery before, damages the baby's head so badly that the baby suffers almost total brain damage and dies

3.5 Points for discussion

Fault liability and the need for reform

Fault liability, particularly in the case of medical negligence as we have seen, seems unfair to claimants because of the problems associated both with amassing evidence and of actually proving fault.

It seems obviously wrong to impose liability on a body such as a Health Authority unless that body can be shown to have done wrong. The fact that the defendant satisfies legal tests on fault is nevertheless scant comfort to a person who places his safety in the hands of professional people and finds himself later to have suffered irreversible and disabling damage.

Fault liability can also be seen as unfair to victims who have suffered harm because the degree to which a person can easily gather evidence, and therefore present a winnable case, may depend on the degree of publicity that the case has produced. Inevitably, people involved in an event gaining media attention or involving a number of claimants may be in a better position to find suitable evidence.

In this way, fault liability can also be unfair to society generally in not providing an adequate means of remedying wrongs, since the fault-based system can create classes of victims who can be compensated and classes who cannot. This can be particularly true of the victims of pure accidents and those suffering from genetic disorders.

It can also be seen as unfair to defendants, since there are no identified degrees of culpability. This, in turn, means that a defendant will not be penalised according to the degree of negligence shown.

The rules concerning the standard of care, as well as the imposing of duties, mean that very often a claimant's ability to recover for the wrong suffered is determined according to the whims of policy and therefore can be subject to arbitrary and often inconsistent reasoning.

In fairness to the fault-based system, its major justification is that it does punish the wrongdoer and so is said to have some deterrent value.

However, no-fault systems have been advocated on a number of occasions. The Pearson Committee in 1978 suggested such a system in the case of personal injury claims, though this has never been accepted or implemented. Two no-fault based medical negligence Bills have also been introduced unsuccessfully. The principle is not without precedent, since such a system has operated in New Zealand.

Activity

Self-assessment questions

1. Who, exactly, is a 'reasonable man'?
2. In what ways does a 'reasonable man' differ from an average man?
3. How big a part does policy play in determining the standard of care in negligence?
4. To what extent must a person owing a duty weigh up the risks associated with his acts and omissions?
5. What, exactly, is the 'thin skull' rule?

6. When will a standard of care be lowered because of the inexperience of the person owing the duty?

7. What standard of care does a child usually owe?

8. What effect does the fact that the acts leading to the damage were common practice have on deciding whether there is a breach of duty?

9. How does the test used for measuring the standard of care appropriate to a professional differ from the normal test?

10. What is the value of expert witness evidence in determining whether or not a professional has breached his/her duty of care?

11. What criticisms can be made of the test used for establishing the standard of care owed by professionals?

12. In what ways has *Bolitho* altered the principle in *Bolam*?

Key Facts

- A breach of duty occurs where a person falls below the standard of care appropriate to the duty (s)he owes.
- The standard of care is that appropriate to the 'reasonable man' (*Blyth v Birmingham Waterworks*).
- The reasonable man is free from both over-apprehension and over-confidence (*Glasgow Corporation v Muir*).
- Policy considerations often govern what the standard will be, e.g. the floodgates argument.
- Many factors are taken into account in determining whether the duty is breached:
  - foreseeability of harm (*Roe v Minister of Health*)
  - the magnitude of the risk (*Bolton v Stone*)
  - the 'thin skull' rule (*Paris v Stepney BC*)
  - the social utility of the act (*Watt v Herts CC*)
  - the practicability of precautions (*Latimer v AEC*).
- Consideration will be made for different types of defendant, e.g.:
  - children are expected to be less cautious (*Mullin v Richards*)
  - the disabled (*Morris v Marsden*)
  - motorists all owe the same duty, even if inexperienced (*Nettleship v Weston*)
  - sportsmen will depend on rules of sport being observed (*Smolden v Whitworth*)

- people lacking specialist skills (*Wells v Cooper*)
- people using equipment (*Makepeace v Evans*).
- The standard appropriate to professionals is judged according to the standards of a competent body of professional opinion (*Bolam v Friern Hospital Management Committee*).
  - This is because the 'reasonable man' does not share those skills.
  - All aspects of medicine are tested against this rule (*Whitehouse v Jordan*).
  - Even complementary medicine is tested against this rule (*Shakoor v Situ*).
  - However, there is no lowering of standard to take account of inexperience (*Wilsher v Essex AHA*).
  - The rule is criticised for allowing doctors to set their own standards, while standards generally are measured according to an objective standard.
  - It is felt that the standard should not be applied to hypothetical situations (*Bolitho v City & Hackney HA*)
- There are alternative systems where no-fault principles operate.

Activity

Legal essay writing

Consider the following essay title:

Consider the extent to which the rules by which the courts determine whether there is a breach of a duty of care actually discourage people from engaging in activities that may harm or damage others.

Answering the question

There are usually two key elements to essays in law:

- Firstly, you are required to reproduce factual information on a particular area of law that is identified in the question.

- Secondly, you are required to answer the question set, which is usually found in some critical element, i.e. you are likely to see the words 'discuss', 'analyse', 'critically consider', etc.

Students, for the most part, seem quite capable of doing the first, and also generally seem less skilled at the second. The important things in any case are to ensure that you deal only with relevant legal material in your answer, and that you do answer the question set, rather than one you have made up yourself.

For instance, in the case of the first element of this essay you might briefly explain that negligence requires the existence of a duty of care, which is breached when a defendant falls below the appropriate standard of care, and damage is caused which is a foreseeable consequence of the defendant's breach. However, you need give no more detail on duty or causation beyond that, since the essay is all about breach of duty.

In the case of the second element, in essence the essay asks you to consider whether this fault liability principle and the rules determining the standard of care make potential defendants act less negligently. So you must give a detailed account of the various rules on standard of care, and evaluate their effectiveness as a deterrent.

Relevant law

- Briefly define the principles of negligence coming from *Donoghue v Stevenson*: existence of a duty of care, breach of that duty, causation in fact and in law.

- Identify the usual test for establishing breach – the 'reasonable man' test – and an objective standard (*Blyth v Birmingham Waterworks*).

- Establish that the test is subject also to various qualifying factors:

  - the foreseeability of the risk (*Bolton v Stone*)

  - the practicability of precautions (*Latimer v AEC*)

  - the likely magnitude of the risk (*Haley v London Electricity Board*)

  - the 'thin skull' rule (*Paris v Stepney Borough Council*)

  - the effect of common practice (*Brown v Rolls-Royce*).

- Establish that there is no lowering of standard for inexperience (*Wilsher v Essex AHA*).

- The test may take into consideration characteristics of certain types of defendant:

- children are less likely to be cautious (*Morales v Eccleston*)

- the disabled are limited by their disability (*Morris v Marsden*)

- motorists are bound by a common standard, whatever their experience (*Nettleship v Weston*), and this even applies where illness prevents them from exercising proper care (*Roberts v Ramsbottom*)

- people engaging in sporting activities are required to exercise the standard of care appropriate to the rules of the sport in question and the circumstances in which it is played, i.e. a greater degree of care is expected of professionals (*Condon v Basi*). Spectators are entitled to whatever protection is reasonable (*Wooldridge v Sumner*), and officials are also under a duty to do what is reasonable to protect participants (*Smolden v Whitworth*)

- people not possessing specialist skills are not expected to exercise the same standard of care as a skilled person, unless appropriate (*Phillips v Whiteley*)

- people using equipment are assumed to know how to use it (*Makepeace v Evans*).

- Some detailed consideration should also be given to the very different method of establishing the standard appropriate to professionals, particularly doctors (the *Bolam* test), measured against a competent body of medical (professional) opinion. This applies not just to selection of treatment, but to advice and information given (*Sidaway v Governors of the Bethlem Royal & Maudsley Hospitals*), but cannot be applied to hypothetical situations (*Bolitho v City and Hackney HA*).

Evaluation and analysis

The commentary in the essay requires a discussion of a very precise point – whether or not the means of measuring the standard of care allows the law of negligence to act as a deterrent:

So, while critical appreciation of all the various rules may be made, comment must ultimately be directed to answering that specific question.

Relevant aspects of the discussion might include:

- whether an objective standard is really possible, or whether judges are merely imposing their own standard

- whether the fact that there is no lowering of the standard based solely on the inexperience of the defendant helps any objectivity to be maintained

- whether the standard being an objective one does actually have a deterrent effect

- whether the deterrent effect is lessened because there are the means of treating different classes of defendant differently

- in particular whether it is appropriate for professionals, particularly doctors, in effect to set their own standards

- whether the difference in tests for professionals and the apparently greater protection enjoyed by doctors contrasts too sharply with the 'reasonable man' test and thus lessens the deterrent effect generally

- whether this different test is dangerous in allowing marginal practices to be legitimised which would not be accepted under the objective test

- whether the existence of insurance means that the deterrent effect is lessened
- whether fault liability in any case places too great a burden on the claimant and in this way lessens the deterrent effect on negligent defendants
- whether use of the criminal law could act as more of a deterrent.

One other interesting comment that could be made also involves criminal law. Since, in many cases, big business negligently causing large-scale injuries or death pays either compensation or fines from corporate money, and no individual responsible suffers, does this justify the introduction of a crime of corporate manslaughter, with imprisonment maybe having a more deterrent effect?

Chapter 4

Negligence: Causation and Remoteness of Damage

4.1 Introduction

Once the claimant has shown the existence of a duty of care and proved that it has been breached by falling below the appropriate standard of care, he or she must still prove that the defendant's negligent act or omission caused the damage.

As with the other two elements, the burden is on the claimant to prove the causal link on a balance of probabilities. This may actually be quite difficult, particularly where the incident has been the result of multiple causes or where the damage suffered is of an unusual type.

Causation is also clearly appropriate to other torts, even those that are strict liability and where the claimant, as a result, is relieved only of the burden of proving fault, but still must show a direct link between the defendant's acts or omissions and the damage suffered.

Causation is necessarily measured against the facts of the individual cases. Nevertheless, as in the other areas, policy can still play a big part in decisions.

Causation is measured in two ways:

- according to the 'but for' test, that the defendant's negligent act or omission did in fact cause the claimant's damage (causation in fact)
- by establishing that the damage is still

sufficiently proximate in law to hold the defendant liable to compensate the victim (remoteness of damage).

The latter of these will be the subject of section 4.7.

4.2 Causation in fact and the 'but for' test

The simplest proposition, and the effective starting point in establishing causation, is to say that the defendant will only be liable in negligence if the claimant would not have suffered the damage 'but for' the defendant's negligent act or omission.

The test was explained simply and precisely by Lord Denning in *Cork v Kirby MacLean Ltd* (1952):

'... if the damage would not have happened but for a particular fault, then that fault is the cause of the damage; if it would have happened just the same, fault or no fault, the fault is not the cause of the damage.'

In many cases the facts allow the test to operate simply and straightforwardly.

> ### Barnett v Chelsea & Kensington Hospital Management Committee (1969)
>
> Three night watchmen from a college went to the casualty ward of the hospital at around 5.00 a.m. on New Year's Day complaining of vomiting and stomach pains after drinking tea. The doctor on duty refused to attend to them and told them to call on their own doctors. A few hours later one of the men died, as it was discovered later, through arsenic poisoning. The hospital was not liable for the failure to treat, even though this was a clear breach of their duty, because it was shown that the man would not have recovered even with treatment.

However, the facts of a case will not necessarily always be straightforward, so there can be difficulties in establishing causation.

4.3 Problems in proving causation

Very often the problem is not purely one of fact, and the process of establishing cause is not so much scientific enquiry as attributing blame. Inevitably, interpretation of the factual evidence may still depend on the value judgments used by the court. For instance, a pedestrian runs on to the road into the path of an oncoming vehicle that is travelling over the speed limit for the area, and is injured. In purest scientific terms the cause of the accident is both parties being present on the road at the same time. It is possible in the circumstances to feel that the pedestrian has done as much as, if not more than, the motorist in causing his own injuries. Inevitably, however, even allowing for a successful claim of contributory negligence, the motorist would be held to have caused the victim's injuries, because he is blameworthy by exceeding the speed limit.

Greater problems may occur where the level of knowledge available to the court makes it impossible to pinpoint a precise cause. This may be particularly appropriate where medicine and medical technology is concerned.

> ### Wilsher v Essex Area Health Authority (1988)
>
> Here, the baby after delivery was given excess oxygen as a result of the admitted error of the doctor and then suffered blindness through retrolental fibroplasia. The House of Lords identified that the excess oxygen was just one of six possible causes of the condition and therefore it could not be said to fall squarely within the risk created by the defendants.

The difficulty of identifying precise cause means that the case law is often inconsistent. The risk, then, is that the decision will appear on the surface to be unfair to the claimant. This again is common where the chance of recovery may have been lost through negligence in medical treatment or diagnosis.

> ### Hotson v East Berkshire Area Health Authority (1987)
>
> A young boy suffered a fractured hip when he fell out of a tree. The hospital negligently delayed a correct diagnosis so that he later developed avuncular necrosis, a deformity of the hip. It was shown that he would have had a 75% chance of the deformity even without the failure to diagnose promptly and the Court of Appeal awarded him 25% of the damages they would have considered appropriate. The House of Lords allowed the Health Authority's appeal and would not consider the slim chance of recovery an issue of causation.

The House of Lords has recently reviewed the law on 'loss of a chance'.

Gregg v Scott (2005)

The claimant had a lump under his arm but his GP wrongly diagnosed it as harmless fatty tissue. The claimant, in considerable pain, then saw another GP nine months later. He was referred to hospital for tests and diagnosed with cancer of the lymph glands which by this time had spread considerably. It was shown that if his condition had been diagnosed by the first GP and treatment started then he would have had a 42% chance of being alive and disease-free in 10 years, whereas as a result of the delay his chances were reduced to 25%. The House of Lords, on a split decision 3:2, followed *Hotson* and refused to award the claimant a proportion of what he would have recovered if the doctor's negligence had in fact caused his premature death.

The reverse possibility is that the court accepts the chance of a causative link between the defendant's acts and the damage, and risks the possibility of unfairly penalising the defendant.

McGhee v National Coal Board (1973)

Here, the claimant worked in a brick kiln where he was exposed to brick dust, a possible cause of the dermatitis he contracted. The Board was not liable for exposure during working hours. They were held liable for increasing the risk of contracting the disease because of their failure to provide washing facilities, even though it could not be shown that he would have avoided the disease if there had been any.

The problems that the courts have in determining cause can be added to by being asked also to decide the possible outcomes of hypothetical situations.

Bolitho v City and Hackney Health Authority (1997)

The doctor here argued that, even if she had attended the child with the breathing difficulties, she would not have intubated and thus the same damage would have occurred. The House of Lords rejected the idea that the Bolam test should be applied to the issue of causation in order that the Health Authority should escape liability.

Nevertheless, there are occasions where the courts appear to take a pragmatic approach where proof of causation is difficult.

Bonnington Castings Ltd v Wardlaw (1956)

The claimant contracted pneumoconiosis after years of working in dusty conditions and without adequate washing facilities. There were two principal causes of dust, the one requiring no extraction system and the other which did, but no extractor was provided. It was impossible to prove accurately which dust the claimant had inhaled most of. Since the dust which should have been extracted legally was at least a partial cause of his illness, the court was prepared to award compensation.

The courts are also at times prepared to accept the chance of a causal connection with the damage, or the chance of damage being avoided without the defendant's negligent act or omission.

Stovold v Barlows (1995)

It was claimed that a house sale was lost through the negligence of the solicitors. The Court of Appeal felt that there was at least a 50% chance that the deal would otherwise have gone through and so awarded half damages.

Equally, courts have been prepared to place too much emphasis on a single cause out of a number of possibilities, leading to unfair treatment of the claimant.

Fairchild v Glenhaven Funeral Services Ltd and others (2001)

Claimants suffered mesothelioma after exposure to asbestos dust over many years working for a number of different employees. While medical evidence identified that inhaling of asbestos fibres was the cause of the disease, in which particular employment the disease was contracted was impossible to say. The Court of Appeal took the view that even a single asbestos fibre could initiate the disease and held that the precise employer responsible could not be identified and so the claim was rejected. It is impossible to say with certainty how the disease begins, but it is possible to identify that prolonged exposure worsens the risk. It seems that the CA applied *Wilsher* inappropriately where *McGhee* would have been more fairly applied. Subsequently in any case the House of Lords has reversed the CA decision.

However, sometimes judges will simply ignore the problems associated with applying the 'but for' test in order to give a just result.

Chester v Afshar (2004)

The claimant, who suffered from back pain, was persuaded to have an operation by a doctor who failed to warn her of a 1–2% risk of nerve damage and paralysis. The operation was not carried out negligently but the claimant did suffer nerve

damage. The claimant argued that she would not have had the operation at that time if she had been warned of the risk, although she probably would have had it at a later stage. Despite the fact that she may still have suffered damage if she had had the operation at a later stage, the House of Lords held that the failure to warn was the cause of the damage.

4.4 The problem of multiple causes

The problem of proving a causal link between the defendant's negligent act and the damage is always made more difficult where there is the possibility of more than one cause. Multiple causes can arise generally in one of two types of circumstances.

4.4.1 Multiple concurrent causes

If the damage is caused by multiple causes that are acting concurrently, then the 'but for' test appears to be incapable of providing an absolute test of causation. The case law demonstrates the difficulties faced by the courts.

The court may decide that the negligence has 'materially increased the risk' (*Fairchild v Glenhaven Funeral Services Ltd and others* (2002)) and that the defendant should therefore be liable for damages.

McGhee v National Coal Board (1973)

Here, as we have already seen, the court was prepared to make the employer liable for the dermatitis suffered by the worker in the brick kiln. It did so because it considered that the risk of the particular damage occurring had been materially increased, even though it was impossible to pinpoint the lack of washing facilities as the exact cause of the condition.

Where the courts use this 'material contribution' test it can be difficult, in any case, determining the exact extent of the defendant's contribution leading to some strange and apparently arbitrary decisions.

Holtby v Brigham & Cowan (Hull) Ltd (2000)

Here, the claimant had been exposed to asbestos dust for more than 40 years working for different employers. When he contracted asbestosis he sued the defendants for whom he had only worked for half that time. The trial judge reduced damages by 25%. The claimant appealed, using *McGhee*, that once having established material contribution by the defendants he was entitled to full damages. The Court of Appeal rejected his argument and upheld the trial judge's award, even though 50% deduction would have seemed more accurate. *McGhee* was distinguished.

In comparison, where there is a number of possible concurrent causes of the damage, and it is impossible to identify the specific one causing the damage, then it is unlikely that the court will hold one cause ultimately responsible.

Wilsher v Essex Area Health Authority (1988)

Here, the court identified that there were at least five other possible causes of the baby's blindness, thus the claimant could not establish the necessary causal link with the defendant's negligence.

4.4.2 Multiple consecutive causes

Where causes leading to the loss or damage suffered come one after the other, then ordinarily the liability will remain with the first event unless subsequent events have added to the damage. The 'but for' test will be applied to the original defendant.

Performance Cars Ltd v Abraham (1962)

The defendant negligently collided with a Rolls-Royce car. When the Rolls was later negligently struck by another car this did not relieve the original defendant of liability for a re-spray that had, in any case, been made necessary by the first collision.

However, a court, in determining where liability lies in the case of consecutive causes, has inevitably at times been influenced by the desire to avoid in any way undercompensating the victim.

Baker v Willoughby (1970)

The claimant was knocked down by a car and suffered a permanent stiff leg as a result. He was then forced to take work on a reduced income. At a later time he was shot in the injured leg during an armed robbery, causing it to need amputation. The House of Lords rejected the driver's claim that he was then only liable for damages up to the point of the amputation. The loss of earnings was a permanent state of affairs and had resulted from the original injury. The armed robbery and amputation of the leg had not altered this fact.

Nevertheless, the picture is even less straightforward because the courts have also, at times, been keen to ensure that the victim is not overcompensated at the expense of the defendant.

Jobling v Associated Dairies (1982)

In 1973, and as a result of his employer's negligence, the claimant slipped on the floor of a refrigerator in his employer's butcher's shop, injuring his back and losing 50% of his earning capacity as a result. Then, in 1976, he developed spondylotic myelopathy, a crippling back disorder unrelated to the fall. The defendant employer was liable for damages only up to the condition developing in 1976. While not overruled, *Baker* was heavily criticised in the case.

The fact that the courts are prepared to consider the impact that future foreseeable tortious acts may have on termination of the claimant's employment is yet another source of complication.

Heil v Rankin (2000)

Here, a police officer who suffered post-traumatic stress disorder following a car crash was discharged from the police force. The court held that it was a foreseeable consequence of such employment that he would, at some point, suffer another foreseeable event that might cause his retirement from the force, and that they were entitled to take this into account when assessing damages.

The House of Lords has recently accepted that in certain circumstances where there are a number of defendants all contributing to the same basic injury, then a modified approach to causation has to be taken.

Fairchild v Glenhaven Funeral Services Ltd and others (2002)

This is a major case involving three joined appeals. They all concerned employees who had contracted mesothelioma as a result of prolonged exposure to asbestos dust with a number of different employers. Because of the difficulty of identifying during which employment the disease was actually contracted, the Court of Appeal rejected the claims. The House of Lords accepted that it is scientifically uncertain whether inhaling a single fibre or inhalation of many fibres causes the disease, so it is impossible to say accurately which employer caused the disease. However, because it is evident that the greater the exposure to the dust, the greater the chances of the disease occurring, then each employer has a duty to take reasonable care to prevent employees from inhaling the dust. Besides this, any other cause of developing the diseases could be ignored in the case. On the basis that the claimants suffered the very injuries that the defendants were supposed to guard against, the House of Lords was prepared to impose liability on all employers. Applying the 'material risk' test from *McGhee*, all of the defendants had contributed to a risk of mesothelioma, and no distinction should be drawn between making a material risk of causing the disease and materially increasing the risk of the disease.

However, the House of Lords has recently modified the principle, leading to even more confusion.

Barker v Corus; Murray v British Shipbuilders (Hydromatics) Ltd; Patterson v Smiths Dock Ltd and Others (2006)

In three joined appeals, one appellant, Barker, died from mesothelioma after exposure to asbestos fibres during three different periods. One period was in the defendant's employment, one in different employment and one while self-employed. The defendant argued that causation could not be proved since the disease might have been contracted during the self-employment. Alternatively, the defendant argued that damages should be apportioned. The House of Lords held that the defendant could be liable only for the share of damages equivalent to the share of the risk of contracting mesothelioma created by his breach of duty, and apportioned damages accordingly. This clearly contradicts *Fairchild*. Special rules were later put in place for mesothelioma victims in the Compensation Act 2006 which reverses the decision in their case only.

Activity

Self-assessment questions

1. What is the difference between causation in fact and causation in law?

2. How does the 'but for' test work?

3. In what ways is causation a problem to a claimant trying to prove medical negligence?

4. What, exactly, is the effect of the judgment in *Hotson v East Berkshire Area Health Authority*?

5. What is the difference in the judgments in *McGhee* and in *Wilsher*?

6. What effect has the case of *Fairchild v Glenhaven Funeral Services* had on proving causation in fact?

7. How do courts react when there are multiple causes for the damage suffered?

8. How do the courts react when the claimant has a pre-existing condition?

9. What is the justification for the decision in *Performance Cars v Abraham*?

10. Why, exactly, are *Baker v Willoughby* and *Jobling v Associated Dairies* decided differently?

11. Do these two judgments represent fair results to both claimants and defendants?

12. In what ways does the case of *Heil v Rankin* cause complications?

Key Facts

- A defendant may be liable in negligence if 'but for' his act or omission the damage would not have occurred (*Barnett v Chelsea & Kensington Hospital Management Committee*).
- It may be difficult at times to prove causation, and courts will not impose liability where the cause is uncertain (*Wilsher v Essex AHA*).
- Courts are very reluctant to base liability on loss of a chance (*Hotson v East Berks AHA*).
- Where there are multiple causes, the court may feel that the defendant's act has materially increased the risk (*McGhee v National Coal Board*).
- Where there are multiple consecutive causes the liability remains with the first defendant, unless the later cause increased the damage (*Performance Cars v Abraham*).
- However, the courts are careful not to undercompensate or to overcompensate (*Baker v Willoughby* and *Jobling v Associated Dairies*).
- However, where a number of defendants all contribute to the risk of harm, no distinction should be drawn between creating a material risk of causing the disease and materially increasing the risk of the disease in determining liability (*Fairchild v Glenhaven Funeral Services and others*).

4.5 *Novus actus interveniens*

4.5.1 Breaking the chain of causation

Even though the defendant can be identified as negligent and the 'but for' test satisfied in some senses, the chain of causation may be broken by a subsequent intervening act. If the court accepts that this intervening act is the true cause of the damage suffered, then the defendant may not be liable despite his/her breach of duty.

Such a plea by the defendant is known as *novus actus interveniens*. Translated it means 'a new act intervenes', and it is an effective defence. If, however, the intervening act is not accepted by the court as being the true cause of the damage, then the chain is unbroken and the defendant remains liable for his/her breach.

Kirkham v Chief Constable of Greater Manchester (1990)

Police who had transferred a prisoner to Risley remand centre had failed to inform the authorities there that the prisoner was a known suicide risk.

When the prisoner did, in fact, commit suicide the police were held liable for their failure to warn the prison authorities. Their plea of *novus actus interveniens* by the prisoner failed, since he was suffering from clinical depression, not in full control, and therefore the suicide was not as such a voluntary act.

The area is full of difficulties and the possibility of the plea succeeding is entirely dependent on the facts of the individual case. The case law seems, however, to fall into three definable categories.

4.5.2 An intervening act of the claimant

This is very closely connected with contributory negligence. Unlike contributory negligence, however, the plea here is that the claimant is actually responsible for his/her own damage and therefore the chain of causation is broken and the defendant has no liability at all.

McKew v Holland & Hannen & Cubitts (Scotland) Ltd (1969)

The claimant suffered an injury to his leg, leaving it seriously weakened, as a result of the defendants' negligence. When he later tried to climb a steep flight of steps with no handrail without asking for help, he fell and suffered further serious injuries. The defendants were not liable for this fall. The claimant's act was a *novus actus interveniens*.

However, if the defendant's original breach is still the operating cause of the later damage and the claimant was not acting unreasonably, then the plea that the chain of causation is broken will fail.

Wieland v Cyril Lord Carpets Ltd (1969)

Mrs Wieland suffered an injury following the defendant's negligence, causing her to have to wear a surgical collar. She wore bifocals and wearing the collar restricted her head movement and meant her use of her spectacles was also seriously impaired. When she then fell down a flight of stairs and sustained further injuries the defendants were liable for those injuries. There was no break in the chain of causation. The risk to Mrs Wieland in the circumstances was said to be foreseeable. The obvious difference with the last case was that the claimant did nothing unreasonable.

So, providing the claimant's actions are reasonable there will not necessarily be a break in the chain of causation.

Lord v Pacific Steam Navigation Co. Ltd (The Oropesa) (1943)

Here, through the negligence of those sailing the Oropesa, another ship was damaged in a collision between the two. The captain of the other ship and some crew members then put to sea in a lifeboat to consult with the captain of the Oropesa as to what to do to save their ship. Some of the sailors drowned. The Court of Appeal held that the decision to take out the lifeboat was perfectly reasonable in the circumstances and so there was no break in the chain of causation.

It will not be a *novus actus interveniens* of the claimant himself if the alleged intervening act is one that the defendant was under a duty to prevent.

Reeves v Commissioner of the Metropolitan Police (1999)

Here, police were holding a prisoner who was a known suicide risk. When the prisoner did commit suicide, while the police accepted that they owed the claimant a duty of care, they nevertheless denied liability arguing a *novus actus interveniens* by the claimant himself. The court rejected the argument as the suicide was the specific act that the police should have been seeking to prevent.

4.5.3 An intervening act of nature

A plea that an act of nature has broken the chain of causation will rarely succeed. The reason is that the claimant in this instance is then left without any means of gaining a remedy for the wrong suffered.

However, the defendant might be relieved of

liability in those situations where (s)he can show that the act of nature (s)he argues is breaking the chain of causation is unforeseeable and independent of his/her own negligence.

Carslogie Steamship Co. v Royal Norwegian Government (1952)

The claimant's ship was damaged following a collision with a vessel of the defendant's navy and through the defendant's fault. After a delay for repairs the ship then embarked on a voyage it would not otherwise have taken. On that voyage it suffered further damage in a heavy storm. The argument that the defendant should be liable for this damage also failed. The storm was a genuine break in the chain of causation.

4.5.4 An intervening act of a third party

In order to succeed with a plea of *novus actus interveniens* in these circumstances the defendant must show that the act of the third party was negligent and is of such magnitude that it does, in fact, break the chain of causation.

Knightley v Johns (1982)

The defendant, through negligent driving, crashed and blocked a tunnel. The police officer in charge at the scene then negligently sent a police officer against the flow of traffic to block off the tunnel at the other end. The defendant was not liable for the injuries sustained by this policeman. They were the fault of the other police officer.

Furthermore, the consequences of the third party's act must be foreseeable.

Lamb v Camden London Borough Council (1981)

Here, the defendant council negligently broke a water main as a result of which the claimants' house suffered water damage and the claimants had to move out. While the claimants were out of the house, squatters moved in and caused much more damage. The council was not liable for the further damage. The actions of the squatters were a *novus actus interveniens*. It was not foreseeable.

Also, the defendant must not have any duty to guard against such an act.

Ward v Cannock Chase District Council (1986)

Here, the defendant council negligently allowed a house to fall into general disrepair. The house adjoined the claimants' house. When they were forced to move out of their house vandals and thieves broke in and damaged it. The council had failed to make proper repairs and act quickly enough in repairing the house next door. This meant that acts of vandalism were almost inevitable. There was no *novus actus interveniens* and the council was liable.

Nevertheless, it is possible that in such circumstances both the defendant and the third party have, in fact, contributed to the damage caused, and will be held individually liable accordingly.

Rouse v Squires (1973)

The defendant driver negligently caused an accident on a motorway in which many vehicles were involved. Another driver then negligently collided with some of the stationary vehicles from the first incident, killing the claimant. Despite the obvious responsibility of the later driver, the chain of causation was held not to be broken. The damage in the second incident was held to be a foreseeable consequence of the first and the first driver was held to be 25% responsible for the death of the claimant.

Activity

Self-assessment questions

1. What, exactly, does the phrase *novus actus interveniens* mean?

2. What are the necessary requirements for a successful claim of *novus actus interveniens* by a defendant?

3. What is the difference between a plea of *novus actus interveniens* and one of contributory negligence?

4. What are the three types of *novus actus*?

5. Which is the least likely to be successful?

6. What happens to the claimant's claim when the defence proves successful?

Key Facts

- A defendant will not be liable where there is a *novus actus interveniens* (a new act intervening).
- This is because the 'chain of causation' is broken.
- An intervening act could be one of three types:
  - an intervening act of the claimant (*McKew v Holland & Hannen & Cubitts*)
  - an intervening act of nature (*Carslogie Steamship Co. v Royal Norwegian Government*)
  - an intervening act of a third party (*Knightley v Johns*).
- There will be no break in the chain of causation where the intervening event is reasonable and foreseeable (*Lord v Pacific Steam Navigation Co. Ltd (The Oropesa)*).
- Nor will there be a break in the chain where the defendant was under a duty to prevent the act that is alleged to have broken the chain of causation (*Reeves v Commissioner of the Metropolitan Police*).

4.6 Contributory negligence and *volenti non fit injuria*

4.6.1 Introduction

Causation also needs to be considered when determining whether or not the claimant has either accepted a risk of harm and voluntarily taken it, or has otherwise contributed to his or her own damage by taking insufficient care for his or her own safety. In this way, a claimant who takes part in sporting activities, particularly in the case of a contact sport, may have voluntarily assumed the risk of injury by taking part and being aware of the nature of the sport. Similarly, in the case of road traffic accidents there may be contributory negligence, for instance where the claimant has failed to wear a seat belt, or in the case of an accident involving a motorbike where the claimant failed to wear a crash helmet.

If, on the other hand, the claimant has contributed so much to the damage suffered as to be entirely responsible, then this will probably result in a successful plea of *novus actus interveniens*.

4.6.2 *Volenti non fit injuria*

Volenti non fit injuria is a complete defence, unlike contributory negligence which only reduces damages. The defence succeeds because there is a voluntary assumption of the risk of harm by the claimant, and a simple translation would be that no injury is done to one who freely consents to the risk.

So, some judges incline to the view that the defence succeeds because there is an express or implied agreement between the defendant and the claimant. However, certain judges believe that the defence can still succeed where the claimant has come upon a danger that has already been created by the defendant.

To succeed, the defendant would have to show three things:

- knowledge of the precise risk involved
- exercise of free choice by the claimant
- a voluntary acceptance of the risk.

So it is not sufficient merely that the claimant has knowledge of the existence of the risk. The defence is *volenti non fit injuria* and not *scienti non fit injuria*. The claimant must fully understand the precise nature of the actual risk and be prepared to run it.

Stermer v Lawson (1977)

The claimant borrowed the defendant's motorbike but was not shown how to use it, so did not appreciate the risks involved. The defendant's claim of *volenti* failed as a result.

Similarly, the risk must be freely taken for the defence to succeed. There will be no defence where the claimant had no choice but to accept the risk.

Smith v Baker (1891)

The claimant drilled rock in a quarry bottom. He was injured when a crane moved rocks over his head and some fell on him. *Volenti* failed in the case because the worker was given no proper warning of when the crane was in use and so was unaware of the danger. He was aware of the risk of stones falling, but there was no voluntary assumption of risk in the circumstances.

If the claimant's behaviour is such that he or she need not have been in any danger then *volenti* is clearly a possibility.

ICI Ltd v Shatwell (1965)

The claimant and his brother were quarry workers. The claimant, following his brother's instructions, ignored his employer's instructions on the handling of detonators and was injured when one exploded. His claim of vicarious liability by the quarry failed. By ignoring his employers and listening to his brother's unauthorised comments he had assumed the risk of injury voluntarily.

Before the defence can be applied successfully it must be shown that the defendant did in fact commit a tort.

Wooldridge v Sumner (1963)

The claimant attended a horse show as a professional photographer. A rider who was riding too fast lost control of the horse which then injured the claimant. The Court of Appeal recognised that the rider owed spectators a duty of care. Nevertheless, they considered that he had been guilty of an error of judgment in his riding of the horse, but not negligence. He had not breached his duty, so *volenti* was not an issue.

The test of *volenti* is a subjective rather than an objective one. It will not help the defendant to argue that the claimant ought to have been aware of the risk. The defence only applies where the claimant does actually know of the risk.

Nevertheless, where a defence of *volenti* may fail for just such a reason, the defendant may still be able to successfully claim contributory negligence and at least reduce the amount of damages that are payable.

4.6.3 Contributory negligence

Contributory negligence was originally a complete defence so that no damages at all were payable if the defence succeeded.

Butterfield v Forester (1809)

Here, the defendant obstructed a road by placing a pole across it. The claimant was injured when his horse collided with the pole while he was violently riding the horse. It was held that the claimant had contributed to his own harm. Taking proper care would have avoided the accident and he was unable to claim any damages.

In the nineteenth century this was particularly harsh on people sustaining injuries while at work.

The Law Reform (Contributory Negligence) Act 1945 changed the nature of the rule so that damages could be altered according to the extent to which the claimant had contributed to his or her own harm. Damages will then be reduced proportionately according to the degree that the claimant contributed to his/her own harm.

Sayers v Harlow Urban District Council (1958)

A lady became trapped in a public lavatory when, through negligent maintenance, the door lock became jammed. She then stood on the toilet roll holder in an effort to climb out of the cubicle. She had to catch a bus so it was reasonable for her to try to get out in the circumstances, and so her act did not break the chain of causation. The council was liable but the damages were reduced by 25% because of the careless manner in which she tried to get out.

The defence has become a common aspect of claims for injuries or damage sustained in road traffic accidents, so that damages can be reduced where a motor cycle passenger fails to take the precaution of wearing a crash helmet.

O'Connell v Jackson (1972)

Here, it was acknowledged that the passenger received much greater injuries because of not wearing a crash helmet, so damages were reduced accordingly.

The defence is also commonly applied to passengers of motor cars who fail to wear seat belts as required by law.

Froom v Butcher (1976)

Again, the passenger suffered greater injuries than would have been the case if wearing a seat belt. Damages were reduced as a result.

A successful claim of contributory negligence depends on the defendant showing that the claimant has been negligent himself and is therefore partly to blame. This will mean that use of the defence, just as in negligence, depends on showing that the behaviour of the claimant meant that harm was foreseeable.

Jones v Livox Quarries Ltd (1952)

The claimant was employed in a quarry and, in defiance of his employer's express instructions, rode on the rear towbar of a 'traxcavator'. The driver was unaware of the claimant and, when another vehicle collided with it the claimant was injured. His damages were reduced by 5%. Lord Denning stated that:

'A person is guilty of contributory negligence if he ought reasonably to have foreseen that, if he did not act as a reasonable, prudent man, he might be hurt himself; and in his reckonings he must take into account the possibility of others being careless'.

Activity

Self-assessment questions

1. What would a defendant have to prove about a claimant for a defence of *volenti* to succeed?

2. Why was the case of *ICI v Shatwell* decided the way it was?

3. What are the basic differences between the defences of *volenti* and contributory negligence?

4. What is the effect of a successful plea of contributory negligence?

5. Why, exactly, did the claimant fail in *Livox*?

6. Why is the defence of contributory negligence so commonplace in road traffic accidents?

Activity   *Quick Quiz*

In the following situations, say which defence would apply, if at all, and why.

♦ Mohammed was injured when he went for a flight in a light aeroplane with Pierre, who he knows does not have a pilot's licence

♦ Helga fell off a horse and was badly injured during a show jumping contest when the horse pulled up at a large fence.

- A defendant will not be liable where there is a voluntary assumption of risk.
- So, for the defence to succeed there must be:
  - knowledge of precise risk involved
  - exercise of free choice by claimant
  - voluntary acceptance of the risk (*Smith v Baker*).

- Damages may be reduced where there is contributory negligence (Law Reform (Contributory Negligence) Act 1945).
- The defendant must show that:
  - the claimant has failed to take reasonable care of himself and
  - this caused the injury or damage (*Sayers v Harlow UDC*).

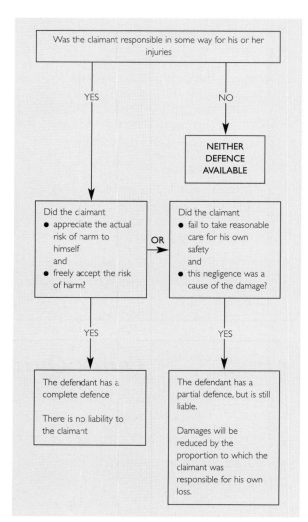

Figure 2 *Flow chart illustrating the availability of defences of volenti non fit injuria and contributory negligence and contrasting their effects*

4.7 Causation in law and testing remoteness of damage

4.7.1 The tests of remoteness

The final element of proof in negligence is whether there is causation in law, otherwise known as remoteness of damage. Even though a causal link can be proved factually according to the 'but for' test, the claimant may still be prevented from winning the case if the damage suffered is too remote a consequence of the defendant's breach of duty.

The test is a matter of law rather than fact and, like other aspects of negligence, is much influenced by policy considerations. The principal justification for the rule is that the defendant should not be overburdened by compensating for damage linked to the breach which is of a kind that is unlikely or unforeseeable.

The original test of remoteness, however, was that the claimant could recover in respect of a loss that was a direct consequence of the defendant's breach, regardless of how foreseeable.

Re Polemis and Furness, Withy & Co. (1921)

Charterers of a ship filled the hold with containers of benzine that then leaked during the voyage, filling the hold with vapour. In port the ship was being unloaded when a stevedore negligently dropped a plank into the hold. A spark then ignited the vapours and the ship was destroyed. The arbitrator held that this was too unlikely a consequence of dropping the plank, though some damage was of course foreseeable. The Court of Appeal held that the charterers, as employers of the stevedores, were liable. Scrutton LJ stated that:

'if the act would or might probably cause damage, the fact that the damage it in fact causes is not the exact kind of damage one would expect is immaterial, so long as the damage is in fact directly traceable to the negligent act.'

The test was then criticised for its failure to distinguish between degrees of negligence. As a result, the test was later changed to one of liability only for damage that was a reasonably foreseeable consequence of the breach.

Overseas Tankship (UK) Ltd v Morts Dock & Engineering Co. (The Wagon Mound (No. 1)) (1961)

Due to the defendant's negligence, bunkering oil was leaked into Sydney Harbour from a tanker. The oil floated on the water to the claimant's wharf, mixing with various flotsam and jetsam, including patches of cotton wadding. Welding was taking place in the wharf and the claimant's manager enquired whether there was a risk of the oil igniting. This was considered unlikely since the oil had an extremely high flash point. Welding then continued and sparks did, in fact, ignite the oil-soaked wadding and then set fire to ships being repaired in the wharf. The oil also caused fouling to the wharf. The trial judge held that, since some damage, the fouling, was foreseeable, the defendants were liable also for the fire damage which was a direct consequence of their breach of duty in allowing the spillage. The Privy Council reversed this decision, holding that the defendant could not be liable for the fire damage since the correct test for remoteness was reasonable foreseeability and, because of the improbability of the oil igniting, the fire damage was unforeseeable.

4.7.2 Applying the 'reasonable foreseeability' test

The critical element of the test is foreseeability of the general rather than the specific type of damage. It is not therefore necessary for the full extent of the damage to be foreseen.

Bradford v Robinson Rentals (1967)

The claimant suffered frostbite when sent on a long journey by his employers in severe winter weather in a van without a working heater. The defendants argued that the type of damage was too remote and unforeseeable. The court disagreed. It was certainly foreseeable that some cold-related illness was a possibility. It was immaterial that the actual damage was frostbite and the defendants were held liable.

It is not, therefore, necessary for the defendant to have contemplated the precise consequences of the negligent act or omission provided he or she is aware of the possibility of damage resulting.

Margereson v J W Roberts Ltd (1996)

The court in this case considered that the owner of an asbestos works should have been aware of the dangers of inhaling asbestos dust even in 1933. In consequence it was prepared to impose liability in respect of mesothelioma contracted by children who played in dust from the factory collecting in and around the entrance to the factory.

Neither is it necessary, when the defendant is negligent, for the precise consequences of the act or omission to be foreseen when damage is a foreseeable consequence.

Hughes v The Lord Advocate (1963)

Post Office employees negligently left a manhole uncovered inside a tent and the tent unattended. They left four lit paraffin lamps at the corners of the tent. A boy entered the tent with a lamp and when it fell into the hole there was an explosion, the boy fell in also and was burnt. This was an unlikely chain of events, but the defendants were nevertheless liable since some fire-related damage was a foreseeable consequence of leaving the scene unattended.

Nor will it matter that the damage is actually more extensive than might have been foreseeable, provided that the kind of damage itself is foreseeable.

Vacwell Engineering Co Ltd v BDH Chemicals Ltd (1971)

Here, the defendants were the suppliers of a chemical product to the claimants. The defendants negligently failed to warn the claimants that the chemical would explode on contact with water. When one of the claimant's scientists did expose the chemical to water there was an alarming explosion causing very extensive damage. The defendants were liable even though the resultant damage to property was far more severe than might have been foreseen.

The 'thin skull' rule will also apply, so that the defendant will be liable for the full extent of the damage if damage of the type is foreseeable.

Smith v Leech Brain & Co. Ltd (1962)

An employee suffered a burnt lip following his employers' negligence. He later died from cancer which had developed following the burn. His lip had actually been in a pre-malignant state at the time of the burn. Harm from the burn was foreseeable, though death from cancer was not, but the defendants were liable.

The test of reasonable foreseeability and claims for personal injury

In general cases, such as the above seem to indicate that the courts take a fairly broad view of what is reasonably foreseeable in the event that the damage suffered is personal injury.

Jolley v London Borough of Sutton (2000)

A council failed to move an abandoned boat for two years. It was well known that children played in the boat and it was a clear danger. A boy of 14 was hurt when he and a friend tried to repair the boat. The Court of Appeal felt that the course of action taken by the boys, and thus the specific type of damage, were not foreseeable. The House of Lords disagreed. The boat was dangerous; it was quite foreseeable that children coming into contact with the boat might suffer some kind of harm.

Nevertheless, there are occasions when the court has taken a narrower view and this appears on the surface to work unfairly on the claimant.

Tremain v Pike (1969)

The claimant, a herdsman, suffered Weil's disease. This is a rare disease contracted only through contact with rats' urine. This, he said, happened when he worked with hay and washed with water that was contaminated with rats' urine. It was accepted that the defendant had allowed the rat population on his farm to grow too large, and that there was some risk of damage from rats. Nevertheless, the defendant was not held liable since the court considered that the disease was so rare in humans that it was unforeseeable.

On occasions it also appears that the test in *Hughes* can be contradicted if the court focuses too closely on the circumstances in which the damage occurs.

Doughty v Turner Manufacturing Co. Ltd (1964)

Here, due to negligence, a cover over a cauldron of heated sodium cyanide was allowed to slide into the liquid. The cover was made of asbestos compound. There was a chemical explosion and the claimant was burned. It was previously unknown that there would be such a chemical reaction between the asbestos and the sodium cyanide and the Court of Appeal held that the defendants were not liable. The chemical reaction was unforeseeable and the damage was thus too remote. However, there certainly seems to be merit in the claimant's argument that damage from the liquid if splashed would be foreseeable.

The test of reasonable foreseeability and claims for property damage

However, judges also apply policy in deciding on reasonable foreseeability.

Corr v IBC Vehicles Ltd (2006)

An employee was badly injured because of his employer's negligence and then suffered post-traumatic stress disorder, resulting in his suicide. The Court of Appeal accepted that depression was a foreseeable consequence of the original negligence and, since suicide is not uncommon in cases of depression, this was also foreseeable, leading to liability.

With the exception of cases such as *Tremain* and *Doughty*, the courts in general appear to adopt a narrower approach to what is foreseeable when the damage in question is to property rather than being personal injury.

Overseas Tankship (UK) Ltd v Morts Dock & Engineering Co. (The Wagon Mound (No. 1)) (1961)

The trial judge acknowledged that some damage was foreseeable in the circumstances. The type of damage that was foreseeable, though, was fouling by the oil, not fire. However, since he believed the fouling was foreseeable he held that the fire damage was also a direct consequence of the defendant's negligence.

Even degree of risk of the type of damage actually caused has been considered narrowly, thus avoiding imposing liability.

Overseas Tankship (UK) Ltd v Miller Steamship Co. Pty (The Wagon Mound (No. 2)) (1967)

The owners of the two ships that were being repaired in the wharf and were damaged in the fire brought this case. The trial judge showed a very narrow approach to foreseeability in relation to an action for property damage. While he accepted, unlike the trial judge in *Wagon Mound (No. 1)* that fire was a foreseeable consequence of the defendants' negligence, he nevertheless felt that it was so remote as to not give rise to any liability. He was reversed by the Privy Council which held that, provided the type of damage was foreseeable, liability must result, and the degree of likelihood is irrelevant.

4.7.3 Points for discussion

It is difficult in some ways to see a real difference between the test based on direct consequences and the test based on reasonable foreseeability. In many instances certainly, damage that is reasonably foreseeable will also be a direct consequence of the defendant's breach. It is similarly difficult to contemplate situations that are totally unforeseeable and yet are still a direct consequence.

Besides this, the difference may well be unimportant. The effect of the 'thin skull' rule is to compensate many victims for damage that the defendant will probably not have contemplated at all. On top of this, many areas of quite remote damage are in any case within the scope of insurance, and so a claimant may still gain some form of compensation.

Activity

Self-assessment questions

1. What are judges trying to achieve with the rule on remoteness of damage?

2. When, precisely, will damage be too remote to be compensated?

3. How does the *Wagon Mound* test differ from that in *Re Polemis*?

4. How, exactly, is reasonable foreseeability measured; in other words, what has to be foreseen?

5. Do the attitudes of the courts generally vary according to the type of damage caused?

6. To what extent are the judgments in *Doughty v Turner Manufacturing* and *Hughes v The Lord Advocate* consistent?

7. What is the effect of a claimant's peculiar sensitivities on the issue of remoteness of damage?

- At one time a defendant was liable for all damage that was a direct consequence of his negligent act or omission (*Re Polemis and Furness, Withy & Co.*).
- Now, the modern test is one of liability for reasonably foreseeable damage (*The Wagon Mound*).
- Only the general, not the actual type of damage needs to be foreseen (*Bradford v Robinson Rentals*).
- Nor do the precise consequences of the negligent act or omission have to be foreseen (*Hughes v The Lord Advocate*).
- The 'thin skull' rule applies (*Smith v Leech Brain*).
- The courts generally, but not always, seem to take a broader view of remoteness in personal injury cases than they do with property damage.

In the Dilemma Board below, consider the accuracy of each of the four statements, A, B, C and D, as they apply to the facts in the central scenario. You only need to give the basic principles. The answer is in the Appendix at the end of the book.

Dilemma Board

Ralph drives his car at 90 miles per hour, at night, on the wrong side of the road, in a dark country lane. Ralph collides with another car, being driven by Susie. Susie's passenger, Theo, is seriously injured in the collision. Susie and Theo were returning from a party where they had both drunk a large quantity of wine. Theo had accepted a lift even though he knew Susie was over the limit and should not be driving.

A.

Theo will have no claim for damages in negligence against Ralph as he does not owe him a duty of care and if he does then he is not in breach of his duty to him.

B.

Ralph will not be liable to Theo in negligence because he will be able to argue that there was a *novus actus interveniens* by Susie.

C.

Ralph may be liable in negligence for Theo's injuries but Ralph will be able to use the defence of *volenti non fit injuria* because Theo accepted a lift from Susie who he knew was unfit to drive.

D.

Ralph may be liable in negligence for Susie's injuries but Ralph will be able to use the defence of contributory negligence to reduce damages.

Chapter 5

Negligence: Proving Damage

5.1 Pleading *res ipsa loquitur*

One of the common threads throughout all law is the general maxim that 'he who accuses must prove'. In this way, the party claiming the negligence has the burden of proof and must show the defendant's breach of the duty of care. The burden of proof can work very harshly on a claimant who will be bound to collect all of the necessary evidence to show the negligence. This can be particularly difficult, for instance, in medical negligence cases where a mass of highly technical evidence may need to be produced.

There are certain rare circumstances in which this burden of proof can be made less demanding. The first of these is under the Civil Evidence Act 1968 by which, under s11, it is possible to introduce criminal convictions as evidence.

A second area that relaxes the burden of proof is an old common law maxim *res ipsa loquitur*. Literally translated, *res ipsa loquitur* means 'the thing speaks for itself'. So it is a mechanism whereby the claimant can be relieved of the burden of proving the negligence, and the court can infer negligence in those situations where the factual circumstances of the case would make proving it almost impossible.

5.2 The effects of the doctrine

There is some argument as to the exact means by which the principle works. In simple terms it is often explained as reversing the burden of proof, and in effect putting the burden on the defendant to prove that he or she was not negligent.

In *Wilsher v Essex Area Health Authority* (1988), on the other hand, it was suggested that the maxim does not in fact reverse the burden of proof. Here, it was suggested that invoking the maxim raises a *prima facie* presumption of negligence. The defendant is then required to rebut that presumption by the introduction of evidence to the contrary. Nevertheless, it was said that the burden remains throughout with the claimant. This, though, does not appear to be the standard view.

Whatever the precise mechanism is, it does at least give a claimant alleging negligence the opportunity to demand some contrary proof from the defendant in circumstances where the collection of evidence is difficult if not impossible.

Henderson v H E Jenkins & Sons (1970)

The claimant's husband was killed when the brakes of a lorry failed while it was on a steep hill. The defendants argued that this was to do with a latent defect causing corrosion in the brake pipes. This could only be detected on removing the pipes, which was a practice not recommended by the manufacturers. The court would not accept this as sufficient rebuttal of the claimant's inference of negligence. The defendants should have gone on to show that there was nothing else in the vehicle's history that could account for the corrosion. So the defendants were required to prove that they were not negligent and had failed to do so.

Inevitably, the effect of the maxim can be equally harsh on the defendant, so the maxim is very narrowly construed and it will only be considered as appropriate if the facts of a case fit specific criteria laid down by the courts.

Scott v London and St Katherine's Dock Co. (1865)

Here, the claimant was standing outside the defendant's warehouse when several large bags of sugar fell on him. There was little or no explanation for the incident and no evidence that anybody had been negligent. The trial judge initially found for the defendant since there was no proof of negligence. On appeal, the criteria for dealing with such claims were established.

5.3 The criteria for claiming *res ipsa loquitur*

There are three specific criteria for successfully pleading *res ipsa loquitur*:

- at all material times the thing causing harm must have been in the control of the defendant
- the incident is of a type that could only have been caused by negligence
- the cause of the incident is not known and there is no other obvious explanation for the incident.

1. The incident was in the control of the defendant

Inevitably, the defendant must be in control of the situation that has led to the damage or there can be no liability.

What falls within the defendant's control is a question of fact in each case, for the court to decide.

Gee v Metropolitan Railway Co. (1873)

A passenger leaned on a train door shortly after it left the station. The door opened and the passenger fell out and was injured. The defendants were responsible for ensuring that all doors were properly closed before the train left the station, so they were in control at the material time and were liable.

Clearly, in some cases circumstances may show that it would be unfair to suggest that the defendant had actual control.

Easson v London and North Eastern Railway (1944)

Here, a boy passenger fell through the door of a train when it was a long way from its last stop. It was possible that another passenger had opened the door. It was certainly felt to be impossible to say that the doors were under the control of the railway company throughout the journey and *res ipsa* could not apply.

It seems only fair that if the defendant is in control of the circumstances in which the damage occurred (s)he should be called on to give some explanation of the incident.

2. The incident is of a type usually associated with negligence

It is crucial also to show that the incident causing the damage is of a type that would not normally occur if proper care were taken. If this is so, then the incident can be seen as one of a type commonly caused by negligence. The absence of a reasonable explanation by the defendant means that it is reasonable to assume that the event occurred because of lack of care.

> ## Scott v London and St Katherine's Dock Co. (1865)
>
> Large bags of sugar are inanimate objects and it is unlikely that they could fall from a hoist without a lack of care being taken.

Res ipsa is often pleaded in medical negligence cases because the claimant is entitled to an explanation of how the damage occurred if not by negligence.

> ## Glass v Cambridge Health Authority (1995)
>
> A man with a normal healthy heart went into cardiac arrest while under a general anaesthetic. The maxim was held to have been appropriately pleaded in the case, although the Health Authority were able to introduce evidence to show why they had not been negligent.

In medical negligence cases the plea may often be used because the precise party responsible is unknown.

> ## Mahon v Osborne (1939)
>
> Here, after an operation a patient later died and a swab was found inside him. It was clear that the swab could not have been there but for negligence, although the person actually responsible could not be identified. Scott LJ, however, felt that some positive evidence of neglect of duty in the operation was needed in such cases.

The maxim in such cases may be used when the claim is that a particular body is vicariously liable for the acts of the tortfeasor.

> ## Ward v Tesco Stores Ltd (1976)
>
> A customer slipped on yoghurt that had been spilt on to the supermarket's floor. Tesco claimed that they had a procedure in place whereby the floors were cleaned regularly throughout the day and staff were instructed to stay with such spillages when they were found until they were cleaned. Nevertheless, the customer was also able to show evidence of other spillages that were not immediately cleaned up. The court accepted that such occurrences could only result from negligence.

3. There is no other explanation for the incident causing damage

The third and final criterion is that it is impossible to give any explanation of the incident. If the circumstances of the incident are capable of explanation by the claimant then the usual burden applies and the claimant should show how the facts prove negligence.

A claim of *res ipsa loquitur* can only apply because there are no other means available to explain the true cause of the incident. It is thus fairer in the circumstances to ask the defendant to introduce some evidence to rebut the presumption that negligence has occurred.

> ## Barkway v South Wales Transport Co. Ltd (1950)
>
> A bus mounted a pavement and resulted in injury to the claimant. A tyre had burst through a defect in the wall of the tyre that could not have been discovered earlier. *Res ipsa* was shown to be inappropriate, however, when it was discovered that

the bus company gave no instructions to drivers to report heavy blows suffered by the tyres. As a result, negligence could be shown and the defendants were liable.

5.4 *Res ipsa loquitur* and medical negligence

We have already seen that there is debate among the judiciary as to the proper role of the maxim in relation to medical negligence.

There is a strong argument to say that the maxim should always apply because the three criteria will generally be satisfied and the claimant may face a very difficult time gathering the appropriate evidence.

The courts have been reluctant to accept such widespread application of the maxim. The Pearson Report in 1978 also rejected general application because of the fear of an escalating number of claims, and the consequent rise in insurance premiums for medical staff.

5.5 Strict liability in negligence

Res ipsa was formerly very often used in cases involving foreign bodies in foodstuffs. Clearly, while it may be difficult to show how the material got there it is nevertheless something that should not happen if proper care is taken.

EU law is fairly explicit on such issues and has traditionally imposed stricter standards than English law. English law is now very much in line with European law since the passing of the Consumer Protection Act 1987, enacted to comply with EU directives. The Product Safety Directive has also subsequently been implemented in the form of regulations.

The Consumer Protection Act allows that any person within the chain of distribution of a product is strictly liable if a consumer suffers harm as the result of defects in the product.

While fault is, in a sense, abolished in the Act, causation is still an issue.

Activity

Self-assessment questions

1. *Res ipsa loquitur* means 'the thing speaks for itself', but what does this mean precisely, in relation to the incident in question?

2. What three elements must always be present for a judge to accept that the doctrine applies in the case?

3. To what extent is it accurate to speak of a reversal of the burden of proof?

4. What sorts of things indicate that the loss or damage suffered could only have been the result of negligence?

5. Why has the doctrine regularly been pleaded in medical negligence cases?

6. What is the effect of the doctrine in consumer protection law?

- *Res ipsa loquitur* means 'the thing speaks for itself'. It is a means of establishing negligence where proof is hard to come by.
- The doctrine, in effect, means that the defendant has to prove that he was not negligent if the plea is raised successfully.
- There are three essential aspects to the plea:
  - at all material times events leading to the damage were under the control of the defendant (*Gee v Metropolitan Railway*)
- the incident is of a type usually associated with negligence (*Scott v London & St Katherine's Dock*)
- there is no other explanation (*Barkway v South Wales Transport*).
- It can be particularly appropriate to medical negligence claims.

Chapter 6

Negligence: Novel Duty Situations

6.1 Introduction

We have already seen how the tort of negligence is based on the existence first of a duty of care owed by the defendant to the claimant. The law has developed over time to include many instances where a duty of care exists.

There are numerous straightforward relationships where we might naturally expect a duty of care to exist. These would include between fellow motorists, between doctor and patient, between employer and employee, between manufacturers of products and their consumers, and many others. We have already seen examples in the case law of all of these.

There are also certain situations that are less obvious which have had to be considered by the courts. They have proved more controversial, but in some of them the courts have held that a duty of care does in fact exist. They include the following four examples.

6.2 Negligent misstatement

6.2.1 Introduction

The law of torts is concerned mainly with compensating for physical damage or personal injury, not for loss that is only economic. The obvious justification for this stance is that economic loss or, for instance, loss of a profit or bargain is more traditionally associated with contract law and the judges have always been eager to separate out the two.

An action for an economic loss caused by a statement was traditionally available in tort, but in the tort of deceit and only in the case of fraudulently made statements.

> ### Derry v Peek (1889)
>
> A representation in a share prospectus that a tram company could use motive power led to loss when the Board of Trade refused the company a licence to use motorised trams. The company had fully expected to be granted the licence, so their misstatement was not considered to be fraudulent.

6.2.2 The origins of liability

That action for economic loss caused by reliance on a negligently made statement should be available was reaffirmed even more recently, although not without some fundamental disagreement being expressed.

> ### Candler v Crane Christmas & Co. (1951)
>
> Accountants negligently prepared a company's accounts and investors then lost money. In the absence of a contractual relationship or fraud the court was not prepared to declare the existence of a duty of care. Lord Denning, dissenting, felt that there should be a duty of care to the investor and to:

> 'any third party to whom they themselves show the
> accounts, or to whom they know their employer is
> going to show the accounts so as to induce them to
> invest money …'

The House of Lords eventually accepted this
dissenting judgment a long time afterwards, and
initially only *in obiter.*

Hedley Byrne v Heller & Partners Ltd (1964)

An advertising company was approached with a
view to preparing a campaign for a small company,
Easipower, with whom they had not previously
dealt. The advertisers then did the most sensible
thing in the circumstances and approached
Easipower's bank for a credit reference. The bank
gave a satisfactory reference without checking on
their current financial standing and the advertisers
produced the campaign. They then lost money
when Easipower went into liquidation. They sued
the bank for their negligently prepared advice. They
failed because the bank had included a disclaimer of
liability in the credit reference. Nevertheless, the
House of Lords, approving Lord Denning's
dissenting judgment in the last case, held that such
an action should be possible, and this has
subsequently been accepted as law.

The interesting point of the court's approval of
the principle in the case is that they were holding
that such a duty could apply despite there being
no contractual relationship, and despite the fact
that, in effect, they were accepting that they could
impose liability for an economic loss.

As a result, the House of Lords in the case laid
down strict guidelines for when the principle
could apply:

- there must be a special relationship between
  the two parties, based on the skill and
  judgment of the defendant and the reliance
  placed upon it
- the person giving the advice must be
  possessed of special skill relating to the type of
  advice given, so the defendant ought to have
  realised that the claimant would rely on that
  skill
- the party receiving the advice has acted in
  reliance on it and, in the circumstances, it was
  reasonable for the claimant to rely on the
  advice.

The subsequent case law has in general followed
these requirements.

6.2.3 The elements of liability
A special relationship

The precise meaning of 'special relationship' was
never really examined in *Hedley Byrne* and so it
has become an area for judicial policy making.
The original leaning was towards a narrow
interpretation that would then only include a
relationship where the party giving the advice
was in the business of giving advice of the sort in
question.

However, it has since been suggested that a
business or professional relationship might in
general give rise to the duty if the claimant is
genuinely seeking professional advice.

Howard Marine & Dredging Co. Ltd v Ogden & Sons Ltd (1978)

Dredging took a lot longer because the hirers of
the barges had misstated the payload weight to the
party hiring them. It was accepted that the
relationship, while a standard business one, could
give rise to a special relationship for the purposes
of imposing a duty.

However, the mere fact that the claimant pays for the advice is insufficient for liability unless there is proximity between the parties.

West Bromwich Albion Football Club Ltd v El-Safty (2005)

The club sent a player with a knee injury to a consultant, on the advice of its physiotherapist. The consultant negligently advised reconstructive surgery which failed and the player had to retire when other treatment would have been more appropriate. The club sued for the economic loss arising from the player's premature retirement, claiming a special relationship existed because it had paid for the treatment. The court held that the person really taking the advice was the player and there was insufficient proximity between the club and the doctor to impose a duty.

A purely social relationship should not normally give rise to a duty of care, but has done when it has been established that carefully considered advice was being sought from a party with some expertise.

Chaudhry v Prabhaker (1988)

A woman asked her friend who, while not a mechanic, had some experience of cars, to find her a good second-hand car that had not been in an accident. When it was later discovered that the car advised on had been in an accident and was not completely roadworthy the friend advising on its purchase was successfully sued.

Common relationships where a duty will be identified, though, are those where valuers or accountants are providing the advice.

Yianni v Edwin Evans & Sons (1982)

A building society surveyor was held to owe a duty to purchasers of a property valued at £12,000 where it was later discovered that repairs worth £18,000 were required. The duty was imposed because it was shown that at the time less than 15% of purchasers would have their own independent survey carried out, and therefore it was foreseeable that they would rely on the standard building society survey.

The real test is whether there is sufficient proximity between the parties for there to be reasonable reliance on the advice. In *Raja v Gray* (2002) the Court of Appeal held that there was insufficient proximity between valuers appointed by receivers and parties with an interest in mortgaged property generally.

The possession of special skill or expertise

Ordinarily, then, a claim is possible only if the party giving the advice is a specialist in the field which the advice concerns.

Mutual Life and Citizens Assurance Co. Ltd v Evatt (1971)

A representative of an insurance company gave advice about the products of another company. The court held that there could be a duty in such circumstances only if the party giving the advice had held him/herself out as being in the business of giving the advice in question.

So, advice given in a purely social context could not usually give rise to liability. So the defendant in *Chaudhry v Prabhaker* was unfortunate in this way, though the result was justified since he should have applied the same caution in advising that he would have if he had been buying it himself.

Reasonable reliance on the advice

It is only fair and logical that, if there has been no reliance placed on the advice given, there should be no liability on the defendant for giving it.

JEB Fasteners Ltd v Marks Bloom & Co. (1983)

A negligent statement of the value of a company's stock did not give rise to a duty. This was because the party buying the company was doing so only to secure the services of two directors, and so placed no reliance on the stock.

So, it will not be foreseeable reliance if the claimant belongs to a group of potential claimants that is too large.

Goodwill v British Pregnancy Advisory Service (1996)

Here, a man had not been properly advised of the possibility that his vasectomy could automatically reverse itself. It was held that there could be no duty of care owed to a future girlfriend of the man.

However, when there is foreseeable reliance on advice given then there will be a duty of care owed.

Smith v Eric S Bush (1990)

A building society valuation had identified that chimney breasts had been removed, but the valuer had failed to check whether the brickwork above was properly secured. It was not and after the

purchase it collapsed. There was a duty of care because, as in *Yianni v Edwin Evans*, even though the contract was between building society and valuer, it was reasonably foreseeable that the purchaser would rely on it.

Foreseeable reliance by the party seeking the advice might also prevent an exclusion of liability clause in a contract from operating successfully.

Harris v Wyre Forest District Council (1989)

Here, in the sale of a council house a negligent survey had been carried out for the local authority. Even though the purchaser did not see the valuation he could rely on it and a disclaimer of liability inserted in the valuation was ineffective because it was not reasonable within the terms of the Unfair Contract Terms Act 1977.

Where a duty to act is imposed by statute, a civil action is only usually available to a party when the type of harm suffered was that anticipated by the statute. This was one of the reasons why the action failed in *Caparo v Dickman*. However, a duty may apply where the public would generally benefit.

Law Society v KPMG Peat Marwick (2000)

Here, the Law Society was owed a duty of care by a firm of accountants hired by solicitors to prepare annual accounts for the Law Society because Law Society compensation to clients of firms would be possible on a bad report.

Policy obviously plays a part in deciding whether there has been reasonable reliance.

> ### Newell v Ministry of Defence (2002)
>
> An army officer made an application for early release and then claimed that he had lost the opportunity of civilian employment because the army had taken an unreasonable time to reply. The court would not accept that the army owed any duty in relation to his civilian affairs.

In contrast, there is much more chance of genuine reliance being accepted in contractual or near-contractual arrangements. In *Commissioner of Police for the Metropolis v Lennon* (2004), acting on advice the claimant took time off before moving to a new force and as a result lost his housing allowance. The police were held liable under *Hedley Byrne*.

6.2.4 The current state of the law

In *Caparo v Dickman* the House of Lords had the opportunity to consider the principles involved in liability under *Hedley Byrne*. The financial booms and rapid development in property markets had not only led to a greater increase in home ownership and share ownership, they had also led on to a great number of claims for negligent misstatement, particularly against property surveyors and accountants.

The House of Lords preferred an incremental approach to establishing the duty of care, as we have already seen. They also made a number of observations regarding the circumstances in which the *Hedley Byrne*-type duty will be owed:

- the advice must be required for a purpose described at the time to the defendant at least in general terms
- this purpose must be made known actually or by inference, to the party giving the advice at the time it is given

- if the advice will subsequently be communicated to the party relying on it, this fact must be known by the advisor
- the advisor must be aware that the advice will be acted upon without benefit of any further independent advice
- the person alleging to have relied on the advice must show actual reliance and consequent detriment suffered.

So, the significant feature of this development of the duty is the express or implied knowledge of the purpose for which the claimant acted in reliance of the statement.

Guidance on the factors to be taken into account in deciding whether a duty of care in fact exists have subsequently been provided by the Court of Appeal.

> ### James McNaughten Paper Group Ltd v Hicks Anderson & Co. (1991)
>
> Here, accountants who drew up accounts at very short notice for the Chairman of a company had no duty of care to the person who acquired the company in a take-over bid, having inspected the accounts. The Court of Appeal identified the factors that should be taken into account in establishing a duty of care as follows:
>
> - the purpose for which the statement was made
> - the purpose for which the statement was communicated
> - the relationship between the person giving the advice, the person receiving the advice, and any relevant third party
> - the size of any class that the person receiving the advice belonged to
> - the degree of knowledge of the person 'giving the advice.
>
> As a result of this final point, *Caparo* has been distinguished in some later cases.

This is a very narrow approach to the duty and subsequent cases have tended to take a more relaxed view.

Some cases certainly seem to be at odds with the general principle, and liability has been imposed apparently to prevent a party being without any remedy.

White v Jones (1995)

Solicitors who negligently failed to draw up a will before the testator's death were held to owe a duty to the intended beneficiaries who consequently lost their inheritance. Any contractual relationship was with the testator, and since a will can be changed a beneficiary is not necessarily ensured the inheritance. Nevertheless, the House of Lords was prepared to identify both a special relationship in the circumstances and reliance.

Although in some instances this is because the court is uncertain whether the principle in *Hedley Byrne* or that in *Donoghue v Stevenson* is the appropriate one to apply. The latter is certainly less restrictive.

Spring v Guardian Assurance plc (1995)

An employee of an insurance company was dismissed and then prevented from gaining a position with another company because of a negligently prepared and highly unfavourable reference provided by the first company. The House of Lords held that the first employers were liable because of the reference, but the House was split on whether *Hedley Byrne* should apply.

The approach to dealing with negligently prepared references has since been developed by the Court of Appeal. In *Bartholomew v London Borough of Hackney* (1999) the court increased the duty to ensuring that information provided is accurate and that the reference does not create any unfair impression.

This test has now been developed further.

Cox v Sun Alliance Life Ltd (2001)

The claimant was a branch manager who was suspended for reasons not related to dishonesty. An allegation of dishonesty was made during negotiations for a termination agreement. However, the investigation that followed was abandoned and Sun Life agreed that in any references they would make no mention of the allegation. However, they did so in one reference which cost the claimant a job and he sued successfully for negligence. Lord Justice Mummery stated that: before divulging information that s unfavourable to an ex-employee in a reference, the employer must believe in the truth of the information, have reasonable grounds for that belief, and make a reasonably thorough investigation before making the statement.

Activity

Self-assessment questions

1. Why did the House of Lords in *Hedley Byrne* alter the previous rule in *Candler v Crane Christmas & Co.*?

2. What exactly is a special relationship?

3. How can the decision in *Chaudhry v Prabhaker* be justified?

4. What level of specialist expertise is required for liability?

5. Against what standards is reasonable reliance measured?

6. How can the *Goodwill v BPAS* case be distinguished from other cases on reasonable reliance?

7. Why was the decision in *Yianni v Edwin Evans* greeted with such shock by building society surveyors?

8. To what extent does the case of *Caparo v Dickman* limit liability under *Hedley Byrne*?

9. How do cases like *White v Jones* and *Spring v Guardian Assurance* fit in with the normal rule?

Key Facts

- Originally, there was only an action available for misrepresentations if they were made fraudulently (*Derry v Peek*).
- An action for negligence was originally specifically rejected in *Candler v Crane Christmas*.
- However, the House of Lords eventually accepted *in obiter* that such an action was possible in *Hedley Byrne v Heller & Partners*.
- This, however, was only the case subject to certain requirements:
  - the existence of a special relationship (*Yianni v Edwin Evans*)
  - where the party giving the advice has specialist skill and knowledge of the type sought (*Mutual Life & Citizens Assurance v Evatt*)
  - the other party acts in reliance of the advice, which is known to the other party (*Smith v Eric S Bush*).
- Limitations on these requirements have since been made (*Caparo v Dickman*).
- A list of important factors to be considered has been identified in *James McNaughten Paper Group v Hicks Anderson*, including:
  - the purpose for which the statement was made and communicated
  - the relationship between all relevant parties
  - the degree of knowledge of the defendant.
- However, there are also cases that do not fit the principle neatly (*White v Jones* and *Spring v Guardian Assurance*).

In the Dilemma Board below, consider the accuracy of each of the four statements, A, B, C and D, as they apply to the facts in the central scenario. You only need to give the basic principles. The answer is in the Appendix at the end of the book.

Dilemma Board

A.

Gillian is liable to Fiona for negligent advice under basic *Donoghue v Stevenson* principles.

B.

Gillian cannot be liable to Fiona because the situation involves pure economic loss.

Fiona intends to buy a house and pays a qualified surveyor, Gillian, to produce a survey. The report on the survey states that there are no structural problems so Fiona buys the house. After she moves in Fiona notices large cracks appearing in certain walls and damp on all outside ground floor rooms. A further survey by another surveyor identifies that this is due to the house having been built on a landfill site making any foundations inadequate, which should have been known to all local surveyors.

C.

Fiona cannot claim from Gillian because there is no special relationship between them.

D.

Fiona cannot claim from Gillian because there was no reason for her to rely on the advice given by Gillian.

6.3 Pure economic loss

6.3.1 The traditional position

The *Hedley Byrne* case introduced the concept that a claimant could recover for economic loss arising from negligently made statements. However, the courts have always distinguished such an action from 'pure economic loss' arising out of negligent acts. The position here was traditionally very clear; there was no liability for a 'pure economic loss'.

In the past this was based on policy and the idea that 'economic loss', for instance a loss of profit, was a concept applicable to contract law rather than tort. The principle has been quite clearly stated and illustrated in past cases.

Spartan Steel v Martin & Co. (Contractors) Ltd (1973)

An electric power cable was negligently cut by the defendants, resulting in a loss of power to the claimants, who manufactured steel alloys. A 'melt' in the claimant's furnace at the time of the power cuts had to be destroyed to stop it from solidifying and wrecking the furnace. The claimants were able to claim for physical damage and the loss of profit on the 'melt' in the furnace. The court refused to allow their claim for lost profits for four further 'melts' they argued they could have completed while the power was still off. The loss was foreseeable. Nevertheless, Lord Denning held that a line must be drawn as a matter of policy, and that the loss was better borne by the insurers than by the defendants alone.

There appears to be an artificial distinction here, created for policy reasons purely for the purpose of restricting any extension of liability. The distinction has the obvious potential to create unfair anomalies in the law. For instance, it might mean that an architect giving negligent advice leading to the construction of a defective building could be liable, where the builder whose negligence leads to a defect in a building may not be.

Nevertheless, other cases have confirmed the principle that a pure economic loss arising from a negligent act is unrecoverable.

Weller & Co. v Foot and Mouth Disease Research Institute (1966)

Auctioneers' regular income from sale of cattle was disrupted as the result of a ban on the movement of livestock following an escape of a virus from the defendant's premises. No liability could be accepted for their loss of profit.

However, there have also been situations where an economic loss was recovered, although in less clear-cut situations where the difference between a negligent statement and a negligent act was less obvious.

Dutton v Bognor Regis Urban District Council (1972)

A local authority was responsible for a negligently carried out building inspection that resulted in defective foundations having to be repaired at great financial cost to the owner of the building. The Court of Appeal held that, since a local authority was under no duty to carry out an inspection, then they could not be held liable for a negligent inspection. Nevertheless, they were prepared to impose liability on the basis of physical damage, that the defective foundations were a risk to the health and safety of the occupants. The claimant, as a result, was awarded damages to restore the building to a state where it was no longer a danger. Clearly it is difficult to distinguish between a negligent inspection (an act) and a satisfactory report based on the inspection (a statement). The case did not fit easily under either *Hedley Byrne* or *Donoghue v Stevenson*, which perhaps explains the court's reasoning.

6.3.2 Pure economic loss and the *Anns* test

Further erosion of the basic principle that pure economic loss is unrecoverable came as a result of Lord Wilberforce's two-part test.

Anns v Merton London Borough Council (1978)

Here, the negligent building inspection had failed to reveal that the foundations were too shallow. On the basis of the two-part test, and that there were no policy grounds to avoid imposing a duty, the tenant was able to recover the cost of making the flat safe, economic loss in other words.

Because of the availability of the *Anns* two-part test, the so-called 'high water mark' was then reached in respect of recovery for a pure economic loss.

Junior Books Ltd v Veitchi Co. Ltd (1983)

The claimants' architects nominated the defendants to lay the floor in the claimants' new print works. As a result, they sub-contracted to the main builders to complete the work. In the event, the defendants laid a thoroughly unusable floor which then had to be re-laid. The claimants could not sue the builders who had hired the floor layers at the claimant's request, and they had no contractual relationship with the floor layers. Nevertheless, they succeeded in winning damages not just for the cost of re-laying the floor, but also for their loss of profit during the delay. There were said to be three key issues:

- the claimant had nominated the defendants and so they relied on the defendants skill and judgment
- the defendants were aware of this reliance at all material times
- the damage caused was a direct and foreseeable consequence of the defendant's negligence.

Lord Brandon dissented and criticised the other judges for creating obligations in a non-contractual relationship only appropriate as between contracting parties.

6.3.3 The retreat from *Anns*

Almost immediately, judges considered that the relaxation of the principle concerning recovery for economic loss had now gone too far. A long line of cases followed in which they tried to limit the scope of the above cases.

Governors of the Peabody Donation Fund v Sir Lindsay Parkinson & Co. Ltd (1985)

The court would not accept that there was liability owed for a negligent council inspection that resulted in a drain having to be re-laid because it did not conform to regulations. The council's duty in inspecting was to protect the health and safety of the public.

The cases had often arisen because an action in contract was not available and the reliance test from *Junior Books* argued.

Muirhead v Industrial Tank Specialists Ltd (1985)

Fish merchandisers bought lobsters while they were cheap, to sell on when their price increased. They bought storage tanks in which to hold the lobsters and lost money when the French-built pumps in the tanks were defective and the lobsters could not be stored. They originally succeeded against the supplier of the tanks in contract, but when they went into liquidation they brought an action in tort against the manufacturers of the pumps. Their claim that the test of proximity and reliance in *Junior Books* applied failed. The court held that reliance had only been possible in that case because the claimants nominated the defendants. The case was therefore distinguished.

The argument that costs of repairing defects in property that could lead to a danger to health or safety, approved in *Anns,* was also gradually rejected.

D & F Estates V Church Commissioners (1989)

Liability against builders was rejected when plaster cracked, fell off walls and had to be replaced as the result of the negligence of sub-contractors. The builders had satisfied their duty by hiring competent tradesmen and, in the absence of injury or an actual risk to health, any loss was purely economic and not recoverable.

These represent only a few of the cases where *Anns* was argued to allow economic loss and rejected, or the case distinguished. The general unease that was felt at Lord Wilberforce's test in *Anns* and at the extension of liability for economic loss, led eventually to the overruling of *Anns,* and

thus back to a more restrictive attitude towards economic loss.

Murphy v Brentwood District Council (1990)

The House of Lords would not impose liability on a council that had approved plans for a concrete raft on which properties were built, which then moved causing cracks in the walls. The claimant was forced to sell the house for £35,000 under its value if not defective, but in the absence of any injury, loss was purely economic. So, the *ratio* in *Anns* was overruled, and the principle of law now is that a local authority will not be liable for the cost of repairing dangerous defects (in the case, gas pipes had broken during the settlement of the property) until physical injury is actually caused. *Junior Books v Veitchi* was not overruled, but was allowed to stand on its own facts. It is unlikely, however, to have much impact on future cases.

The principles in *Murphy* have subsequently been followed.

Department of the Environment v Thomas Bates & Sons Ltd (1990)

Here, the claimant failed to recover the cost of repairing a building that had been built of concrete that was of insufficient strength to support its intended load, although it was not dangerous to carry its existing load. Such cost was purely economic and thus unrecoverable.

So, the present policy of the courts in relation to economic loss appears to be that recovery for such loss should be through the normal insurance of the injured party rather than through the courts using negligence.

Marc Rich & Co. v Bishop Rock Marine Co. Ltd (1995)

A vessel was negligently classed as seaworthy and then sank. The classification society did not owe a duty of care to the owners of a cargo that sank with the ship. This was economic loss. The House of Lords applied the three-part test from *Caparo v Dickman* and determined that it was not just and reasonable in the circumstances of the case to impose a duty.

Activity

Self-assessment questions

1. What, exactly, is a 'pure economic loss'?

2. Why are the courts more willing to accept an economic loss caused by a negligently made statement than one resulting from a negligent act or omission?

3. Why were judges in later cases nervous about the judgment in *Junior Books*?

4. What is the difference between physical damage to property and the cost of repairing defects in property?

5. How would the courts now prefer a claimant to recover compensation for an economic loss?

6. Why did the judges in *Murphy* decide not to overrule *Junior Books*?

- The courts have always been reluctant to allow liability for 'pure economic loss' because it is felt that it is more to do with contract (*Spartan Steel v Martin*).
- However, claims have been successful where there has been a risk also to health (*Dutton v Bognor Regis UDC*).
- The position on economic loss was drastically relaxed as the result of Lord Wilberforce's two-part test in *Anns* (*Junior Books v Veitchi*) although this was because of a 'near contractual' relationship between the two parties.
- Later, judges were never really happy with *Anns* or the two-part test and these were eventually overruled in *Murphy v Brentwood DC*.

6.4 Nervous shock

6.4.1 Introduction

This is another area of negligence that has been the subject of uncertain development. The extent to which liability has been imposed has expanded or contracted according to:

- the state of medical knowledge, i.e. psychiatric medicine and the recognition of psychiatric disorders has developed dramatically over the past 100 years – the great concern expressed in recent years over soldiers who were executed in the First World War is an interesting example
- policy considerations on the part of judges, particularly the 'floodgates' argument, that to impose liability in a particular situation may lead to a rush of claims, and so should be avoided whatever the justice of the case.

Actions failed in the last century for three reasons:

- Because of the state of medical knowledge, psychiatric illness or injury was not properly recognised, so there could be no duty if the type of damage concerned was not recognised.
- Another problem, of course, was the fear that a person making such a claim could actually be faking the symptoms.
- Finally, there was the 'floodgates' argument, that once one claim was accepted it would lead to a multitude of claims.

> ## *Victoria Railway Commissioners v Coultas (1888)*
> Nervous shock resulting from involvement in a train crash did not give rise to liability, not least because of the 'floodgates' argument.

Even from the start there were two aspects to determining whether liability should be imposed:

- Firstly, the injury alleged must conform to judicial attitudes of what constitutes nervous shock, a recognised psychiatric disorder.
- Secondly, the person claiming to have suffered nervous shock must fall into a category accepted by the courts as being entitled to claim.

6.4.2 Definition of 'nervous shock'

The claim must, then, involve an actual, recognised psychiatric condition capable of resulting from the shock of the incident, and recognised as having long-term effects.

> ## *Reilly v Merseyside Regional Health Authority (1994)*
> No liability was found when a couple became trapped in a lift as the result of negligence and suffered insomnia and claustrophobia after they were rescued.

In the modern day, conditions such as post-traumatic stress disorder and acute anxiety syndrome would be recognised where the courts would be reluctant to allow a claim purely for a temporary upset, such as grief or distress or fright, which we all suffer from at times.

> ## *Tredget v Bexley Health Authority (1994)*
> Unusually, parents of a child born with serious injuries following medical negligence and then dying two days later, succeeded in their claim. They were held to be suffering from psychiatric injuries despite the argument that their condition was no more than profound grief.

The courts in recent times have been prepared to accept a claim that is partly caused by grief and partly by the severe shock of the event.

> ## *Vernon v Bosley (No. 1) (1997)*
> Here, a father had witnessed his children being drowned in a car negligently driven by their nanny. He recovered damages for nervous shock that was held to be partly the result of pathological grief and bereavement, but partly also the consequence of the trauma of witnessing the events.

6.4.3 Development of a test for who can recover

Originally, claims were first allowed purely on the basis of foreseeability of real and immediate fear of personal danger (the so-called 'Kennedy' test) so that the class of possible claimants was at first very limited.

> *Dulieu v White & Sons (1901)*
>
> The court accepted a claim when a woman suffered nervous shock after a horse and van that had been negligently driven burst through the window of a pub where she was washing glasses. She was able to recover because she had been put in fear for her own safety.

This limitation was later extended to include a claim for nervous shock suffered as the result of witnessing traumatic events involving close family.

> *Hambrook v Stokes Bros (1925)*
>
> A woman recovered damages for nervous shock when she saw a runaway lorry going downhill towards where she had left her three children, and then heard that there had indeed been an accident involving a child. The court disapproved the 'Kennedy' test and considered that it would be unfair not to compensate a mother who had feared for the safety of her children when she could have claimed if she only feared for her own safety.

This principle was even extended, at one point, to include shock suffered on witnessing events involving close but not related people.

> *Dooley v Cammell Laird & Co. (1951)*
>
> A crane driver claimed successfully for nervous shock when he saw a load fall and thought that workmates underneath would have been injured.

Indeed, claims have even been allowed where harm to the person with whom the close tie exists would be impossible.

> *Owens v Liverpool Corporation (1933)*
>
> Here, relatives recovered for nervous shock when the coffin fell out of the hearse that they were following.

One restriction on this development was to prevent a party from recovering who was not within the 'area of impact' of the event.

> *King v Phillips (1953)*
>
> A mother suffered nervous shock when, from 70 yards away, she saw a taxi reverse into her small child's bicycle and presumed him to be injured. Her claim failed because the court said she was too far away from the incident and outside of the range of foresight of the defendant.

In contrast, the same principle of reasonable foresight has allowed recovery for nervous shock where the damage was to property.

> *Attic v British Gas (1987)*
>
> A woman who witnessed her house burning down when she arrived home was able to claim successfully for nervous shock. She was within the

area of impact. The claim was said to be within the reasonable foresight of the contractors who negligently installed her central heating, causing the fire.

An alternative measure to the area of impact test is whether the claimant falls within the area of shock

---

Bourhill v Young (1943)

A pregnant Edinburgh fishwife claimed to have suffered nervous shock after getting off a tram, hearing the impact of a crash involving a motorcyclist, and later seeing blood on the road, after which she gave birth to a still-born child. The House of Lords held that, as a stranger to the motorcyclist, she was outside of the area of foreseeable shock.

It has also been well established in the case law that a rescuer will be able to recover when suffering nervous shock.

Chadwick v British Railways Board (1967)

When two trains crashed in a tunnel a man who lived nearby was asked, because of his small size, to crawl into the wreckage to give injections to trapped passengers. He was able to claim successfully for the anxiety neurosis he suffered as a result. This was largely explained on the basis that he was a primary victim, at risk himself in the circumstances.

Usually only professional rescuers will be able to claim, or those present at the scene or the immediate aftermath.

Hale v London Underground (1992)

A fireman claimed successfully for post-traumatic stress disorder he suffered following the King's Cross fire.

However, claims for shock suffered at the scene of disasters will not be successful in the case of those people considered only to be bystanders.

McFarlane v EE Caledonia (1994)

A person who was helping to receive casualties from the Piper Alpha oilrig failed in his claim because he was classed as a mere bystander rather than a rescuer at the scene.

As we have seen, the tests developed above involve the proximity of the claimant in time and space to the negligent incident, or the closeness of the relationship with the party who is present. The widest point of expansion of liability came under the two-part test from *Anns*, and allowed for recovery when the claimant was not present at the scene but was at the 'immediate aftermath'. Inevitably, the meaning of 'immediate aftermath' was open to an interpretation based on policy.

McLoughlin v O'Brian (1982)

A woman was summoned to a hospital about an hour after her children and husband were involved in a car crash. One child was dead, two were badly injured, all were in shock and they had not yet been cleaned up. The House of Lords held that since the relationship was sufficiently close and the woman was present at the 'immediate aftermath' she could claim. Lord Wilberforce identified a three-part test for secondary victims that was approved later in *Alcock*.

More recently, the courts have been prepared to accept that the shocking event itself might last over a considerable period of time.

North Glamorgan NHS Trust v Walters (2002)

Doctors negligently failed to diagnose that a baby with hepatitis needed a liver transplant. The baby then suffered a major fit and was transported with the mother to a hospital in London for a liver transplant. On arrival it was discovered that the baby had suffered severe brain damage. The parents' permission was asked to switch off life support and the baby died in his mother's arms. The whole episode took 36 hours. The defendant countered the claimant's claim for nervous shock by arguing that it was not as a result of witnessing a single traumatic event. The Court of Appeal disagreed and held that there was a continuous chain of events.

The Court of Appeal referred to the case in *Atkins v Seghal* (2003) where a mother was told of her daughter's death by a police officer but did not see the body until two hours later. The court accepted that this still fell within the immediate aftermath.

Even the House of Lords has reached some surprising conclusions on this issue.

W v Essex and Another (2000)

The claimants agreed to foster a 15-year-old boy, having been assured by the defendant's officers that the child did not have a record as a child abuser or was not suspected of such. In fact, the child had been cautioned for indecent assault and was currently under investigation for rape. He then committed serious sexual assaults on the children of the family and when the parents found out the marriage eventually broke down and the parents suffered depression as a result of discovering the abuse. The House of Lords rejected the defendant's argument that the injury was not the result of witnessing the shocking event, and would not strike out the claim.

6.4.4 Restrictions on the scope of the duty

The House of Lords has subsequently had the opportunity to review all aspects of the duty and to identify fairly restricted circumstances in which a claim can succeed.

Alcock v Chief Constable of South Yorkshire (1992)

At the start of a football match police allowed a large crowd of supporters into a caged pen, as a result of which 95 people in the stand suffered crush injuries and were killed. Since the match was being televised, much of the disaster was shown on live TV. A number of claims for nervous shock were made. These varied between those present or not present at the scene, those with close family ties to the dead and those who were merely friends. The House of Lords refused all of the claims and identified the factors important to consider in determining whether a party might recover. These were:

- the proximity in time and space to the negligent incident – there could be a claim in respect of an incident or the immediate aftermath that was witnessed or experienced directly; there could be none where the incident was merely reported
- the proximity of the relationship with a party who was a victim of the incident – a successful claim would depend on the existence of a close tie of love and affection with the victim, or presence at the scene as a rescuer

---

- the cause of the nervous shock – the court accepted that this must be the result of witnessing or hearing the horrifying event or the immediate aftermath.

The case then identifies, for the future, the classes of claimants who will be successful and those who will not:

- **Primary victims** – those present at the scene and themselves injured.

Page v Smith (1996)

Here, Page was involved in a car accident caused by the defendant's negligence. Although he actually suffered no physical injury he suffered a recurrence of 'chronic fatigue syndrome' which he had suffered some years before. The House of Lords held that the defendant was liable for the psychological injury caused to the claimant.

In this way courts apply the 'thin skull' rule in the case of primary victims even though the psychiatric injury may appear to be unforeseeable.

Simmons v British Steel (2004)

The claimant was injured through his employer's negligence and then suffered a worsening of his psoriasis, a stress-related skin disease, and of a depressive illness, also leading to a personality change. This resulted from his anger at his employer's lack of apology and lack of support, rather than from the injury itself. However, the court still imposed liability as the claimant was a primary victim.

- **Primary victims.** An alternative is those who were present at the scene and whose own safety was threatened, as in *Dulieu v White*, where the woman could have been hurt by the horse coming through the glass window, and did in fact suffer a miscarriage.
- **Secondary victims.** These are people who are not primary victims of the incident, but who are able to show a close enough tie of love and affection to a victim of the incident and witnessed the incident or its 'immediate aftermath' at close hand. The probable limit of this is in *McLoughlin v O'Brian*. In *Alcock*, the judges were reluctant to allow claims there in respect of both proximity in time and space to the incidents at Hillsborough, and turned down claims from people who had identified bodies in the morgue some time after the events of the match. Indeed, the courts have engaged in some fairly fine distinctions as to what can acceptably be called 'the immediate aftermath' in later cases.

Taylor v Somerset HA (1993)

The claimant's husband suffered a fatal heart attack while at work. She was told only that he had been taken to hospital, and when she arrived at the hospital she was told that he was dead. She was so shocked that she would not believe he was dead until she identified his body in the mortuary. She later suffered a psychiatric illness and claimed against the hospital. Even though she was at the hospital within an hour, her action failed. The court held that the actual purpose for her visit was to identify the body, so it was not to do with the cause of his death.

- **Rescuers.** These may well, of course, be primary victims and at risk in the circumstances of the incident causing the nervous shock.

Hale v London Underground (1992)

A fireman who had been involved in the rescue of victims at the King's Cross fire suffered post-traumatic stress disorder and recovered damages for nervous shock.

However, the question of who qualifies as a rescuer seems uncertain.

Duncan v British Coal (1990)

There was, surprisingly, no liability where a miner saw a colleague crushed in a roof fall, the fault of the employers, and tried to resuscitate him.

The House of Lords certainly seems to be hostile towards claims by the emergency services for psychological injury suffered while dealing with the aftermath of a disaster in the course of their duties. A rescuer will be able to claim only where (s)he is a genuine 'primary victim'.

White v Chief Constable of South Yorkshire (1999)

Police officers who claimed to have suffered post-traumatic stress disorder following their part in the rescue operation at the Hillsborough disaster were denied a remedy by the House of Lords. The reasoning seems to be that they did not actually put themselves at risk, and that public policy prevented them from recovering when the relatives of the deceased in the disaster could not.

More recently the courts have been willing to accept that a rescuer can also claim as a secondary victim, but only where the rescuer conforms to all of the requirements for secondary victims in *Alcock*.

Greatorex v Greatorex (2000)

Here, a fire officer attended the scene of an accident caused by the negligence of his son. He was required to attend to his son and claimed afterwards to suffer from nervous shock. The court would not accept the claim because of the conflict that it would cause between family members, but had the son not been the cause of the accident a claim may have been possible in the circumstances.

- **Secondary victims watching the events on live TV** in contravention of broadcasting standards may claim from the broadcasting authority.

6.4.5 Those who cannot claim

Bystanders

The law has always made a distinction between rescuers or people who are at risk in the incident, and those who are merely bystanders and have no claim. This point goes back as far as *Bourhill v Young*.

McFarlane v EE Caledonia Ltd (1994)

A person on shore receiving survivors from the Piper Alpha oilrig disaster was not classed as a rescuer and therefore had no valid claim.

No close tie of love and affection

Workmates who witness accidents involving their colleagues will not be able to claim because any ties are not close enough to involve foreseeable harm.

Robertson and Rough v Forth Road Bridge Joint Board (1995)

Three workmates had been repairing the Forth Road Bridge during a gale. One of them was sitting on a piece of metal on a truck when a gust of wind blew him off the bridge and he was killed. His colleagues who witnessed this were unable to claim. They were held not to be primary victims and had insufficient ties with the dead worker for injury to be foreseeable.

Gradual rather than sudden shock

If the psychological injury is the result of a gradual appreciation of events rather than a sudden shock then there will be no liability.

Sion v Hampstead Health Authority (1994)

A father claimed to have suffered psychological injury as the result of watching his son, over the space of 14 days, gradually deteriorate and then die, when there was the possibility of the death resulting from medical negligence. There could be no claim because there was no sudden appreciation of a horrifying event.

No causal link between the incident and the damage

If the psychological injury can be attributed to an event other than the horrifying incident in question, then there is no causal link and no possible claim.

Calascione v Dixon (1994)

The defendant was responsible for the death of a 20-year-old in a motorcycle accident. He was not liable, however, for the psychological injuries suffered by the mother of the young man. It was shown that the psychiatric illness was more the result of the stress of the inquest and a private prosecution rather than the incident itself.

6.4.6 Comment

Clearly, the area of recovery for psychological injury (nervous shock) has been subject to an erratic development. There is no doubt that secondary victims have been treated harshly by comparison with primary victims, although, taken the kind of harm suffered, they are just as likely to suffer harm. Even in the case of bystanders it seems that it is policy reasons rather than the foreseeability of harm that has led to a denial of liability.

The need for reform in the area has been identified by the Law Commission in a Report (Law Com. No 249) in 1998. Their chief recommendations are:

- to retain the requirement of a close tie of love and affection to the primary victim in the case of secondary victims
- to remove the requirements for such claimants to show proximity in time and space, and that the event has been witnessed by the claimant's own unaided senses
- that the injury should be accepted even where not caused by a sudden trauma.

The proposals seem to be much fairer. However, it is not clear whether or not there is any likelihood of them becoming law. In the light of recent response to Law Commission proposals it may be unlikely, at least in the near future.

Activity

Self-assessment questions

1. What, exactly, is 'nervous shock'?

2. Why were courts originally reluctant to allow a claimant to recover for nervous shock, and why has this changed?

3. How broad is the definition of 'psychological injury'?

4. Has there been any logical development to nervous shock?

5. What is the 'area of impact', and what is the 'area of shock'?

6. What is the difference between a 'primary victim' and a 'secondary victim'?

7. In what specific ways is a primary victim in a better position to claim than a secondary victim?

8. What are the three essential features of a successful claim by a secondary victim?

9. How have the courts defined the meaning of 'immediate aftermath' in the decisions of cases?

10. To what extent is policy a determining factor?

11. To what extent does *McLoughlin v O'Brian* fit in with other cases?

12. In what way is *Attia v British Gas* a strange case?

13. Why did the House of Lords in *White* reverse *Frost v Chief Constable of South Yorkshire*?

Activity

Multiple choice questions

In each of the following series of situations, suggest which of the statements may raise a successful claim of nervous shock

1. a) James is present when his dog is run over by Carl's negligent driving, and suffers nervous shock.
   b) James hears that his mother was run over by Carl's negligent driving four days ago, and suffers nervous shock.
   c) James is a passenger in a car when his friend Andrew, the driver, is killed by Carl's negligent driving, and suffers nervous shock.
   d) James hears screams when Carl crashes his car, and suffers nervous shock.

2. a) Sally hears that a friend has died in a car crash caused by negligence, and suffers from profound grief.
   b) Sally sees her friend killed in an accident at work caused by the employer's negligence, and cannot sleep.
   c) Sally is called to the hospital to identify her mother's body after a car driver has negligently run her over, and it makes her very angry.
   d) Sally is with her father when he drowns as a result of negligence when a ferry sinks, and she suffers post-traumatic stress disorder.

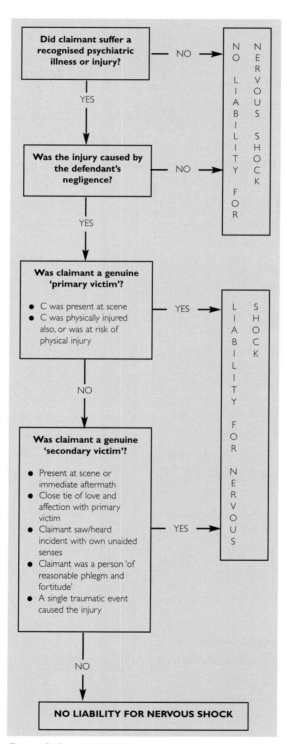

Figure 3 *Flow chart illustrating the means of determining liability for nervous shock*

Key Facts

- A contract is made where there is an agreement between two parties
- Originally, courts were unwilling to allow actions for nervous shock (*Victoria Railway Commissioners v Coultas*).
- This was because of the primitive state of psychiatric medicine.
- So, the key requirement is always that the illness amounts to a recognised psychiatric disorder (*Vernon v Bosley*).
- An action was first accepted only because the claimant was also in physical danger (*Dulieu v White*).
- However, this was then extended to include a person who was in the area of shock, i.e. witnessed the accident and had some close tie with the victim (*Hambrook v Stokes*).
- The widest extent of the duty was to include witnessing the immediate aftermath of the accident (*McLoughlin v O'Brian*).
- Strangely, a claim has been allowed for nervous shock on witnessing property damage (*Attia v British Gas*).
- Now, basic rules identify a restricted range of people who can claim (*Alcock v Chief Constable of South Yorkshire*) which include:
  - primary victims – present and either injured or at risk
  - secondary victims – close tie of love and affection to the victim, and a witness of the incident or its immediate aftermath
  - rescuers – where the rescuer is either a genuine primary victim (*White v Chief Constable of South Yorkshire*) or a genuine secondary victim (*Greatorex v Greatorex*), but there is now no general category of liability to a rescuer
  - those witnessing it on live TV in contravention of broadcasting requirements.
- There are a number of classes of people who could not claim:
  - mere bystanders (*McFarlane v EE Caledonia*)
  - secondary victims without close ties to the victim (*Robertson and Rough v Forth Road Bridge Joint Board*)
  - those not suffering a recognised psychiatric disorder (*Reilly v Merseyside Regional Health Authority*)
  - those outside of the area of foreseeable shock of the accident (*Bourhill v Young*).
- The Law Commission has suggested relaxing the rules for claims by secondary victims, so that they should only need to prove the close tie of love and affection with the primary victim.

Activity

Consider the following essay title:

Compare and evaluate the rules applied by the courts to different types of claimants in cases of nervous shock.

Answering the question
There are usually two key elements to essays in law:

Legal Essay Writing

- Firstly, you are required to reproduce a series of factual information on a particular area of law as identified in the question.

- Secondly, you are required to answer the question set, which is usually found in some critical element, i.e. you may see the words 'discuss', 'analyse', 'critically consider', 'explain', etc.

Students, for the most part, seem quite capable of doing the first, and also generally seem less skilled at the second. The important points in any case are to ensure that you only deal with relevant legal material in your answer, and that you do answer the question set, rather than one you have made up yourself, or the one that was on last year's paper.

For instance, in the case of the first element of this essay you might say the following: 'Nervous shock is an area of negligence. Negligence requires proof of the existence of a duty of care and breach of that duty, and damage caused by the defendant that is not too remote a consequence of the breach.' But you do not need to treat the examiner to everything that you know about the standard of care, or the 'but for' test, etc, because none of that is relevant.

In the case of the second element, the essay asks you to 'compare and evaluate' the rules applicable to different types of claimant in nervous shock cases. This clearly indicates that you must compare the different rules for dealing with primary and secondary victims, and since you are asked to evaluate you will need to pass some sort of comment on whether the law treats both fairly, adequately, etc.

Relevant law
- Nervous shock is one of those novel duty situations in negligence and thus all the other rules of negligence apply.
- Nervous shock involves recognised psychiatric illnesses such as PTSD, but not mere grief or other distress – compare *Reilly* and *Tredget*.

- The rules on who can recover in what situation are now contained in *Alcock*.

- The law distinguishes between primary victims (those present at the scene of an incident and directly affected or injured by the defendant's negligent act or omission) – and secondary victims (those indirectly affected by the trauma caused by the defendant's negligent act or omission).

- Primary victims can recover if they suffer physical as well as psychological injury, or if physical harm is foreseeable and they suffer nervous shock as a result (*Dulieu v White* or *Page v Smith*).

- Secondary victims must prove a close tie of love and affection with a primary victim, and close proximity in time and space to the traumatic event or its immediate aftermath (*McLoughlin v O'Brian*), or be a professional rescuer (*Chadwick v British Railways Board* and *Hale v London Underground*). Note also that such people must be of reasonable fortitude (*Bourhill v Young*) and that the psychological injury must result from the trauma being witnessed by their own unaided senses, either seeing or hearing

Evaluation
The commentary in the essay requires you to compare the treatment of primary and secondary victims and to evaluate their treatment. Relevant comments might include:

- that the range of injuries that will allow liability is limited, although the floodgates argument and state of medical knowledge may justify this, and it has had some expansion (*Vernon v Bosley*)

- that primary victims generally have no problem recovering

- consideration that, since *White v Chief Constable of South Yorkshire*, professional rescuers must be identifiable as genuine primary victims in order to claim

- consideration that, according to *Greatorex v Greatorex*, a rescuer could also claim if he or she could be classed as a genuine secondary victim, i.e. conform to all of the requirements in *Alcock*

- that a close tie of love and affection is quite limited in scope (*Alcock*)

- and, perhaps unfairly, does not include close friendships or working relationships (*Robertson and Rough v Forth Road Bridge* and *Duncan v British Coal*)

- that 'immediate aftermath' is quite narrowly defined (*Alcock*) and the widest point predates the test now (*McLoughlin v O'Brian*)

- that bystanders are treated unfairly in comparison with professional rescuers, although they might suffer the same psychological injuries (*McFarlane v EE Caledonia*)

- that professional rescuers were originally treated more fairly in determining liability than were the relatives of primary victims (*Alcock*), but that the courts recognising the possible injustice have changed their stance on professional rescuers in relation to the 'Hillsborough' litigation – compare *Frost v Chief Constable of South Yorkshire* in the Court of Appeal and the House of Lords, and also the different approach in *White v Chief Constable of South Yorkshire*

- that public policy plays an important role in deciding on liability in nervous shock, particularly the 'floodgates' argument

- that numerous cases seem to be out of line with the 'strict' rules – e.g. *Attia v British Gas* and nervous shock following witnessing damage to property; *Owens v Liverpool Corporation* and primary victim being a corpse; *Dooley v Cammell Laird* and primary victim being a work colleague of the claimant; *Tredget v Bexley Health Authority*, where the nervous shock seemed to be based on profound grief at the death of a child; *Hevican v Ruane*, where the nervous shock followed the claimant being informed of the death of his son and witnessing the body was long after the immediate aftermath.

In the Dilemma Board below, consider the accuracy of each of the four statements, A, B, C and D, as they apply to the facts in the central scenario. You only need to give the basic principles. The answer is in the Appendix at the end of the book.

Dilemma Board

A.

Charlie can claim successfully for nervous shock as a primary victim.

B.

Charlie will be unable to claim for nervous shock as he did not suffer a recognised psychiatric injury.

Through his employer's negligence, Brett is crushed under a collapsed machine at work, suffering multiple injuries. Charlie, Brett's father and fellow employee, stays with Brett until the paramedic arrives but suffers grief and severe depression as a result of seeing Brett's extensive injuries. Dalvinder, a paramedic, is called to the scene, tries, unsuccessfully, to save Brett's life and suffers post-traumatic stress disorder after seeing the extent of Brett's injuries. The collapsed machine was no danger to either Dalvinder or Charlie.

C.

Dalvinder will have an automatic right to claim for nervous shock as a primary victim since he is a professional rescuer.

D.

Dalvinder can claim successfully as a secondary victim.

6.5 Liability for omissions

English law distinguishes between:

- misfeasance – the infliction of damage or injury by a positive act; and
- non-feasance – causing harm by failing to prevent it or allowing it to happen.

The law does not include any general liability for non-feasance, or failing to act. There are, of course, those who believe in the idea of a 'good neighbour' principle, but this idea has generally not been accepted.

There are two fairly obvious reasons for this historically:

- The problem of showing causation – showing that somebody failed to prevent harm is much more difficult than showing that they caused it.
- The problem of imposing onerous burdens – it is hard to define the burdens on a defendant and when they should act, and there is the distinct possibility of unfairness in doing so. For instance, should a person who sees someone drowning be obliged to jump in to attempt a rescue, even if he cannot swim himself?

The law has, however, recognised a number of exceptions. These have all been identified and categorised.

Smith v Littlewoods Organisation Ltd (1987)

The defendants bought a cinema to demolish and rebuild as a supermarket. It was then left empty and vandals broke in and set fire to it, the fire spreading and causing damage to adjoining property. There was no liability since the defendant was not responsible for the acts of strangers. As Lord Goff in the House of Lords stated:

'In such a case it is not possible to invoke a general duty of care; for it is well recognised that there is no general duty of care to prevent third parties from causing such damage.'

Further than this, he discussed the situations in which the law will impose a duty for a failure to act.

The defendant owes a duty by a contractual or other undertaking

The defendant may owe a contractual duty to act.

Stansbie v Troman (1948)

A decorator was given the key to the premises he was decorating and told to lock the door when he left. He failed to do so and a thief entered the house and stole property. The decorator was liable for failing to lock the door.

The duty might also arise from the character of an undertaking.

Barnett v Chelsea & Kensington Hospital Management Committee (1969)

Here the hospital casualty department undertook to diagnose ailments and injuries and treat their patients. They were therefore in breach of their duty when the doctor negligently failed to diagnose the condition of a patient who later died of arsenic poisoning.

However, policy considerations may prevent a duty from being imposed at all.

Hill v Chief Constable of West Yorkshire (1988)

A powerful argument by the mother of the Yorkshire Ripper's last victim that her murder might have been avoided with adequate policing was rejected. It was held that the police have no duty to the victims of crime to prevent the crime, or to catch the criminal according to any set time scale.

The defendant owes a duty because of a special relationship with the claimant

Clearly, in certain situations the nature of the defendant's duty arises because of the potential danger to the public presented by the activity carried out by the defendant. This could be so particularly of public bodies. In such cases the defendant may have a duty to act.

Home Office v Dorset Yacht Co. Ltd (1970)

Borstal boys escaped due to the negligence of the warders. These young offenders then did considerable damage to neighbouring property. The Home Office was then liable for their employees' failure to control the offenders in their charge.

There can be a duty in such a relationship leading to liability for its breach, despite the fact that the claimant has contributed to his/her harm.

Barrett v Ministry of Defence (1995)

Employers were liable for the death of a naval airman who became so drunk on cheap alcohol provided in the mess that he fell into a coma and drowned in his own vomit. The Court of Appeal would not impose liability for supplying the drink since the claimant had a responsibility for his own safety. The defendants were liable, however, for a failure to call a doctor or to look after him properly when he had collapsed. Damages were reduced by two-thirds to account for the man's contributory negligence.

Public bodies which fail to carry out statutory duties have also been the subject of claims.

D v East Berkshire Community Health NHS Trust (2005)

Doctors and social workers investigated parents where they suspected child abuse. The investigations revealed that the suspicions were unfounded. The parents then argued that the original suspicion was negligent and claimed damages for psychiatric injury. The House of Lords held that there was no duty owed to the parents since this would conflict with the statutory duties owed to the children to investigate.

The defendant owes a duty because of damage caused by a third party who is within his/her control

If the defendant can, in fact, be said to be responsible for a third party then there may be liability for a failure to properly exercise that control.

Haynes v Harwood (1935)

A driver left his horse-drawn van unattended in a street. Boys then threw stones at the horses, which bolted, injuring a policeman trying to prevent harm to pedestrians. The driver was liable. He had failed to leave the horses in a secure state and the boy's act was entirely foreseeable.

Again, this principle might operate in relation to public officials, such as the duty a prison officer has to control prisoners. So, the damage done by the Borstal boys in *Home Office v Dorset Yacht Co* is an example of a failure to exercise proper control.

The principle also has an obvious context in the case of sports officials. In both *Smolden v Whitworth and Nolan* (1997) and *Vowles v Evans and Another* (2003) courts imposed liability on rugby football associations. Failure by referees properly to control scrummages or apply the rules properly risked the safety of players.

Another obvious example where the duty might arise is in an employer's duty to his employees to hire competent staff for them to work with.

Hudson v Ridge Manufacturing Co Ltd (1957)

Here, an employee was injured following an incident involving a fellow employee who was a known practical joker. The employer had failed to deal with this employee's activities in the past, so was liable on this occasion.

The defendant owes a duty because of control over land or some other dangerous thing

If the defendant is in control of premises then there is a duty to ensure that visitors to the premises use them safely without risk to others.

Cunningham v Reading Football Club Ltd (1992)

Here, the football club was liable for the injuries caused by football hooligans breaking lumps of concrete off the premises and using them as missiles. They had failed to exercise proper control over these visitors.

In this way a defendant might owe a duty even for damage caused by acts of nature where he has failed properly to deal with the hazard arising.

Goldman v Hargrave (1967)

Here, a tree was struck by lightning on the defendant's land and ignited. When the defendant failed to deal with the fire and it spread to neighbouring property he was liable.

Activity

Self-assessment questions

1. What, exactly, is 'non-feasance'?

2. Why did English law traditionally reject the idea of liability for a failure to act?

3. In which situations will courts impose liability where there has only been an omission to act?

4. What is the common factor in those situations where the courts will impose such liability?

5. What significant warning does the case of *Hudson v Ridge Manufacturing* provide for employers?

Activity

Quick Quiz

Which of the following is an omission creating a duty of care?

1. A man sees another man bleeding to death in the street and walks past.

2. A doctor refuses to attend to a sick patient who then dies.

3. An electrician paid to fit new lights for a householder leaves some bare wires overnight and a child of the house is electrocuted.

4. A person who has borrowed a book from a friend leaves the book on the bus and it is lost.

5. I could help my nephew revise for his A Level Law but I do not and he fails.

6. Sparks from my barbecue are blown by a high wind and set fire to my next-door neighbour's shed.

Key Facts

- There is no general liability for a failure to act.
- However, there can be liability where there is a positive duty to act.
- A defendant may be liable for an omission where:
  - there is a contractual duty to act (*Stansbie v Troman*)
  - there is a duty based on a special relationship (*Home Office v Dorset Yacht Co.*)
  - the defendant has a duty to control another's acts (*Haynes v Harwood*)
  - the defendant has a duty to control events on his land (*Goldman v Hargrave*).

In the Dilemma Board below, consider the accuracy of each of the four statements, A, B, C and D, as they apply to the facts in the central scenario. You only need to give the basic principles. The answer is in the Appendix at the end of the book.

Dilemma Board

A.

Raj cannot claim any damages from Stan for the £20,000 theft, as leaving the door open was not a negligent act.

B.

Stan will not have to pay damages to Raj for the £20,000 theft because he was in great pain when he failed to lock the door after him.

Stan, a painter and decorator, is decorating Raj's hall and has been left with the keys to the house to lock up when he finishes because Raj works late. Stan falls off his stepladder, injures his arm in the fall and goes off to hospital, failing to lock the door after him. The house is burgled after Stan leaves and £20,000 worth of goods stolen. At the hospital Dr Blunder fails to x-ray Stan's arm, which has a complex fracture. As a result of the failure to diagnose the injury, Stan suffers permanent disability, preventing him from working.

C.

Dr Blunder will not be held liable for Stan's permanent disability because Dr Blunder owed no duty to Stan to x-ray Stan's arm.

D.

Dr Blunder will not be liable to Stan for his permanent disability because Dr Blunder did not cause the injury to Stan's arm.

Chapter 7

Torts Affecting Land: Occupiers' Liability

7.1 Liability to lawful visitors

7.1.1 Introduction and origins

Occupiers' liability concerns the liability of an 'occupier' of land for the claimant's injury, or loss or damage to property suffered while on the occupier's 'premises'. Therefore, it must be distinguished from damage caused by the defendant's use of his or her land, which the claimant suffers on his or her own land. This would lead to an action in nuisance, or possibly *Rylands v Fletcher*.

It is a fairly recent tort, and is found in two statutes: the Occupiers' Liability Act 1957 (concerned with the duty of care owed to lawful visitors) and the Occupiers' Liability Act 1984 (concerned with the duty owed to trespassers).

While, in statutory form, the tort has developed out of negligence, so much of the terminology and many of the principles are the same. Indeed, although the Acts do contain extensive definition, where definitions are not supplied in the Acts these are to be found in the common law.

Inevitably there is some overlap with negligence. The basic liability arises from the loss or injury caused by the 'state of the premises'. Loss or damage that arises other than because of the state of the premises should be claimed for under negligence where this is possible.

> ### Ogwo v Taylor (1987)
> Here, there was no liability under the 1957 Act when a fireman was injured in a fire on the defendant's premises. The fire did not result from the state of the premises, so liability was in negligence.

It is possible to argue that the Act should apply in the case of damage caused other than by the state of the premises since s1(1) states that the 1957 Act should apply

'in respect of dangers due to the state of the premises or to things done or omitted to be done on them'.

While the 1957 Act has been described as a particularly well-drafted statute, it possibly suffers from under-use. While the Pearson Report recognised that as many as 27% of reported accidents occur in the home, very few claims follow domestic accidents.

7.1.2 Who is an occupier? (potential defendants)

Potential defendants are the same under either Act: occupiers of premises.

There is in fact no statutory definition of 'occupier'. S1(2) of the 1957 Act merely states that the rules apply *'in consequence of a person's occupation or control of premises . . .'*.

The established test for determining occupation, then, is found in common law.

> ## Wheat v E Lacon & Co. Ltd (1966)
>
> A manager of a public house was given the right to rent out rooms in his private quarters even though he had no proprietary interest in the premises. When a paying guest fell on an unlit staircase, the House of Lords held that both the manager and his employers could be occupiers for the purposes of the Act. In the event, neither had breached their duty since it was a stranger who had removed the light bulb.

So, there can be dual or multiple occupation of premises, and the identity of the defendant, which party was in control of the premises, may depend on the circumstances in which the damage or injury was suffered.

> ## Collier v Anglian Water Authority (1983)
>
> Here, a promenade formed part of the sea defences for which the water authority was responsible. The local authority owned the land and was responsible for cleaning the promenade. When the claimant was injured as a result of its disrepair, it was the water authority rather than the local authority which was liable, though both were occupiers.

Occupation does not require either proprietary interest or possession, so the position is quite different from trespass. All that is required for liability is that the defendant has sufficient control of the premises at the time that the damage was caused to be responsible for it.

> ## Harris v Birkenhead Corporation (1976)
>
> Here, a four-year-old child had been injured in an empty house, which was not boarded up or secured in any way. Even though the council had not yet taken possession of the house they were liable since they had served a compulsory purchase notice and were effectively in control of the premises.

In the final analysis, the identity of the defendant will be influenced by the ability to meet a successful claim whether through insurance or other means.

7.1.3 Premises

The Acts are again relatively silent on the meaning of 'premises'. Some limited reference is given in s1(3)(a) which refers to a person having occupation or control of any *'fixed or moveable structure, including any vessel, vehicle and aircraft . . .'*.

So the common law again applies, and besides the obvious, such as houses, buildings and the land itself, premises has also been held to include:

- ships in dry dock (*London Graving Dock v Horton* (1951))
- vehicles (*Hartwell v Grayson* (1947)
- lifts (*Haseldine v Daw & Son Ltd* (1941)
- and even a ladder (*Wheeler v Copas* (1981).

7.1.4 Potential claimants under the Occupiers' Liability Act 1957

The 1957 Act was passed in order to simplify a fairly complex common law, whereby the duty owed to a person entering premises varied according to the capacity in which that person entered. The Act introduced a common duty to be applied to all lawful visitors.

By s1(2) the classes of people to whom the occupier owes a duty remains as it was under common law. These are called visitors under the Act, and as a result of s1(2) include:

- All invitees – these can be, for example, friends making a social call, but they could also include people invited on to land for a purpose, e.g. to give a quote for work.
- Licensees – or people whose entry is to the material interest of the occupier, e.g. customers. They can include anyone with permission to be on the premises for whatever purpose (licensees were treated somewhat harshly by the common law, being entitled to no more than warnings of danger). Visitors under an implied licence will need to prove that the conduct of the occupier amounted to a grant of a licence.

Lowery v Walker (1911)

Certain members of the public used a short-cut across the defendant's land for many years. While he objected he took no legal steps to stop it. When he loosed a wild horse on the land, which savaged the claimant, he was liable. The claimant, by the defendant's conduct, had a licence.

- Those entering under a contractual agreement – in which case the terms of the contract might determine the extent of the duty.
- Those not requiring permission to enter because of a legal right to enter, e.g. meter readers, police officers, etc.

No duty is owed under the 1957 Act to trespassers. A more limited duty is owed to trespassers under the Occupiers' Liability Act 1984. Certain other categories of entrants are also not covered by the 1957 Act. These include:

- those using a private right of way
- those entering under an access agreement under the National Parks and Access to the Countryside Act 1949 (both of the above classes are also dealt with under the 1984 Act)
- those using a public right of way – these are excluded by both Acts and will fall under common law with the tortfeasor being liable for misfeasance but not non-feasance.

McGeown v Northern Ireland Housing Executive (1994)

The claimant lived in a cul-de-sac owned by the defendants. She was injured on a footpath which had become a public right of way. The reason for the injury was a failure to maintain the footpath and her action failed.

Activity   *Quick Quiz*

Consider which of the following potential claimants would be able to class themselves as visitors for the purposes of the OLA 1957 and why.

1. Trevor is a milkman delivering milk to Archie's door.
2. Kurt is a milkman who picks flowers in Archie's garden after delivering the milk.
3. Gordon, a football fan with a season ticket for the Wanderers, arrives at the ground on Wednesday night for the match with United.
4. Hannah regularly crosses Farmer Giles' field using a well-known public path.

5. Greg is at Mavis's house on Monday morning, as agreed, to paint the outside.

6. Ali is a police officer who has called at Brian's house for some routine enquiries.

7. Tom regularly climbs over his neighbour's back fence and comes through his back garden on his way home, knowing that his neighbour works late so will be out.

8. Parminder calls at her friend Baljinder's house, as arranged, to enjoy a meal together.

9. Baljinder is at her friend Parminder's house for a meal and enters Parminder's bedroom and takes a valuable ring.

10. Yuri is an employee of British Gas and has called at Ojukwu's house to read the gas meter.

7.1.5 The scope of the occupier's duty under the 1957 Act

The extent of the duty of care is set out in s2(1):

'An occupier owes the same duty, the common duty of care, to all his visitors except insofar as he is free to do and does extend, restrict, modify or exclude his duty to any visitors by agreement or otherwise.'

The nature of the duty is found in s2(2). The duty is to:

'take such care as in all the circumstances ... is reasonable to see that the visitor will be reasonably safe for the purpose for which he is invited ... to be there ...'.

Three key points need to be made straightaway.

- Firstly, the standard of care is that generally applied in negligence, the standard of the 'reasonable man'. As a result, the occupier is merely obliged to guard against the foreseeable.

- The duty in the 1957 Act applies only so long as the visitor is carrying out activities that are authorised within the terms of the visit. So, if the visitor strays (s)he may lose protection under the 1957 Act, although the 1984 Act might still apply.

- The duty is to keep the visitor safe, not necessarily to maintain safe premises. If the latter were the case it would make industry unworkable. But because of the scope and potential limitations of the duty, the Act sensibly makes some different rules for different classes of visitor.

7.1.6 Children and the 1957 Act

Under s2(3) the occupier *'must be prepared for children to be less careful than adults ...'* and, as a result, *'... the premises must be reasonably safe for a child of that age ...'*, demonstrating that in the case of children the standard of care is measured subjectively.

The reasoning is perfectly logical – what may pose no threat to an adult may nevertheless be very dangerous to a child.

> ### *Moloney v Lambeth LBC (1966)*
> Here, a four-year-old fell through a gap in railings guarding a stairwell and was injured. An adult could not have fallen through the gap so such an injury would have been impossible. The occupier was liable.

Similarly, a child is unlikely to appreciate risks as an adult would, and indeed might be attracted to the danger. As a result, an occupier should guard against any kind of 'allurement' which places a child visitor at risk of harm.

Glasgow Corporation v Taylor (1922)

Here, a seven-year-old child ate poisonous berries in a botanical gardens and died. The shrub on which the berries grew was not fenced off in any way – the occupier should have expected that a young child might be attracted to the berries, and was liable.

Nevertheless, the mere existence of an allurement on its own is not sufficient ground for liability.

Liddle v Yorkshire (North Riding) CC (1944)

A child was injured jumping off a soil bank while showing off to his friends. The defendant was not liable since the child had been warned away from the bank on numerous previous occasions.

In fact, even though an allurement exists there will be no liability on the occupier if the damage or injury suffered is not foreseeable.

Jolley v London Borough of Sutton (1998) CA and (2000) HL

The council failed to move an abandoned boat for two years. Children regularly played in the boat and it was clearly a potential danger. When two young boys of 14 jacked the boat up to repair it, the boat fell on one, injuring him. In the Court of Appeal the action for compensation failed, since it was held that, while the boat was an obvious allurement, the course of action taken by the boys, and therefore the specific type of damage, were not foreseeable. The House of Lords reversed this. As Lord Hoffmann said: 'the [trial] judge's broad description of the risk as being that children would "meddle with the boat at the risk of some physical injury" was the correct one to adopt ...'.

In any case, the courts will sometimes take the view that very young children should be under the supervision of a parent or other adult. In this case the occupier might find that (s)he is relieved of liability.

Phipps v Rochester Corporation (1955)

A five-year-old child was injured when it fell down a trench dug by the defendant where the child frequently played. The defendant was not liable because the court concluded that the parents should have had the child under proper control.

7.1.7 People carrying out a trade or calling on the occupier's premises and the 1957 Act

Sensibly, the Act also has a more particular attitude to professional visitors, taking the view that, by s2(3)(b), in relation to activities carried on within their trade, they should *'appreciate and guard against any special risks ordinarily incident to it ...'.*

So, an occupier will not be liable where tradesmen fail to guard against risks which they should know about.

Roles v Nathan (1963)

There was no liability on the occupiers when chimney sweeps died after inhaling carbon monoxide fumes while cleaning flues. The sweeps should have accepted the advice of the occupiers to complete the work with the boilers off.

However, tradesmen might still have an action against their employer if the latter has agreed to an unsafe system of work.

General Cleaning Contractors v Christmas (1953)

Occupiers were not liable for an injury sustained when a window cleaner fell after a window closed on him, but the employers were.

However, the existence of a skill is not proof *per se* that the occupier is not liable. It depends whether the normal safeguards associated with the trade could have averted the loss or injury.

Salmon v Seafarers Restaurants Ltd (1983)

Owners of a chip shop were liable for the injuries caused to a fireman, which were unavoidable because of the character of the fire.

7.1.8 Liability for the torts of independent contractors under the 1957 Act

Generally, the occupier will be able to avoid liability for loss or injuries suffered by his/her visitors when the cause of damage is the negligence of an independent contractor hired by the occupier. This is under s2(4).

It is a sensible rule because a reputable contractor will, in any case, be covered by his/her own insurance, and so the claimant will still be able to recover compensation.

However, three requirements will apply:

- Firstly, it must be reasonable for the occupier to have entrusted the work to the independent contractor.

Haseldine v Daw & Son Ltd (1941)

Here, the occupier was not liable for negligent repair of a lift, a highly specialist activity.

- Secondly, the contractor hired must be competent to carry out the task.

Ferguson v Welsh (1987)

Demolition contractors hired by the local authority employed the claimant. When he was injured as a result of their unsafe working systems the local authority was liable.

One indication that a contractor is competent is the possession of insurance.

Bottomley v Todmorden Cricket Club (2003)

The club hired a contractor to carry out a fireworks display. The contractor used gunpowder, propane and petrol for the display rather than traditional fireworks and used the claimant, who had no experience, to run it. The claimant was badly burnt when the display went wrong. The club was liable because the contractor carried no insurance, an indication of incompetence.

- Thirdly, if possible the occupier must check the work. (Obviously, the more complex and technical the work and the less expert the occupier, the less reasonable it is to impose this obligation.)

Woodward v The Mayor of Hastings (1945)

Occupiers were liable when a child was injured on school steps which were negligently left icy after cleaning off snow. The danger should have been obvious to the occupiers.

One aspect of inspection could be checking whether the contractor has appropriate insurance.

Gwillam v West Hertfordshire NHS Trust (2002)

The Trust hired a 'splat wall' from contractors for a fund-raising event (where a person wears a Velcro suit and sticks to a wall after jumping from a trampoline). The claimant was injured because the contraption was negligently assembled by the contractors. The Trust had checked that the contractors had insurance but this ran out four days before the incident. The court held that there was a duty to check insurance but the Trust had discharged it in this case.

The obligation may not apply if there are other accepted means of assessing the independent contractor's competence.

Naylor (t/a Mainstream) v Payling (2004)

The claimant was thrown out of a nightclub and negligently injured by a door attendant supplied by an independent contractor. The claimant argued that the club had failed to check whether the independent contractor had insurance. The Court of Appeal held that there was no obligation to check whether the independent contractor was insured since the nightclub had complied with a local scheme supported by both the local authority and the police for establishing whether door attendants were suitably qualified for the work.

7.1.9 Avoiding liability under the 1957 Act

As we have already seen in s2(1), the occupier is free to extend, restrict, modify or exclude his duty to visitors. The occupier may achieve this in one of three ways.

1. Warnings

Under s2(4)(a) a warning will not absolve the occupier of liability unless *'in all the circumstances it was enough to enable the visitor to be reasonably safe'*. What is sufficient warning, then, will be a question of fact in each case.

Sometimes, for instance, a mere warning may be insufficient to safeguard the visitor and the occupier may be obliged to set up barriers instead.

Rae v Mars (UK) Ltd (1990)

A warning was ineffective in respect of a deep pit inside the entrance of a dark shed, so the occupier was liable.

However, a choice of words, which are nothing more than an attempt to avoid liability, will not be accepted as a warning.

Some risks are possibly so obvious that no additional warning is needed.

Staples v West Dorset DC (1995)

Danger of wet algae on a high wall at Lyme Regis should have been obvious.

This is certainly the case where the occupier has taken reasonable steps to avoid harm.

Beaton v Devon County Council (2002)

The claimant was injured while riding his bicycle through a tunnel. The tunnel was well lit and in good condition. Two gullies that ran through it were well known. The court held that the occupier had done everything practical to keep the visitor safe.

2. Exclusion clauses

These are allowed by s2(1), so they can be a term in a contractual licence.

> ### Ashdown v Samuel Williams & Sons Ltd (1957)
>
> The claimant was unable to recover for injuries sustained in a shunting yard because notices excluding liability were sufficiently brought to her attention and she was no more than a contractual licensee when she entered.

Use of exclusion clauses will, however, be subject to various restrictions:

- they will be unavailable in the case of persons entering under a legal right
- they will not apply in the case of strangers, e.g. a tenant's visitors, because they will have had no chance to agree the exclusion
- they will probably fail against children, who may be unable to read or to understand their implications fully
- they will not be allowed in respect of death or personal injury caused by the occupier's negligence because this will be prevented by s2(1) Unfair Contract Terms Act 1977
- there is also an argument that, since OLA 1984 imposes a minimum standard of care owed to trespassers, then this minimum standard should be beyond exclusion, or trespassers have better rights than lawful visitors.

3. General defences

There are two possibilities:

- the claimant's contributory negligence – under the Law Reform (Contributory Negligence) Act 1945 this has the effect of reducing awards of damages

- *volenti non fit injuria* (consent) – s2(5) allows that the occupier'*... has no liability to a visitor in respect of risks willingly accepted as his by the visitor ...*'.

The risk must, however, be fully understood by the visitor.

> ### Simms v Leigh RFC (1969)
>
> There was no liability to a Rugby Football player when the injury was sustained within the normal rules of the game.

- Mere knowledge of the risk is also insufficient – it must be accepted.

> ### White v Blackmore (1972)
>
> General knowledge that 'Jalopy Racing' was dangerous did not mean that the claimant had accepted inadequate safety arrangements.

- If the claimant has no choice, then their consent cannot be used as a defence.

> ### Burnett v British Waterways Board (1973)
>
> A claimant entering the defendant's dry dock on a barge had no choice but to be there, so consent was unavailable as a defence.

- Express warnings that the claimant enters at his/her own risk may well be caught by the Unfair Contract Terms Act 1977.

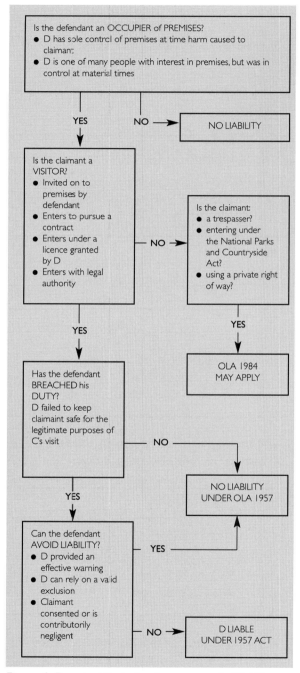

Figure 4 *Flow chart illustrating the assessment of liability under the Occupiers' Liability Act 1984*

Activity

Self-assessment questions

1. Who, exactly, is a visitor?

2. What sorts of people are non-visitors?

3. What decides whether a person is an occupier?

4. Why is the duty called 'the common duty of care'?

5. What, exactly, is the duty owed by the occupier?

6. Why should children have a different duty of care applied to them?

7. What, exactly, is 'allurement'?

8. What protection does the case of *Phipps v Rochester Corporation* give to an occupier?

9. When will a tradesman be able to sue an occupier successfully?

10. When will an occupier be liable for the negligent acts or omissions of people who have carried out work on his premises?

11. How can an occupier avoid being liable to a lawful visitor?

12. When will a warning sign protect an occupier from liability and when will it not?

13. When is an exclusion clause likely to be used and what will prevent it from succeeding?

- Occupiers' liability is covered by two Acts: the Occupiers' Liability Act 1957 in the case of lawful 'visitors', and the Occupiers' Liability Act 1984 in the case of trespassers.
- An 'occupier' is anybody in actual control of the land (*Wheat v Lacon*).
- 'Premises' is widely defined and has included even a ladder (*Wheeler v Copas*).
- By s2(1) 1957 Act a 'common duty of care' is owed to all lawful visitors.
- By s2(2) the duty is to ensure that the visitor is safe for the purposes of the visit.
- Under s2(3) an occupier must take extra care for children, who are less careful than adults, and not put extra danger in their path (*Taylor v Glasgow Corporation*).
- This will be in respect of any foreseeable danger to the child, regardless of what injury is actually caused (*Jolley v London Borough of Sutton*).
- However, it is assumed that parents should keep control of young children (*Phipps v Rochester Corporation*).
- A person carrying out a trade or calling on the occupier's premises must prepare for the risks associated with the trade (*Roles v Nathan*).
- The occupier will not be liable for damage which is the result of work done by independent contractors if:
  - it is reasonable to entrust the work
  - a reputable contractor is chosen
  - the occupier is not obliged to inspect the work – compare *Haseldine v Daw* and *Woodward v Mayor of Hastings*.
- It is possible to avoid liability where:
  - adequate warnings are given (*Rae v Mars*)
  - exclusion clauses can be relied on – subject to the Unfair Contract Terms Act
  - defences of consent or contributory negligence apply.

7.2 Liability to trespassers and non-visitors

7.2.1 The background to the 1984 Act and the 'common duty of humanity'

The 1984 Act was introduced to provide a limited duty of care mainly towards trespassers. The Act came about because traditionally at common law an occupier owed such entrants no duty at all, other than possibly to refrain from deliberately or recklessly inflicting damage or injury.

> ### Bird v Holbreck (1828)
> This case finally outlawed mantraps.

However, an occupier was still entitled to act reasonably in his own protection.

> ### Clayton v Deane (1817)
> This case accepted that an occupier was entitled to use reasonable deterrents to keep trespassers out, in this case broken glass on top of a wall, as long as it was reasonably visible.

The common law could be particularly harsh when applied to child trespassers.

> ### Addie v Dumbreck (1929)
> Children frequently played on colliery premises and near to dangerous machinery. When one was injured there was no liability since he was a trespasser.

Because of the increase in the number of dangerous premises, and taking into account the difficulties of making children appreciate danger, the law was changed.

BR Board v Herrington (1972)

A six year old was badly burned when straying on to an electrified railway line through vandalised fencing. The House of Lords, using the Practice Statement, established the 'common duty of humanity', a limited duty owed when the occupier knew of the danger, and of the likelihood of the trespass.

Because of some of the impracticalities of the rule, the 1984 Act was passed.

7.2.2 The scope and nature of the 1984 Act

By s1(1)(a) a duty applies in respect of people other than visitors (who are covered by the 1957 Act) for:

'injury on the premises by reason of any danger due to the state of the premises or things done or omitted to be done on them.'

Thus, the 1984 Act provides compensation for injuries only. Damage to property is not covered, reflecting an understandable view that trespassers are deserving of less protection than are lawful visitors.

The occupier will only owe a duty under s1(3) if (s)he:

'(a)   ... *is aware of the danger or has reasonable grounds to believe it exists;*

(b)   *... knows or ... believes the other is in the vicinity of the danger; and*

(c)   *the risk is one against which ... he may be expected to offer ... some protection.'*

The character of the duty owed is, by s1(4) to *'take such care as is reasonable in all the circumstances ...'* to prevent injury to the non-visitor.

So, the standard of care is an objective negligence standard. What is required of the occupier depends on the circumstances of each case. The greater the degree of risk, the more precautions the occupier will have to take. Factors to be taken into account include the nature of the premises, the degree of danger, the practicality of taking precautions and, of course, the age of the trespasser.

Tomlinson v Congleton Borough Council (2002)

The local authority owned a park, including a lake. Warning signs were posted prohibiting swimming and diving because the water was dangerous, but the council knew that these were generally ignored. The council decided to make the lake inaccessible to the public, but delayed start on this work because of lack of funds. The claimant, aged 18, dived into the lake, struck his head and suffered paralysis as a result of a severe spinal injury. His claim under the 1984 Act succeeded. Here, all three aspects of s1(3) were satisfied. The court felt that the gravity of the risk of injury, the frequency with which people were exposed to the risk, and the fact that the lake acted as an allurement all meant that the scheme to make the lake inaccessible should have been completed with greater urgency. However, the judge reduced damages by two-thirds because of the contributory negligence of the claimant.

The mere fact that the occupier has taken precautions or fenced the premises does not, in itself, indicate that the occupier knew or ought to have known of the existence of a danger.

White v St Albans City Council (1990)

Here, the claimant had taken an unauthorised short cut over the council's land. He fell from a narrow bridge that had been fenced. The court did not feel that this was sufficient to make the council liable.

There is no liability if the occupier had no reason to suspect the presence of a trespasser.

Higgs v Foster (2004)

A police officer investigating a crime entered the occupier's premises for surveillance and fell into an uncovered inspection pit behind coaches, suffering severe injuries which caused him to retire from the police force. The police officer was a trespasser and the occupier could not have anticipated his presence so there was no liability.

There is also no liability if the occupier was unaware of the danger or had no reason to suspect the danger.

Rhind v Astbury Water Park (2004)

The claimant ignored a notice stating 'Private Property. Strictly no Swimming', jumped into a lake and was injured by objects below the surface of the water. The occupier had no reason to know of the dangerous objects so there was no liability.

7.2.3 Avoiding the duty in the 1984 Act

Again, as with the 1957 Act, it is possible for the occupier to avoid liability.

Under s1(5) (s)he could do so by taking 'such steps as are reasonable in all the circumstances ...'. This might, in the case of adult trespassers, be achieved by use of effective warnings.

Westwood v The Post Office (1973)

A notice that 'Only the authorised attendant is permitted to enter' placed on the door of a motor room was held a sufficient warning for an intelligent adult.

But again, it is unlikely that such warnings will succeed in the case of children.

S1(6) also preserves the defence of *volenti*. Again, the claimant must appreciate the nature and degree of the risk, not merely be aware of its existence.

Ratcliffe v McConnell (1999)

A warning notice at the shallow end of a swimming pool read: 'Deep end. Shallow dive'. The pool was always kept locked after hours and the claimant knew that entry was prohibited at this time. He was a trespasser, so when he was injured diving into the shallow end his claim failed. The court held that he was aware of the risk and had accepted it.

There is no reference to exclusions in the Act. It is argued that exclusions should be impossible since the Act creates a minimum standard of care which would then be thwarted. However, this creates the unhappy situation where a trespasser might be entitled to more care than a lawful visitor.

Activity

Self-assessment questions

1. What protections, if any, did the law traditionally offer to trespassers?

2. Is it possible for an occupier legitimately to protect against intruders?

3. What type of damage is compensated under the 1984 Act?

4. Does the 'duty of common humanity' and the duty owed to trespassers under the 1984 Act differ at all?

5. What factors must be present in order to impose a duty on the occupier under the 1984 Act?

6. What difficulties are created by the minimum standard of care in the 1984 Act?

Activity   Problem

Consider the following problem on occupiers' liability.

Alsopp Towers is a large pleasure theme park. At the entrance gate there is a sign that reads *'All of the rides are dangerous and customers enter entirely at their own risk'*.

Consider any liability that Alsopp Towers may incur for the following customers:

a) Jasbir catches her heel in a gap between the boards while getting off 'The Screw', falls several feet, and injures herself badly.

b) Sean, who is a delivery driver, leaves his lorry to pick flowers from one of the ornamental borders and tears his shoe and sock and cuts his foot quite badly on broken glass.

c) Pedro, an electrical contractor who is repairing one of the rides, is electrocuted and badly burnt when Daisy, who operates the ride, carelessly plugs it in.

d) Tom and Jerry, two ten-year-old boys, have sneaked in by climbing over a fence. They are both injured when they walk across the rails on one of the rides and are hit by one of the cars.

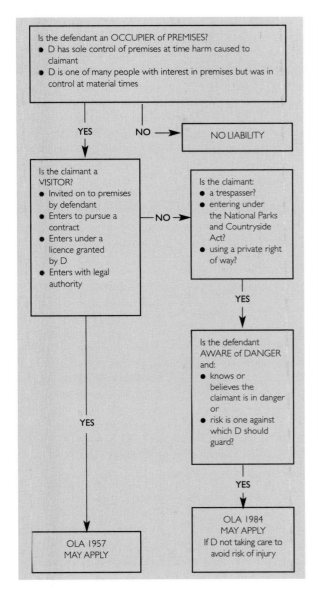

Figure 5 *Flow chart illustrating the assessment of liability under the Occupiers' Liability Act 1984*

- The law originally provided only limited protection to trespassers – the duty was not to deliberately cause them harm (*Bird v Holbreck*).
- Because of the harshness of the rule as it applied to children, a common duty of humanity to trespassers was introduced (*BR Board v Herrington*).
- This was given statutory force in the 1984 Act.
- The occupier only owes a duty under s1(3) if (s)he:
  - is aware of the danger or has reasonable grounds to believe it exists
  - knows or believes the other is in the vicinity of the danger and
  - the risk is one against which he may be expected to offer some protection.
- Compensation is only available in respect of personal injury or death, not personal property.
- The greater the risk, the more precautions must be taken (*Tomlinson v Congleton Borough Council*).
- Under s1(5) the occupier can defend if he has taken reasonable steps to avoid harm – so warnings may succeed, but not against children (*Westwood v The Post Office*).
- By s1(6) *volenti* is also possible if the trespasser is fully aware of the risk (*Ratcliffe v McConnell*).

Activity

There are always four essential ingredients to answering problem questions:

- Firstly, you must be able to identify which are the key facts in the problem, the ones on which any resolution of the problem will depend.
- Secondly, you will need to identify which is the appropriate law that applies to the particular situation in the problem.
- The third task is to apply the law to the facts.
- Finally, you will need to reach conclusions of some sort. If the question asks you to advise, then that is what you need to do. On the other hand, if the problem says 'Discuss the legal consequences of ...' then you know that you can be less positive in your conclusions.

Problem
Homer, his wife Marge, and children Bart and Lisa go to the Springfield Holiday Camp for two weeks in August. In their holiday contract is the following clause: '*Neither the Springfield Holiday Camp nor their servants or agents will be liable for death or injury to visitors, howsoever caused.*' A large notice to the same effect is placed at the entrance to the camp. The camp is owned and managed by Springfield Leisure Co.

Late one night, while returning to the holiday chalet, which is high up on a slope, Homer falls down the steep steps that lead to the chalet from the road below. There is no guardrail to the steps and the steps are unlit. Homer suffers severe head injuries in the fall.

Marge is electrocuted and badly burnt when she plugs in the kettle in the chalet's

Answering problem questions

kitchenette. The socket has actually been left live due to the negligence of Shoddy Electric Co. who recently rewired the chalet.

Bart cuts himself badly and wrecks his jacket with a sharp knife when he sneaks into the kitchen in the camp restaurant to make himself a sandwich. The door is not locked, but a notice on the door of the kitchen reads: 'Danger. Staff only.'

Lisa suffers an upset stomach when she eats berries on a bush growing by the chalet front door. The berries are poisonous.

Advise Homer, Marge, Bart and Lisa of any remedies they might have for their injuries, and against whom.

The facts
It is important to have a clear idea of what the principal facts are, particularly, as here, where there a number of different people and different problems involved. The main facts seem to be:

1. Springfield Leisure Co. own and manage the Springfield Holiday Camp.
2. Homer, Marge and their children, Bart and Lisa, contract for a holiday at the camp for two weeks in August.
3. The contract contains an exclusion of liability for death or injury, however caused.
4. A notice to the same effect is posted at the entrance to the camp.
5. Homer is injured when he falls, at night, down steep, unlit steps with no hand rail that lead to his chalet.

6. Marge is electrocuted and badly burnt when plugging in the kettle.

7. The socket is live due to the negligence of Shoddy Electric Co. who rewired it.

8. Bart cuts himself on a knife in the restaurant kitchen.

9. A notice on the kitchen door reads: 'Danger. Staff only.'

10. Lisa is poisoned when she eats berries growing on a bush by the front door.

11. Bart and Lisa are both children.

The appropriate law

It is very important when answering problem questions that you use only the law that is relevant to the precise facts, if for no other reason than that you are not getting any marks for using law that is irrelevant, so you are wasting valuable writing time. By looking at the various facts we can say that the following law may be relevant in this problem:

1. The area involved is the Occupiers' Liability Acts.

2. a) The 1957 Act covers liability towards 'visitors' – those lawfully on the premises.

   b) The 1984 Act concerns trespassers and is appropriate only to personal injury, not property damage.

3. There are three key issues:

   a) what counts as premises

   b) who is an 'occupier' and so who can be sued

   c) who can claim under the Acts and under which one.

4. There is no real definition of 'premises' in either Act – the common law applies, and is widely defined (i.e. wide enough to include a ladder in *Wheeler v Copas*).

5. Occupier is not defined in either Act – again, the common law applies (an occupier is 'anybody who is in control of the premises' – *Wheat v Lacon*).

6. Under the 1957 Act a 'visitor' is anybody with a lawful right to be on the premises.

7. Under s2(1) a 'common duty of care' is owed to all visitors.

8. Under s2(2) the duty is to take all reasonable care to keep the visitor safe for the purposes for which (s)he has legitimately entered the premises.

9. The standard of care is as for negligence, so the same sorts of principles apply.

10. a) Under s2(3) an occupier must be prepared for children to be less careful than adults would be.

    b) The occupier must not do anything to 'allure' the child into danger (*Taylor v Glasgow Corporation*).

    c) An occupier may be able to rely on the duty of parents to supervise very young children (*Phipps v Rochester Corporation*).

11. An occupier will not be liable for the harm caused by the work of independent contractors provided that:

    a) it is reasonable for the occupier to entrust the work to someone else (*Haseldine v Daw*)

b)   a competent contractor is hired
     (*Ferguson v Welsh*)

c)   the occupier carries out checks on
     the work if appropriate (*AMF v
     Magnet Bowling*).

12. An occupier may avoid liability
    under s2(1) in a number of ways:

    a)   warning notices, provided they are
         effective (*Rae v Mars*), and nothing
         short of a barrier may possibly be
         sufficient for children

    b)   exclusion clauses in contracts, but
         these would be subject to the Unfair
         Contract Terms Act, and a clause
         excluding liability for death or injury
         caused by negligence is invalid under
         s2(1)

    c)   the defences of contributory
         negligence and consent (not relevant
         here).

13. The 1984 Act applies by s1(1)(a) to
    persons other than visitors.

14. Under the 1984 Act an occupier is liable
    under s1(1) in respect of dangers 'due to
    the state of the premises or things done
    or omitted to be done on them'.

15. Under s1(3) the occupier will be liable if:

    a)   he is aware of the danger

    b)   he knows that the trespasser may
         come into the vicinity of the danger
         and

    c)   the risk is one against which the
         occupier might be expected to
         provide some protection.

Applying the law to the facts

1.   We know that Springfield Leisure Co. own
     and manage the holiday camp, so we can
     feel that they 'control' the premises and
     are occupiers and therefore defendants
     under the Act.

2.   We know also that Homer and his
     family have paid for their holiday and so
     will be 'visitors' and therefore may claim
     under the 1957 Act. The common duty of
     care applies to them all and they are
     entitled to expect the same standard of
     care.

3.   'Premises' presents no problems here –
     the holiday camp clearly is.

4.   It is easier past this point to take each
     individual in turn:

     Homer:
     •   The question is whether not providing
         a hand rail on the steep steps and not
         having them lit is a breach of
         Springfield's duty. It would certainly
         seem to fall below an appropriate
         standard of care, and the facts in any
         case seem to resemble those in
         Wheat v Lacon.

     •   The exclusion clause cannot
         apply because of s2(1) of UCTA.

     •   Similarly, the warning notice outside
         the camp would fail to relieve liability
         unless it covered specific risks (*Rae v
         Mars*).

     Marge:
     •   Leaving sockets 'live' clearly falls below
         an appropriate standard of care.

- The question here is whether it is Springfield or Shoddy who is responsible.

- It will obviously depend on whether Shoddy is a reliable contractor or not.

- Clearly, it is appropriate for Springfield to delegate that type of work, and they do not have the expertise to check it – they are relying on the contractors (*Haseldine v Daw*).

- The exclusion clause and warning notice would fail for the same reasons.

Lisa:
- Lisa is a child, so under s2(3) is entitled to expect greater care than an adult.

- The bush appears to be a possible 'allurement', certainly if we compare it with the facts in *Taylor v Glasgow Corporation*.

- It would be difficult to expect the parents to take full responsibility here where the bush is outside the front door, so is unlikely that *Phipps v Rochester Corporation* could apply in the circumstances.

- Again, the exclusion clause cannot apply and the notice is even less appropriate here because Lisa is a child.

Bart:
- Bart has entered a part of the premises from which he is barred – this may make him a trespasser.

- Bart is a child and a kitchen may well be an allurement to a hungry child – Springfield may expect some risk of trespassers to such parts of the premises if they do not keep them locked up (*BR Board v Herrington*).

- Furthermore, kitchen implements, sharp knives, etc. are clearly dangerous if unattended.

- The notice on the door is unlikely to be sufficient warning since it is imprecise in respect of the risk and, in any case, Bart is a child.

- The 1984 Act applies only in respect of injuries, so Bart may be unable to claim in respect of his damaged jacket

Conclusions

We have shown how the law applies to each of our four central characters, and would be able to advise them to sue with confidence.

- Homer and Lisa could both sue Springfield for their injuries under the 1957 Act.

- Marge can sue for her injuries, but unless Shoddy are disreputable contractors whom Springfield should not have hired then her action will be against Shoddy rather than Springfield.

- Bart is a trespasser and will sue Springfield under the 1984, Act, but for his injuries only, not for his other damage.

In the Dilemma Board below, consider the accuracy of each of the four statements, A, B, C and D, as they apply to the facts in the central scenario. You only need to give the basic principles. The answer is in the Appendix at the end of the book.

Dilemma Board

Hector is a paying guest at the Feelbetta Healthfarm. Before he goes to bed at midnight he goes to the pool for a swim. A sign on the door reads: 'Opening hours 9.00 a.m. to 9.00 p.m. No entry to guests outside of these hours. Pool dangerous when unattended.' Hector reads but ignores the sign and enters. He cannot find the light so he dives into the pool. The pool has been emptied and Hector is badly injured and blood from his injuries ruins his Armani swimwear which cost £200.

A.

Hector will be unable to claim damages under the Occupiers' Liability Act 1984 because of the warning notice.

B.

While Hector may be able to claim for his injury under the Occupiers' Liability Act 1984, Feelbetta will have a successful defence of *volenti*.

C.

Hector can claim damages successfully under the Occupiers' Liability Act 1957.

D.

Hector can claim damages successfully for his ruined Armani swimwear.

Chapter 8

Torts Affecting Land: Trespass to Land

8.1 The character and purpose of trespass

Trespass is one of the oldest torts, originating with the medieval writ *quare clausum fregit*, literally meaning 'by way of taking an enclosed area'. So even within the general heading of trespass, a trespass to land is still the oldest form of the tort.

The tort is defined fairly straightforwardly: a trespass to land occurs where there is an intentional (or negligent), unlawful entry on to, or a direct interference with, the land in the possession of another.

Again, the purposes of bringing an action in trespass to land seem quite straightforward:

- a claimant may wish to remove unwanted intruders from his or her land
- there may be a dispute as to title
- the claimant may be seeking to regain entry to land from which he or she has been unlawfully ejected
- and, above all of these, the claimant may be seeking an award of damages for any loss or physical damage caused by the trespasser.

Before identifying the various essential ingredients of the tort there are a number of important general points to make:

- Trespass is actionable *per se*. This means that there is actually no need for the claimant to prove that (s)he has suffered any damage – it is enough, merely, that the defendant has trespassed on to the land.

- Nevertheless, if damage has occurred then the claimant is entitled to make a claim for compensation.
- While usually a trespass is committed consciously and intentionally, it does not have to be – a negligent trespass might occur, for example, where picnickers stop on land on which they are unaware they have no right to be.
- A defendant in a trespass claim might have entered on to the land perfectly lawfully, but become a trespasser by going beyond the legitimate purpose for which he or she is on the land (this is particularly appropriate where a licensee exceeds the proper limits of the licence).

8.2 Land, claimants and defendants

8.2.1 What counts as land for the purposes of trespass?

There is no single definition of what counts as land that a claimant can then protect legitimately against a trespass. It will quite obviously include the land itself and any structure that has been erected upon it. Significantly, it can also include the boundary, as seen in *Westripp v Baldock* (1938).

A traditional principle applied to rights in land is *cujus est solum ejus est usque ad coleum et ad inferos*. Roughly translated, this means that the rights in the land extend to the air space above the land as well as to the subsoil below it.

In the case of air space, it has been held to be a trespass where:

- signs overhang land (*Kelsen v Imperial Tobacco Co.* (1957))
- cranes swing out over land (*Woolerton & Wilson v Costain* (1970))
- cables overhang land (*Wandsworth Board of Works v United Telephone Co.* (1884)), although, of course, in modern times this would be subject to any statutory authority.

However, balloons passing overhead have been held not be a trespass. (*Pickering v Rudd* (1815) and *Saunders v Smith* (1838)).

It has been further considered that rights over air space cannot extend so far as to interfere with proper, legitimate use of air transport.

Lord Bernstein of Leigh v Skyviews & General Ltd (1977)

Here, aerial photographers flew over the claimant's land, took photographs, and then tried to sell them to him. It was held not to be a trespass. The claimant's rights over air space should only extend to a height *'reasonably necessary for the enjoyment of the land'*.

This point is also confirmed in the Civil Aviation Act 1982. Generally, as a result of legislation, aircraft are immune from actions for trespass where they pass over land. However, it has been suggested that things that fall from an aircraft may amount to a trespass, as would be the case of the aircraft making an unauthorised landing.

In the case of the subsoil, where subterranean rights were crucial to the growth of industry in the eighteenth and nineteenth centuries, most under-soil activities are now authorised specifically by statute.

However, some interesting principles have developed within the common law, so that undersoil rights might extend under a highway which passes through the claimant's land.

Harrison v The Duke of Rutland (1893)

The Duke held grouse shoots on his land. When protesters who were on the highway tried to scare off the grouse they were held to be trespassing.

This principle has also been extended where the defendant has been using an adjoining highway for improper purposes, rather than merely for entry on to land. The point is that the highway can be freely used until its use is an abuse of a landowner's rights.

Hickman v Maisey (1900)

There was a trespass where the defendant used the highway to spy on the claimant's race horses in training.

However, it will obviously not apply where a trespass follows a legitimate use of the highway.

Randall v Tarrant (1955)

The defendant trespassed on to the claimant's land. The defendant parking on the nearby road prior to the trespass in this case was not classed as a trespass.

8.2.2 Claimants and defendants

Deciding who is eligible to sue in trespass to land can seem quite complex, since it is not based on pure ownership or on pure possession. If the owner of land only could sue, then this would prevent a legitimate tenant from ejecting trespassers or suing for damage they may have caused. If the right to sue came purely with possession, then this might prevent a rightful owner from recovering land from a squatter or even on termination of a lease.

Possession involves some form of occupation or physical control over the land. Any action in trespass, then, is said to be in favour of a person in possession at the actual time of the trespass as against the wrongdoer. So, the right to sue implies some superior right over the land enjoyed by the possessor in comparison with the defendant or alleged trespasser.

So, it is generally possible to use trespass against someone with a lesser right to be on the property.

> ## Graham v Peat (1861)
>
> The claimant was allowed to sue despite his lease being void by statute.

However, an action against a party with superior rights of occupation would fail.

> ## Delaney v T P Smith & Co. (1946)
>
> Under an oral agreement the claimant would acquire a tenancy of the defendant's property. Before the lease was executed the claimant secretly entered the premises. When the claimant was ejected he sued in trespass and failed. The agreement had not been reduced to writing and the defendant still had superior rights of occupation.

Since exclusivity of possession is necessary it would, for instance, be possible for a tenant to use trespass against the freehold owner but impossible for a lodger to succeed against a landlord, since the lodger has only a licence.

> ## White v Bayley (1801)
>
> The claimant was paid £75 a year for managing and living in premises rented by his employers. When the defendants gave the claimant notice to quit and took possession, the claimant forcibly re-entered. The defendants sought an injunction. The claimant's counter action in trespass failed. He was entitled to 'the use but not the occupation of the premises...'.

However, because the tenant rather than the landlord is in possession it is usually the tenant rather than the landlord who would sue. The landlord might still be able to sue when it is possible to show some harm to the reversionary title.

> ## Portland Management Ltd v Harte (1977)
>
> The landlord here brought an action against alleged squatters. It was held that this was acceptable providing the landlord could show title to the land and an intention to regain possession.

8.3 What acts amount to trespass?

The first and most significant point about a trespass to land is that the interference, whatever it is, must be direct. Indirect interference may well be actionable, but generally this will be as either nuisance or negligence, not as trespass.

Esso Petroleum Co. v Southport Corporation (1956)

Oil discharged into an estuary when a tanker beached, while possibly the result of negligence, was felt by Lord Denning to be too indirect to amount to a trespass.

Clearly there has to be some entry on to the land. Trespass must involve direct contact with the land. So, if there is no direct entry then there is no trespass.

Perera v Vandiyar (1953)

The claimant's gas and electricity meters were situated in the defendant's cellar. When the defendant switched off both supplies, while there was a clear interference with the claimant's premises, there was no direct entry so there was no trespass.

So, as long as an entry is wrongful it will be a trespass.

Entick v Carrington (1765)

Here, officers of the Crown broke into the claimant's house searching for documents. In their defence they argued that they were operating under a warrant granted by the Secretary of State. The court held that the Secretary of State had no jurisdiction to issue such warrants, so the entry was unlawful.

It does not, however, have to be the claimant who is responsible for the entry.

Smith v Stone (1647)

Stone successfully defended a trespass action when he had been carried on to the land by force.

So, any unwanted presence on the land might amount to a trespass. This might include walking, running, riding, cycling or driving on the land.

Besides these, however, it is always possible for a trespass to occur where the defendant is responsible for things being placed or even thrown on to the land.

Holmes v Wilson (1839)

The defendants had trespassed on to the claimant's land to erect buttresses as support for a road that was sinking. The claimant was able to sue again when the defendants failed to remove the buttresses.

It is interesting to note then that, while rocks or balls thrown on to the land might be a trespass, rubbish which is blown on to the land might not be. Compare *Smith v Stone* and *Esso Petroleum Co. v Southport Corporation* in this respect.

It will be common for the trespass to involve an active interference.

Basely v Clarkson (1681)

Here, the cutting and carrying away of a neighbour's grass was held to amount to a trespass even though it was carried out by mistake.

It could, however, involve a mere passive state of affairs.

Kelsen v Imperial Tobacco Co. Ltd (1957)

The trespass here involved an advertising hoarding which overhung the neighbouring land.

Even this could be a purely temporary state of affairs.

Woolerton & Wilson v Richard Costain Ltd (1970)

In this case the defendant's crane swung out over the claimant's land and was sufficient to amount to a trespass.

Indeed, even the merest contact might be seen as a trespass.

Westripp v Baldock (1938)

A ladder leaning against the claimant's wall was a trespass.

Finally, a trespass might occur even though the original entry on to the land was lawful, as when a postman veers off the path to pick flowers from the garden.

Trespass to land protects proprietary interests in land. However, while there are no strict privacy laws there are clearly invasions to people's privacy that prove annoying, including the activities of the paparazzi.

Privacy is protected under Article 8 of the European Convention on Human Rights. It may be that, following incorporation of the Convention in the Human Rights Act 1998, this is a better avenue to follow.

Activity   *Quick Quiz*

Consider whether I have trespassed on land in the following situations:

1. While playing 'frisbee' with my small nephew, the frisbee has landed in my next-door neighbour's garden.
2. While waiting for a bus I have sat on a garden wall next to the bus stop.
3. In a high wind my washing has blown off the washing line and on to my neighbour's garden.
4. While paragliding I have flown over a farmer's land.
5. To remove a tree on the boundary of my land I dig a hole underneath it that stretches under my neighbour's lawn.
6. Roofers replacing tiles on my roof have erected scaffolding that juts out over my neighbour's land.
7. I hide in a tree near to the house of a famous actress to take pictures of her sunbathing.

8.4 Trespass *ab initio*

One final problem concerning trespass is the old common-law doctrine of trespass *ab initio*.

As we have seen already, wherever a person abuses the limits of their right of entry on to land that person might become a trespasser from that point on.

The common-law doctrine of trespass *ab initio* was developed in relation to those people who entered on to land with a legal right, rather than by the claimant's permission.

Where such a person, for instance a police officer, enters the land, if the person exercising the right of entry does go beyond the legitimate purpose then (s)he will be said to have trespassed from the beginning (*ab initio* – the *Six Carpenters* case (1610)).

This legal fiction operates quite simply in order to protect the claimant from abuses of authority.

> ## Oxley v Watts (1785)
>
> Here, the doctrine was used when the defendant improperly worked a horse that he had taken under a distraint order.

The doctrine, however, will not apply where the action of the defendant is still justified in some way.

> ## Elias v Pasmore (1934)
>
> Police took documents that would help them in their case when they arrested the claimant. There was no trespass *ab initio* because the arrest was lawful.

Lord Denning has cast doubt upon this principle and upon the doctrine itself.

> ## Chic Fashions Ltd v Jones (1968)
>
> Removing goods for evidence that were believed stolen was held by the Court of Appeal not to be a trespass *ab initio*, and CA also doubted the continued existence of the doctrine.

However, the same judge in a later case applied the doctrine to mini-cab drivers touting for business (*Cinnamond v British Airport Authority* (1980)).

8.5 Defences and remedies

8.5.1 Defences

A number of specific defences may apply in the case of a trespass.

A customary right to enter

This might apply where rights have been gained according to prescription or long use. It is similar to the defence of prescription used in nuisance.

> ## Mercer v Denne (1905)
>
> The owner of a beach was prevented from building on it because local fishermen had a customary right to dry their nets on it.

A common law right to enter

This right itself may be lost if the legitimate entrant goes beyond his or her legal rights.

> ## Clissod v Cratchley (1910)
>
> Here, a solicitor entered land to enforce collection of a debt owed to his client. Since, unknown to the solicitor, the debt had already been paid there was a trespass.

Statutory right to enter land

This could apply, for instance, where a police officer enters to search under the Police and Criminal Evidence Act 1984, or to exercise a warrant for arrest. It may also include where gas and electricity meter readers enter under the Rights of Entry (Gas and Electricity Boards) Act 1954 to read meters. Another statutory licence operates in respect of neighbours under the Access to Neighbouring Land Act 1992. Under this statute, where neighbouring properties are so close that, in order to maintain the properties, decorate, etc. a trespass is inevitable, then this trespass may be excused.

Volenti non fit injuria (consent)

The basic principle here is that it is always possible to come on to land with the permission of the owner.

Necessity

This defence may operate, for instance, where the defendant comes on to land to avert a worse disaster, e.g. coming on to the land to rescue a child from a fire in the house.

Rigby v Chief Constable of Northamptonshire (1985)

Here, police officers fired CS gas into the claimant's shop where a dangerous psychopath was hiding. The shop then burned down. The police claimed necessity in that their actions were designed to get the man out of the shop. Their defence to trespass succeeded as they were responding to an emergency. However, they were still liable in negligence for failing to have the fire brigade in place when they fired the CS gas into the shop.

Licences

People are constantly granted licences in a variety of contexts, e.g. visiting the cinema or a football match, buying from a shop, visiting friends, contractors doing work. It must be remembered, though, that the licence ends where the person entering goes beyond its strict terms. Also, the licence will usually be limited to particular activities so that the person entering land who exceeds the terms of their licence will still be a trespasser.

It is always possible to revoke a licence.

However, this may prove to have other consequences if the landowner's revocation prevents the other party from completing a contractual obligation. This may then amount to an unlawful repudiation and a breach of contract by the landowner.

8.5.2 Remedies

Different remedies may be available, depending on whether the land is in the possession of the claimant or the defendant at the time the trespass is complained of.

Generally, if the claimant is in possession of the land then he or she will be suing for the interference with his or her rights of possession, and also for any loss that has arisen as a result of the trespass. In this case the claimant might recover damages for the loss and also an injunction to prevent further trespasses.

If the defendant is in possession of the land then the claimant will probably want to sue for ejectment of the defendant and recovery of the land, as well as claiming for any consequent loss, in this instance known as mesne profits. However, much more common and quicker remedies are found under straightforward procedural orders of the High Court and the County Court.

It is possible to claim purely nominal damages, and exemplary damages are also possible. In relation to specific losses damages can be based on actual deterioration. They can also take into account any costs of repossession.

Two further remedies are worthy of mention. Distress damage feasant is an old common-law remedy that involves keeping an object associated with damage caused to the land until such time as the damage is made good. This could, for instance, apply in the case of straying livestock, though in this case the police must be notified within a specific time.

A declaration can be obtained from the court where rights are unclear or uncertain.

Acton BC v Morris (1953)

A door was locked which deprived the occupiers access to their upper-floor flat. Rights of entry were then established by declaration of the court.

Activity

Self-assessment questions

1. What damage, if any, must a defendant cause to be liable for trespass?

2. Must a claimant claiming in trespass be the owner of the land?

3. Does a trespass have to be a conscious act?

4. In what circumstances can a defendant be liable for trespass without a positive action?

5. How far above and below the land itself do the claimant's rights extend?

6. What remedy will usually be the most appropriate in trespass?

7. When will it be possible to become a trespasser, despite having entered the land for a legitimate purpose?

8. What, exactly, is trespass *ab initio*?

9. Does it still have any practical significance?

10. When would a person be able to go on to land without the owner's permission?

11. What sort of things will limit the scope of a license to enter land?

Key Facts

- Trespass is a direct interference with someone's land.
- Anybody with an interest can sue a person with an inferior interest in the land, but a person cannot sue someone with a superior interest (*Delaney v T P Smith*).
- There must be a direct entry on to the land (*Perera v Vandiyar*).
- However, it may be only temporary (*Woolerton & Wilson v Richard Costain*).
- Trespass is actionable *per se*, so no damage need be done.
- The land can include the subsoil (*Harrison v the Duke of Rutland*).
- It can also include the air space above, except in the case of preventing air traffic (*Lord Bernstein of Leigh v Skyviews*).
- Trespass *ab initio* is an ancient doctrine which means that an entry on to land can be considered as a trespass even though it began as legitimate entry (*Oxley v Watts*).
- Defences include: a customary or a common-law or a statutory right to enter, consent, necessity and licences.
- Remedies include: a right of ejectment, repossession and damages.

Dilemma Board

In the Dilemma Board below, consider the accuracy of each of the four statements, A, B, C and D, as they apply to the facts in the central scenario. You only need to give the basic principles. The answer is in the Appendix at the end of the book.

Dilemma Board

Karl and Jacques own adjoining semi-detached houses. Karl has planning permission to build an extension at the rear of his house and Jacques allows Karl to walk on his back garden while work is in progress. However, Karl leaves building materials on Jacques' garden which damage his plants and also Karl erects scaffolding which overhangs the fence into Jacques' garden by several metres. Jacques complains to Karl who refuses to do anything to remedy the situation.

A.
Karl cannot be liable to Jacques because Jacques gave Karl permission to enter Jacques' land.

B.
Jacques can only claim in trespass to land because of the damage to his plants.

C.
The scaffolding overhanging Jacques' land does not amount to a trespass because it is not touching Jacques' land.

D.
Jacques can only claim in trespass to land against Karl because Karl owns the land.

Chapter 9

Torts Affecting Land: Nuisance

9.1 The character and purpose of private nuisance

9.1.1 Introduction

The tort of nuisance is the second tort to deal with interference with the land. However, in this case it involves indirect rather than direct interference.

Nuisance is sometimes seen as a quite complex tort. There are a number of reasons for this.

- Firstly, there are two distinct types – private nuisance and public nuisance. These are very different from one another. Besides this, many aspects of nuisance are now found in statutory form. So, strictly speaking, there is a third type also.
- Secondly, the tort covers a more diverse range of situations than do most other torts.
- Thirdly, the tort has itself, in specific circumstances, been developed to create the separate tort of *Rylands v Fletcher*.
- Finally, many of the situations involved can appear to be indistinguishable from those which might now be covered by the tort of negligence. In fact, it is probably simpler and more convenient to bring an action under negligence.

9.1.2 Definition and purpose

The usual definition of private nuisance is that in Winfield:

'... *an unlawful interference with a person's use or enjoyment of land or some right over, or in connection with it.*'

To this must be added the word 'indirect', because any direct interference would be actionable under trespass.

Nuisance is very much a tort of neighbourhood. It will almost always involve the competing claims of neighbours to do as they wish on their own land. Usually, but not always, it will involve adjoining properties. A number of points stand out in this respect.

- Firstly, neighbourhood is a continuous state of affairs, and clearly a problem created by one neighbour could affect another neighbour over a period of time.
- Secondly, it is not unreasonable to expect to be able to do whatever you like on your own land. Problems only arise when this affects your neighbour's ability to enjoy his land.
- Thirdly, disputes between neighbours can be as trivial as disputes within families. It would be an intolerable waste of court time to have to deal with all complaints, no matter how trivial they were.

For these reasons nuisance is often called the 'law of give and take'. It involves balancing the competing interests of individuals and, as Rogers says:

'*each of us must put up with a moderate amount of inconvenience caused by others as the price of being able to inflict some inconvenience upon others in the conduct of our own activities.'*

So, not every intentional interference with the enjoyment of land will be classed as a nuisance, only that which is also classed as unreasonable. What is reasonable in this respect, then, depends not so much on the conduct of the defendant, but on whether the interference caused by that conduct is sufficient to give rise to a legal action.

9.2 Claimants and defendants in private nuisance

9.2.1 Who can sue in private nuisance? (potential claimants)

Since nuisance involves the competing rights of neighbours to use their land how they wish, then the basic rule is that anyone who has the use or enjoyment of the land and is affected by the interference may claim. This will obviously include an owner and an occupier, but also can be any holder of a legal or equitable title.

It could then include an owner not in possession who is suing with respect to permanent damage done to the land by the interference.

A tenant can also sue, though there are some gaps in the law here regarding landlords' responsibilities to their tenants for the condition of the property.

Habiteng Housing Association v Jones (1994)

Here, a tenant was unable to claim compensation for damage caused by a cockroach infestation when there was no vermin control responsibility in the tenancy agreement and the tenant was unable to prove that the infestation began in the landlord's flat.

The Law Commission, in its Report No. 238 in 1966, recommended that the implied covenant of fitness for human habitation in the Landlord and Tenant Act 1985 should be updated to cover such eventualities.

Traditionally it was felt that, while the tenant would be able to bring an action, his or her family could not.

Malone v Laskey (1907)

Here, the wife of the householder was unable to sue in respect of personal injury sustained when vibrations from machinery caused the cistern to fall on her in the lavatory.

A recent innovation modified this principle somewhat.

Khorasandjian v Bush (1993)

The right to sue was granted to an occupier's family where they had suffered harassing telephone calls.

However, the House of Lords has overturned this principle in *Hunter and Another v Canary Wharf* (1997) preferring the principle that the right to sue in nuisance is linked to a proprietary right in the land.

9.2.2 Who can be sued in private nuisance? (potential defendants)

Clearly, the creator of the nuisance can be a defendant, and this might be the case whether or not the creator of the nuisance is also occupier of the land.

Southport Corporation v Esso Petroleum Co. Ltd (1953)

Here, the defendant's oil tanker beached in the estuary and leaked oil that subsequently drifted to local beaches. The court held that there was no reason why a defendant who is not the occupier of neighbouring land but misuses it so as to cause a nuisance should not be liable.

Even though an occupier has not created the nuisance, (s)he might nevertheless be liable in law for authorising it.

Tetley v Chitty (1986)

Here, a landlord was liable in nuisance by permitting go-kart racing on his premises.

However, the authorisation must apply to the nuisance, not just to the use of land by the creator of the nuisance.

Smith v Scott (1973)

A local authority was not liable for letting a flat to a 'problem family'. The lease specifically prohibited the creation of nuisances by tenants.

In other circumstances where the occupier is not responsible for creating the nuisance, (s)he might still be liable as a result of 'adopting' the nuisance, i.e. of failing to deal with the nuisance.

This principle can apply where a stranger has created the nuisance.

Sedleigh Denfield v O'Callaghan (1940)

Here, strangers had blocked a culvert pipe on the defendant's land. He knew about it but failed to deal with it, so that when it led to flooding on the claimant's land he was liable.

It can also apply even where the nuisance is the result of natural causes.

Leakey v National Trust (1980)

Here, following heavy rain, a large natural earth mound on a hillside slipped and damaged the claimant's cottage. The defendants were liable because they were aware of the possibility of it happening and did nothing to prevent it.

Liability is because the defendant is aware of the nuisance but does nothing about it.

Anthony and Others v The Coal Authority (2005)

The defendant took on responsibility for former bodies that had tipped waste from mining onto a tip on its land. This was later partly landscaped and passed into private hands. Later, spontaneous combustion of the coal started a fire which lasted for three years. The claimant sued for the interference caused by the fumes and smoke. The defendant was held liable because it was aware of the problem while the tip was still in its control but failed to prevent the nuisance.

This principle of a landlord being liable for adopting the nuisance by actually failing to deal with it quite commonly applies to local authorities acting as landlords.

> ### Page Motors Ltd v Epsom & Ewell Borough Council (1982)
>
> Here, the council was liable in nuisance for failing to deal with gypsies who camped out on council land and then interfered with the claimant's business.

This would apply whenever the council failed to prevent gypsies or other groups from congregating on council land and using it as a base from which to carry out any illegal activities (*Lippiatt v South Gloucestershire County Council* (1999)).

There are also a number of more complex provisions under landlord and tenant law, which are connected with the obligation to repair.

9.3 The essential elements of private nuisance

9.3.1 Introduction

There are three key elements in proving the existence of a nuisance:

- an unlawful (meaning unreasonable) use of land
- which leads on to an indirect interference
- with the claimant's use or enjoyment of land.

9.3.2 The unreasonable use of land

Mere interference on its own is insufficient to found an action. The claimant must prove that the defendant's activity amounts to an unlawful use of land. 'Unlawful' is not used here in the usual sense of 'illegal', but rather means that the court accepts that the defendant's use of land is unreasonable in the way that it affects the claimant.

The proper question for the court is 'In all of the circumstances is it reasonable for the claimant to have to suffer the particular interference?'. The courts, in assessing the defendant's conduct, are really analysing fault but with a more flexible approach than might be the case with negligence.

> ### Solloway v Hampshire County Council (1981)
>
> Here, the council was not liable for trees on the highway that damaged the claimant's property because they lacked the resources to do anything about it.

However, the opposite answer has been given in *Hurst & Another v Hampshire County Council* (1997) for consistency with other cases.

Because the tort is all about balancing competing interests, a number of factors will have to be considered by the court in deciding whether the use of land by the defendant is unreasonable.

a) Locality

Nuisance has to do with use of land, and land can be used in very different ways according to the area concerned. Thus, as Thesiger LJ stated it in *Sturges v Bridgman* (1879), '*what would be a nuisance in Belgrave Square would not necessarily be so in Bermondsey*'.

- Thus, the nuisance might be as simple as an acceptable activity carried out in the wrong area.

> ### Laws v Florinplace Ltd (1981)
>
> Here, the claimant succeeded in gaining an injunction where a shop in a residential area was converted into a sex shop and cinema club.

- So, the customary use of the area is important in determining liability.

Murdoch v Glacier Metal Co. Ltd (1998)

The claimant failed in showing that his use and enjoyment of land was interfered with when he lived close to a busy by-pass.

- Usually, the result may be different in an industrial area where claimants might naturally expect noise and pollution, though this will not prevent success in a nuisance action where damage is caused rather than mere interference with comfort.

St Helens Smelting Co. v Tipping (1865)

Copper smelting, even in an industrial area, could be classed as a nuisance when it resulted in smuts from the process damaging the claimant's shrubs.

- Often, in any case, it is possible for the court to reach a compromise between the competing interests of the two parties.

Dunton v Dover District Council (1977)

Here, the opening hours of a local authority playground were reduced following a successful complaint by a neighbouring old people's home.

b) The duration of the interference

To be actionable the interference should be continuous. In this way a noisy one-off party to celebrate A Level results may not be a nuisance, where the continuous vibration of machinery may.

- Usually it will be necessary for both the interference as well as its cause to be continuous for there to be liability.

Bolton v Stone (1951)

There was no liability when a cricket ball hit Miss Stone where the pitch was 78 yards from the road, she herself was 100 yards away, and the fence was 17 feet above the pitch. Significantly, it was shown that only six balls had been hit out of the ground in 28 years.

- However, isolated instances have been accepted as nuisances where they arose from a continuing state of affairs

Spicer v Smee (1946)

Fire that began as the result of faulty wiring spread to a neighbour's house. This was accepted as nuisance, the faulty wiring being a continuous state of affairs.

- The fact that the interference is only temporary is not, on its own, sufficient to avoid a claim of nuisance if the interference is of a kind and at times when it is an unacceptable interference.

De Keyser's Royal Hotel Ltd v Spicer Bros Ltd (1914)

Here, building work, including the use of pile drivers, was carried out at night and interfered with the claimant's sleep. Despite the fact that it was only a temporary state of affairs, the court granted an injunction to prevent the building work taking place at night.

- These principles have more recently been extended to cover an event lasting no more than 15 or 20 minutes.

> ### Crown River Cruises Ltd v Kimbolton Fireworks Ltd (1996)
> Here, a barge was set alight by flammable debris resulting from a firework display lasting only 20 minutes.

- Indeed, *Rylands v Fletcher* has been described as a specific form of nuisance covering isolated escapes.

> ### Cambridge Water Co. v Eastern Counties Leather plc (1994)
> Here, chemicals from the tanning process eventually filtered through the ground and polluted the claimant's bore hole.

c) The seriousness of the interference

The law sensibly makes a distinction here between mere inconvenience and actual physical damage.

- In the case of mere discomfort or inconvenience, the test is all about balancing the competing interests and about what is reasonable. The appropriate test is whether the interference is:

  > *'an inconvenience materially interfering with the ordinary comfort physically of human existence, not merely according to elegant or dainty modes and habits of living, but according to plain and sober and simple notions among the English people.'*

  Knight Bruce V-C in *Walter v Selfe* (1851).

- Generally, where the interference causes damage to the claimant it will be sufficient to class the use of land as unreasonable.

> ### Halsey v Esso Petroleum Co. Ltd (1961)
> Here, the claimant was successful in complaining about the noise coming from the defendant's depot, but also in relation to the damage which smuts caused to the washing.

- However, even damage may be insufficient cause to claim if the activity is for the public benefit.

> ### Miller v Jackson (1977)
> The majority of the Court of Appeal held cricket balls coming onto Miller's land from the local cricket club to be a nuisance. Nevertheless, they were not prepared to grant an injunction since it was not in the public interest.

- The use of land in any case might not be considered unreasonable where such use is an absolute right.

> ### Stephens v Anglian Water Authority (1987)
> Because the right to appropriate water is an absolute right, it could not be classed as unreasonable, even though it caused subsidence in the claimant's property.

d) The sensitivity of the claimant

The claimant cannot engage in a use of land that in itself is hypersensitive, and then complain of damage caused by normal activities.

Robinson v Kilvert (1889)

There was no liability when the heat required in the manufacture of the defendant's boxes downstairs in a building damaged the brown paper made by the claimant upstairs, as it would not damage any other paper.

Recently, the law has moved away from the concept of 'abnormal sensitivity' to a general test of foreseeability.

Network Rail Infrastructure v Morris (2004)

Morris ran a recording studio near to a railway line. The railway company installed new track circuits which interfered with the claimant's amplification system, causing him to lose business. The Court of Appeal ignored the issue of abnormal sensitivity but held that the interference was not foreseeable.

e) Malice shown by either party

- Deliberately harmful acts will ordinarily be nuisances.

Hollywood Silver Fox Farm v Emmett (1936)

The defendant, objecting to the claimant's use of his land as a mink farm, fired shotguns near to the property. Normally this would not be unreasonable use of land. However, mink eat their young when frightened. The act was meant to cause harm and was unreasonable.

- Acts of revenge taken in response to unreasonable behaviour can themselves be

classed as unreasonable and therefore a nuisance, and any action that might have been brought may in turn be defeated.

Christie v Davey (1893)

The defendant became annoyed by the noise from music lessons next door and responded by banging on the walls, beating trays and shouting. An injunction was granted against him.

f) The state of the defendant's land

- It is not possible for the defendant to simply ignore nuisances that arise on his or her land, however they are created.

Leakey v The National Trust (1980)

The defendants were liable when a large mound, the Burrow Mump, on their land subsided and damaged the claimant's cottages.

- So, defendants owe a duty to prevent the spread of those things on their land which might create a nuisance.

Bradburn v Lindsay (1983)

The owner of a semi-detached property was held to be liable to his neighbour for the spread of dry rot which he should have prevented.

- However, they will not be liable merely because a natural event is occurring that might create a nuisance, unless they are also aware of the actual danger created by the natural event.

Holbeck Hall Ltd v Scarborough Borough Council (2000)

The claimant's hotel was situated close to the sea near to a cliff. The local council owned the land between the hotel and the cliff top. After a long period of steady erosion there was a major landsl p that undermined the foundations of the hotel, meaning it had to be demolished. The Court of Appeal held that the council was not liable. They were unaware of the danger of the major landslip and it could not be presumed from the previous erosion. They had neither adopted the nuisance, nor had they created it.

g) The actual cause of the nuisance

Where an activity is obviously an interference, but the cause of the harm is another factor, there is no actionable nuisance.

Southwark LBC v Mills and others; Baxter v Camden LBC (1999)

In joined appeals, tenants in blocks of council flats complained about normal daily noises coming from the neighbouring flat. The reason that the noises could be heard at all was the poor soundproofing of the flats. It was held that the noise was not unreasonable in this context and could not be a nuisance.

h) The impact on the claimant's human rights

Since incorporation of the European Convention on Human Rights it may be possible for a claimant to argue that his human rights are also affected by the nuisance.

Marcic v Thames Water plc (2002)

Here, through the failures of the defendants, the claimant's home became flooded with sewage on numerous occasions. The Court of Appeal held that this amounted to an actionable nuisance, but was also a breach of Art 8 – the right to respect for private and family life, home and correspondence.

9.3.3 An indirect interference

The boundaries between trespass to land are found in the character of the interference.

If the interference involves a direct physical intrusion then the action should be fought in trespass. Nuisance will only be available where the interference is indirect.

In this way, a variety of things have been held to be actionable as nuisances:

- fumes drifting over neighbouring land (*Bliss v Hall* (1838))
- loud noises including gunfire (*Hollywood Silver Fox Farm v Emmett* (1936))
- vibrations from industrial machinery (*Sturges v Bridgman* (1879))
- hot air rising into other premises (*Robinson v Kilvert* (1889))
- smuts from factory chimneys (*Halsey v Esso Petroleum* (1961))
- fire (*Spicer v Smee* (1946))
- continuous interference from cricket balls (*Miller v Jackson* (1977))
- pollution of rivers (*Pride of Derby & Derbyshire Angling Association v British Celanese* (1953)).

9.3.4 The use and enjoyment of land

We have already seen how courts will draw a distinction between an interference with the mere enjoyment of the land and actual physical damage.

In this way, there has been some judicial control over the extent to which enjoyment of land is protected within the tort. This is where the courts are called on most often to balance competing interests. It means that certain activities will be beyond protection.

Generally, the courts have refrained from protecting purely aesthetic interests.

Bridlington Relay Ltd v Yorkshire Electricity Board (1965)

Here, there was no nuisance when overhead power cables ruined television reception.

This is because, as Lord Hoffmann has stated, the inconvenience involved in such cases should be in relation to the land itself, rather than merely the landowner.

Hunter v Canary Wharf Ltd (1997)

Families of tenants were denied an action in private nuisance where they complained of dust and poor television reception caused by the erection of a tall building nearby, because they lacked *locus standi*. The House of Lords overruling the Court of Appeal, also stated that such interference could not be classed as a nuisance.

It is logical to assume, therefore, that there could be no action for lowering the tone of a neighbourhood, and yet that seems to be the substance of the case in *Laws v Florinplace* (1981).

In a recent verdict, interference with a functional use of land supporting a purely entertainment or leisure purpose has been identified as an interest capable of protection (*Crown River Cruises Ltd v Kimbolton Fireworks Ltd* (1996)).

Activity   *Quick Quiz*

Consider whether there is a possible claim for nuisance in the following situations:

1. Raj and Jas recently received successful A Level results and held a very noisy party that lasted till 3.00 a.m. Ada and Florence, who live next door, were kept awake and were quite annoyed.

2. Tara lives next door to Albert, an amateur short-wave radio enthusiast. When he is using his equipment it causes interference to both sound and vision on Tara's television.

3. Ricky, a music promoter, proposes to hold an open-air pop concert, lasting one week, in parkland at the head of a residential cul-de-sac.

4. Norris is annoyed because Rita's cat regularly comes into his garden and messes on his flowers, some of which have died.

5. Residents in a private home for the elderly object to the noise from junior football matches played on local authority playing fields near to the home.

9.4 Defences and remedies in private nuisance

9.4.1 Defences

A number of defences may be particularly appropriate to an allegation of private nuisance.

a) Statutory authority

Since many of the activities that are likely to be the cause of a nuisance are now regulated or licensed by environmental or other laws, statutory authority is likely to be one of the most effective defences.

> ## Hammersmith Railway v Brand (1869)
>
> V brations from trains were an inevitable consequence of the existence of the railway. As Lord Cairns said, it would be a *reductio ad absurdam* to grant injunctive relief since this would prevent the railway from operating.

However, the defence may not be available where discretion to act is exercised improperly.

> ## Metropolitan Asylum District Hospital v Hill (1881)
>
> Here, there was a general power to build a smallpox hospital. The defence was unavailable when it was sited in a place that would cause a nuisance.

The defence will not be available, either, where there is negligence.

> ## Dorset Yacht Co. Ltd v Home Office (1970)
>
> In this case the Home Office could not avoid liability for the damage done by borstal boys who had been taken to Poole by their warders.

b) Local authority planning permission

This can, in some circumstances, act as lawful justification for a nuisance.

> ## Gillingham Borough Council v Medway (Chatham) Dock Co. (1993)
>
> Planning permission was granted to use part of a dockyard as a commercial port. Neighbours then suffered disturbance from heavy vehicles using the access 24 hours a day. It was held not to be an actionable nuisance because of the planning permission.

However, local authorities have no power to authorise nuisances, so planning permission will only be granted where the nuisance is the inevitable result of a change in the character of a neighbourhood that Parliament itself has expressly authorised.

> ## Wheeler v Saunders (1996)
>
> A pig farmer was granted planning permission to expand by building two more pig houses, each containing 400 pigs. One pig house was only 11 metres from the cottage of a neighbour, who then took action in nuisance. The defendant's appeal on the point of planning permission failed because the defence was said to operate only in respect of those nuisances that Parliament had authorised.

c) Prescription

This is a defence that is unique to nuisance. If the nuisance has continued for 20 years without complaint, then the right to complain will lapse.

> ## Sturges v Bridgman (1879)
>
> The vibrations from the defendant's machinery disturbed the claimant who had bought land next door and was using it as a doctor's consulting room. The defence of prescription actually failed, since the court held that the nuisance only began when the consulting room was built.

d) Act of a stranger

This means the act of a trespasser may be a defence. This will not apply, however, where the defendant adopts the nuisance (*Sedleigh Denfield v O'Callaghan* (1940)).

e) *Volenti non fit injuria*

A claimant may always consent to the nuisance.

Kiddle v City Business Properties Ltd (1942)

A tenant will generally be said to consent to the risk of nuisances arising from the condition of the premises that are not the result of the landlord's negligence. Here, the tenant failed in his action when gutters had become blocked and flooded over on to the tenant's stock.

f) Public policy

The tort, as we have said, is about competing interests. The courts will not, then grant, a nuisance action where it is not in the public interest.

Miller v Jackson (1977)

Here, the court refused to grant an injunction to the neighbour of a cricket ground that had been in existence for more than 70 years, despite the damage the claimant had suffered, rather than lose a recreational facility.

However, the mere fact that something is of public benefit does not mean that it will automatically escape liability for nuisance.

Adams v Ursell (1913)

A fish and chip shop in a residential area was still a nuisance despite the fact that it was patronised by local people.

g) The claimant coming fresh to the nuisance is not a defence

Bliss v Hall (1838)

The claimant bought a house close to the defendant's candle works. This had been there for three years but was still held to be a nuisance.

Activity   *Quick Quiz*

Consider whether any defence to a claim for nuisance is possible in the following situations:

1. The noise from a busy railway line distresses homeowners living in houses next to the railway line.

2. Burglars break into Ravinder's home while he is spending six months in India and leave his radio, TV and hi-fi all playing on maximum volume.

3. Anna lives in the flat beneath Roger in a block of flats. Anna is very distressed because she has to get up at six to go to work, and when Roger returns from his work at around 1.00 a.m. she can hear his footsteps walking around for hours.

4. Residents of a small estate want to have a nearby local authority playground shut down because of the noise from children playing.

5. For more than 15 years Archie has kept pigs in his back yard. His neighbour, Reggie, eventually objects to the smell.

9.4.2 Remedies

Damages are available as a remedy where the claimant has suffered some loss. The test of remoteness will be that in *The Wagon Mound (No. 2)*, based on reasonable foreseeability. The claimant will be able to recover for any physical loss, for depreciation in value and for a business loss.

The common remedy for nuisance will be an injunction. This will be prohibitory, ordering the defendant to refrain from the nuisance. The injunction may be coupled with damages where a loss has occurred.

One further remedy available to a claimant is 'abatement'. This may well involve entering the defendant's premises in order to prevent further nuisance. In this way a claimant might enter a defendant's land in order to chop down overhanging branches, although these would need to be returned to the defendant.

One possible difficulty with this remedy is that it could lead to a counter injunction, as in *Stanton v Jones* (1995), which involved a dispute over a high hedge.

The remedy, in any case, may not always be possible.

Disputes between neighbours can lead to very strained relations, and indeed television shows have been devoted to the subject of disputes that got out of hand. The courts, in recent times, have encouraged the use of Alternative Dispute Resolution (ADR) in general in civil disputes. Mediation is one way of neighbours approaching the problem from a more productive standpoint than resorting to court actions.

The criminal law also has introduced measures for the protection of people who are the victims of bad behaviour by neighbours as well as by others. These might include antisocial behaviour orders, introduced in the Crime and Disorder Act 1998, and criminal offences under s2 and s4, as well as the possibility of a civil claim under s3 of the Protection from Harassment Act 1997.

Since Art 8 of the European Convention on Human Rights concerns the right to privacy and the respect for family life, it is possible also to use human rights law now, particularly since the incorporation of the Convention in the Human Rights Act 1998. Indeed, such a course of action has already proved successful.

> ### Burton v Winters (1993)
>
> In a dispute over a boundary, a wall was found to be a few inches over the boundary. When the injured party was awarded damages instead, and then damaged the other party's garage, she was prosecuted for criminal damage.

> ### Marcic v Thames Water plc (2002)
>
> Here, the claimant's land was repeatedly flooded with sewage as a result of the defendant's failure to control it. The Court of Appeal, while acknowledging the claim as an actionable nuisance, also accepted that it amounted a breach of Art 8. The House of Lords reversed this decision and held that there was no actionable nuisance and no breach of Art 8 since the interests of the general public were greater.

9.4.3 Alternatives to an action in nuisance

Civil actions of course are costly to bring, and despite the Woolf reforms may still be slower than other forms of action.

Activity

Self-assessment questions

1. Why is the law of nuisance sometimes referred to as 'the law of give and take'?

2. When will an action in nuisance be unavailable to a person who has suffered from the nuisance?

3. In what ways will locality affect an action for nuisance?

4. In what circumstances is it possible for an act that is not continuous to be an actionable nuisance?

5. What is the effect of malice in the tort of nuisance? How does this compare with other torts?

6. In what ways is *Hunter v Canary Wharf* a disappointing judgment?

7. Why should a person's excessive sensitivity prevent them from claiming?

8. In what circumstances is a person liable in nuisance for a nuisance actually caused by someone else?

9. What is generally the most effective defence in nuisance, and why?

10. What factors will determine a claimant's choice of remedy in nuisance?

11. Why would a claimant bring an action in nuisance rather than negligence?

9.5 Public nuisance and statutory nuisance

9.5.1 The definition and character of public nuisance

Public nuisance is very different to private nuisance. For one thing it extends beyond neighbours.

It has been defined as:

'something which affects a reasonable class of Her Majesty's citizens materially or in the reasonable comfort and convenience of life.'

Romer LJ in *A-G v PYA Quarries Ltd* (1957).

Public nuisance does not have to be an interference with the use and enjoyment of land, so it is not based on proprietary rights. For this reason it has also developed as a crime, in which respect it will commonly be prosecuted by the Attorney-General.

9.5.2 Requirements for proving public nuisance

It is essential for an action to be successful in public nuisance for there to be a substantial class of people affected by the nuisance.

Attorney-General v PYA Quarries Ltd (1957)

Here, the nuisance complained of was the noise and vibrations caused by quarrying. The defendant's argument that too few people were affected failed. It was sufficient that a representative class was affected.

To succeed, a claimant must be able to show special damage suffered over and above that which other members of the class have suffered.

> ## Tate & Lyle Industries Ltd v Greater London Council (1983)
>
> The House of Lords characterised an interference with navigation rights in the River Thames as physical damage, making it actionable public nuisance.

- Special damage might include personal injury.

> ## Castle v St Augustine Links (1922)
>
> A taxi driver was hit in the eye by a sliced golf ball. The golf club was liable. In comparison with *Bolton v Stone*, the links straddled the highway so the risk of harm was much greater.

- It can also include damage to goods, as with the washing in *Halsey v Esso Petroleum Co. Ltd* (1961).
- It can also include financial loss.

> ## Rose v Miles (1815)
>
> The defendant's barge blocked a navigable river. As a result, the claimant was forced to empty his barge and pay for alternative transport. The defendant was liable for the cost.

- One further example of special damage might be a loss of trade connection, as when shops lose trade during a long-term blockage of the highway, such as road repairs (*Wilkes v Hungerford Market Co.* (1835)).

Most commonly, the tort involves use and abuse of the highway. Interference can be in a number of ways.

- It might involve obstructions to the highway. This might occur as the result of queues for which the defendant is responsible, as at a football match or concert or theatre performance (*Lyons v Gulliver* (1914)).
- It may apply to a picket line (*Thomas v National Union of Mineworkers (South Wales Area)* (1985)).
- It can apply to projections over the highway that cause damage. These could be clocks, hoardings, signs and other artificial structures. In this case an occupier is liable to ensure that structures do not fall into disrepair. In the case of natural things, the position may be less clear.

> ## Noble v Harrison (1926)
>
> Here, a branch from a tree on the defendant's land fell on to a bus. The defendant was not liable because the defect in the tree was latent and probably beyond his control.

- It will also apply to the condition of the highway, particularly since a local authority will usually have a duty to maintain the highway.

> ## Griffiths v Liverpool Corporation (1967)
>
> Here, it was a nuisance when a person tripped on a flagstone that was standing up by half an inch.

9.5.3 Statutory nuisance

Parliament has declared that certain activities are nuisance by statute.

They are usually part of public health reform and so prejudicial to health more than prejudicial to land, e.g. Clean Air Act 1956. But they may also include provisions designed to protect the environment generally, e.g. the Environmental Protection Act 1990, the Environment Act 1995. They may also include statutes that regulate particular industries, such as nuclear power.

They provide a means of stopping the nuisance and save the victim the cost and inconvenience of taking a civil action.

In all cases they are quasi-criminal and therefore enforced by local authorities through the use of abatement notices.

Offenders failing to comply are then tried in Magistrates' Court, with a range of potential sanctions available, but usually fines.

Activity

Self-assessment questions

1. What are the significant differences between private and public nuisance?

2. Who, exactly, are '*a reasonable class of Her Majesty's citizens*'?

3. What, exactly, is special damage in public nuisance?

4. In what way is the 'highway' so important to public nuisance?

5. What areas in particular does statutory nuisance more effectively control?

Key Facts

- It is possible to have private nuisance, public nuisance, and now statutory nuisance also.
- A private nuisance is defined as an unlawful, indirect interference with a person's use or enjoyment of his land.
- 'Unlawful' means 'unreasonable', and what is unreasonable can depend on:
  - locality – what is a nuisance in Belgravia need not be a nuisance in Bermondsey (*St Helens Smelting Co. v Tippin*)
  - duration of the nuisance – whether the nuisance is continuous or only short lived (*Bolton v Stone*)
  - sensitivity of the claimant (*Robinson v Kilvert*)
  - the seriousness of the nuisance – whether or not damage is caused, or merely inconvenience (*Halsey v Esso Petroleum*)
  - malice can also play an important role (*Christie v Davey*).
- The interference must be indirect; direct interference would be a trespass.
- It is insufficient that the interference is with a purely recreational use of land (*Hunter v Canary Wharf*).
- Defences include: statutory authority, prescription, act of a stranger, consent and public policy.
- Public nuisance is defined as an interference with the material comfort of a class of Her Majesty's subjects.
- It must involve damage to the defendant over and above that caused to the public generally (*Tate and Lyle v GLC*).
- It involves the highway, i.e. damage caused by obstructions to the highway, projections over the highway, and the condition of the highway.
- In many instances, particularly environmental protection, statute has intervened to control nuisances, e.g. Clean Air Act, Environment Act, Environmental Protection Act.

Activity

Answering Problem Questions

Remember, there are four essential ingredients to answering problem questions.

- Firstly, you must be able to identify which are the key facts in the problem, the ones on which any resolution of the problem will depend.

- Secondly, you will need to identify which is the appropriate law that applies to the particular situation in the problem.

- The third task is to apply the law to the facts.

- Finally, you will need to reach conclusions of some sort. If the question asks you to advise, then that is what you need to do. On the other hand, if the problem says 'Discuss the legal consequences of', then you know that you can be less positive in your conclusions.

Problem

Les recently received planning permission from Weatherville UDC to add an extension to his terraced cottage. He has kept his next-door neighbours, Norman and Emma, awake over many nights while he has drilled and hammered till very late. As both go early to bed and are very light sleepers they have been easily disturbed by the noise. Les has gathered together a large amount of building rubbish and left it in his yard on top of bags of kitchen rubbish. The rubbish has begun to smell dreadfully, and the fumes from spilt tins of paint stripper among the rubbish have caused valuable plants in Norman and Emma's garden to wilt and die. Les has ignored all requests to behave more reasonably. Emily, another neighbour of Les, is so upset by Les's behaviour

that she has begun to leave Radio 2 on at full volume during the middle of the night in retaliation.

Advise Les of any possible claims against him.

The facts

It is important to have a clear idea of the principal facts, particularly here, where there many people and many problems involved. The main facts seem to be:

1. Les is extending his terraced home.

2. Les has local authority planning permission to do so.

3. Les drills and hammers till very late at night, keeping his neighbours, Norman and Emma, awake.

4. They are both light sleepers.

5. Les has also left building rubbish on top of rotting rubbish.

6. This causes smells that upset the neighbours, and fumes from a chemical in the rubbish kill valuable plants of Norman and Emma's.

7. Les does not respond to requests to behave more reasonably.

8. Emily, another neighbour, retaliates by playing loud music in the early hours.

The appropriate law

It is very important when answering problem questions that you use only the law that is relevant to the precise facts, if for no other reason than that you are not getting any marks for using law that is irrelevant, and so you are wasting valuable writing time. By looking at the various facts we can say that the following law may be relevant in our problem here:

1. The appropriate area of law appears to be nuisance.

2. Private nuisance is defined as unlawful (unreasonable) indirect interference with a person's quiet use and enjoyment of their land.

3. So anyone may sue who has use or enjoyment of land, but they must also generally have a proprietary interest in the land (*Hunter v Canary Wharf*).

4. Unreasonable use of land depends on many factors, e.g.:
   * locality – a nuisance in a built-up or industrialised area is less likely to be actionable (*Sturges v Bridgman*)
   * though physical damage caused by the nuisance may make locality irrelevant (*St Helens Smelting Co. v Tipping*)
   * continuous duration – a one-off event is less likely to be a nuisance (*Bolton v Stone*)
   * over-sensitivity of a claimant may defeat a claim (*Robinson v Kilvert*)
   * malice may indicate a nuisance or may, if by the claimant, defeat any possible action – compare *Christie v Davey* and *Hollywood Silver Fox Farm v Emmett.*

5. Nuisance must be indirect – any direct interference would be trespass – so includes, smells, fumes, noises etc.

6. Potential defendants can be a person causing the nuisance (*Esso Petroleum v Southport Corporation*), or a person adopting a nuisance (*Sedleigh Denfield v O'Callaghan*), and also the owner or occupier of land.

7. Possible defences include:
   * local authority planning permission (*Gillingham BC v Medway (Chatham) Docks*)
   * but see the qualification to this defence in *Wheeler v JJ Saunders*
   * public policy may also be an issue since, if an injunction were sought, it is unlikely that a court would wish to defeat homeowners' chances to extend or improve.

8. Possible remedies include:
   * injunctions – to prevent the person from continuing the nuisance (see the effect in *Miller v Jackson*)
   * damages – to compensate for loss already suffered as a result of the nuisance.

Applying the law to the facts
1. Les is an occupier of the land and presumably also the owner, since he is extending the property, so he can be the defendant in any possible nuisance action.

2. Norman, Emma and Emily are all neighbours – if the issue of proprietary interest is not a problem they would all appear to be potential claimants.

3. Norman and Emma and the drilling and hammering:
   * Here it would appear that the interference is with use and enjoyment of land, so locality could be relevant,

although it is commonplace for people to build extensions.

- The interference is indirect – noise.
- Les appears to have some defence in his planning permission.
- Les also appears not to have acted with malice initially, but his refusal to 'be reasonable' may be malice.
- It is at least arguable whether Norman and Emma are 'over-sensitive,' since they go to bed early and are very light sleepers.

4. Norman and Emma and the smell from the rubbish:

- Again, interference is indirect.
- The issue again is interference with enjoyment or pleasure, so the same points apply.
- There may also be a possibility of a statutory nuisance.

5. Norman and Emma and the damaged plants:

- Here again, the interference is indirect – fumes.
- However, because damage is caused, locality is irrelevant and a successful claim is most likely.

6. Emily:

- Emily began with the possibility of a claim, from the noise of the drilling and hammering and from the smell of the rubbish.
- However, the facts in her case seem to mirror those in *Christie v Davey*.

- Emily seems to have defeated any possible claim by her own acts of malice.

7. Possible remedies:

- The effects of an injunction should be considered, i.e. the argument in *Miller v Jackson*.
- Damages would be appropriate in relation to the destroyed plants.

Conclusions

We have shown how the law applies to each of our four central characters, and would be able to advise Les that he may be subject to some actions:

- Norman and Emma could take action against Les in nuisance, for the interference with their quiet use and enjoyment of their land, although they may not succeed because of Les's planning permission and their own characteristics, being very light sleepers.
- Norman and Emma could also take action in respect of the smells from the rubbish – and the same factors may apply – although there may be an environmental issue in relation to the smell also, so statutory provisions might be applied.
- Norman and Emma are in any case likely to succeed for their claim where the, apparently toxic, fumes have killed their plants, because there is quantifiable damage.
- Emily is unlikely to succeed in any claim against Les because he can counter with her own acts of malice.

Dilemma Board

In the Dilemma Board below, consider the accuracy of each of the four statements, A, B, C and D, as they apply to the facts in the central scenario. You only need to give the basic principles. The answer is in the Appendix at the end of the book.

Dilemma Board

Albert has recently moved into the adjoining semi-detached house next door to Brenda. Albert keeps tropical fish in a tank on the wall adjoining Brenda's house. The pump for the fish tank makes a loud noise and causes vibrations. Brenda retaliates by playing music very loud. The vibrations from the pump cause a painting to fall off Brenda's wall, hitting her ten-year-old daughter Candice on the head and injuring Candice.

A.
Brenda can claim against Albert for public nuisance.

B.
Brenda can claim successfully against Albert for private nuisance.

C.
Brenda can claim against Albert in private nuisance but Albert will have a defence of prescription.

D.
Candice can claim against Albert in nuisance for the injury caused to her when the painting fell on her head because of the vibrations.

Torts Affecting Land: *Rylands v Fletcher* and Strict Liability

10.1 The character and purpose of the tort

The tort actually comes from the case of *Rylands v Fletcher*. The rule was defined in the case in the Court of Exchequer Chamber by Blackburn J. He said:

'We think that the true rule of law is, that the person who, for purposes of his own, brings on his land and keeps there anything likely to do mischief if it escapes, must keep it in at his peril, and, if he does not do so, he is prima facie answerable for all the damage which is the natural consequence of its escape.'

This basic definition contains the major ingredients of the tort. Lord Cairns then added to these, in the appeal to the House of Lords, the further requirement that for the claimant to succeed the thing brought on to the land must then amount to a 'non-natural' use of land.

The tort is identified as a form of strict liability to deal with dangerous activities and dangerous substances. However, it is arguable how much it can actually be seen as a tort of strict liability, or how much it is a particular type of nuisance dealing with isolated but hazardous escapes, rather than with continuous interference.

Whichever it is, the tort is not straightforward and it is not simple to bring an action. In fact, there are so many defences available to a claim that it is hard to see that it is strict liability at all.

Traditionally, it could be said that the liability was strict because there was no particular requirement to show fault, and the defendant could be made liable even if he or she had taken care to avoid the escape. The tort was also seen as distinguishable from nuisance because there was a requirement in nuisance that harm of the type caused by the nuisance should be foreseeable, but no such requirement is apparent in *Rylands v Fletcher*.

This is not now the case, since the House of Lords has identified the tort as a type of nuisance and subject, therefore, to the same test of foreseeability.

Cambridge Water Co. v Eastern Counties Leather plc (1994)

The claimants were a water company that used a borehole from which to extract water for domestic consumption and use. The defendants owned a nearby tannery where they used a solvent for degreasing the animal skins. Sometimes this solvent would spill on to the concrete floor. Unknown to the defendants, over a period of time the spilt solvent seeped into the ground and eventually filtered through into the borehole contaminating the water. Since the contamination was not foreseeable at the time of the spillages the House of Lords held that there could be no liability.

There are other factors that make the tort difficult to prove. Lord Cairns added the requirement that there be a non-natural use of land. So the simplest way to defeat a claim is to show that the use of land in question is a natural use.

Moreover, the judges have shown hostility to the general principle of strict liability in the tort and have restricted the application of the rule still further.

- Firstly, according to *Read v J Lyons & Co. Ltd* (1947), there can only be liability where the thing brought on to the defendant's land escapes from that land.
- Secondly, according to *Rickards v Lothian* (1913), there must be a '... *special use of land bringing with it increased danger to others'*.
- Thirdly, there has recently been a return to foreseeability of type of damage, as in *Cambridge Water Co. v Eastern Counties Leather plc* (1994).

In spite of all this, the tort can still not be seen as a straightforward extension of nuisance. Claimants have recovered damages despite not being occupiers of land, as in *Hale v Jennings Bros* (1938). The tort has similarly been said to apply to both accidental and intentional releases of the thing that 'causes mischief' (*Crown River Cruises Ltd v Kimbolton Fireworks Ltd* (1996)).

10.2 Essential elements of the tort

10.2.1 Introduction

There are essentially four elements that must be proved in order for there to be a successful claim under the tort of *Rylands v Fletcher*:

- a bringing on to the land and accumulating
- of a thing likely to cause mischief if it escapes
- which amounts to a non-natural use of the land
- and which does escape and causes damage.

In the case itself, all elements were present and the defendants were liable.

Rylands v Fletcher (1868)

The defendant, a mill owner, hired contractors to create a reservoir on his land to act as a water supply to the mill. The contractors carelessly failed to block off disused mineshafts that they came across during their excavations. Unknown to the contractors, these shafts were connected to other mineworks on adjoining land. When the reservoir was filled, water flooded the neighbouring mines. All elements of the modern tort were present. The large volumes of water were not naturally present in that form, but were brought on to the land. Such a large volume of water could quite obviously do damage if it escaped. Lord Cairns identified that storage of water in these quantities did amount to a non-natural use of land. Finally, in the event, the water did escape through the mineshafts causing considerable damage to the claimant.

Each of the four elements requires proof and so should be considered individually.

10.2.2 The bringing on to the land

Clearly, the starting point here is that if the thing in question is already naturally present on the land then there can be no liability.

Pontardawe RDC v Moore-Gwyn (1929)

In this case there was no liability for the damage caused by the escape of rocks in an avalanche.

Neither could there be liability if the thing in question was already growing on the land. There must be a bringing on to land for liability.

Giles v Walker (1890)

There was no liability for weeds spreading on to neighbouring land.

Neither will there be liability for a thing that naturally accumulates on the land.

Ellison v The Ministry of Defence (1997)

Rainwater that accumulated naturally on an airfield at Greenham Common did not lead to liability when it escaped and caused flooding on neighbouring land.

However, it is still possible for there to be an action in nuisance where the defendant is aware of the thing causing the nuisance and has, in effect, 'adopted it' by failing to do anything about it.

Leakey v The National Trust (1980)

Here, a mound of loose earth on a hill was particularly subject to cracking and slipping in bad weather. When the mound did in fact slip and cause damage to neighbouring land, the defendants were liable because they knew of this possibility and yet failed to do anything to prevent it.

Besides this, the person who brings the thing on to the land does not have to be the owner or occupier of the land. In this way a mere licensee could come within the scope of the rule.

Charing Cross Electric Supply Co. v Hydraulic Power Co. (The Charing Cross Co. case) (1914)

Here, the defendants had a statutory power to lay water mains, which were then situated above electric cables. They were liable to the claimants, however, when the water main burst and flooded the electric cable, causing a blackout in large parts of London.

The thing brought on to the land must be brought on to the land for the defendants' purposes.

Dunne v North Western Gas Board (1964)

The Gas Board was bound by statute to supply gas to its consumers. It was held, however, not to have collected the gas on to land for its own purposes, so there was no liability.

But the fact that the thing is brought on to the land for the purposes of the defendant does not mean that it has to be accumulated there for the defendant's benefit.

> ### *Smeaton v Ilford Corporation (1954)*
>
> A local authority collected sewage under a statutory authority. It was held that it did so for its own purposes, even though it was accepted that it derived no benefit from collecting the sewage.

One final, and quite significant, point here is that the thing that is brought on to the land does not necessarily have to be the thing that escapes and causes mischief.

> ### *Miles v Forest Rock Granite Co. (Leicestershire) Ltd (1918)*
>
> The claimant brought the action in respect of injuries suffered when rocks flew on to the highway from the defendants' land where they were blasting. It was the explosives that had been brought on to land that actually caused the rock to escape, but there was still liability.

10.2.3 The thing likely to do mischief if it escapes

It is not the escape itself that must be likely, only that mischief is likely if the thing brought on to land does escape.

> ### *Musgrove v Pandelis (1919)*
>
> Here, the rule was applied when a garaged car with petrol in its tank caught fire and the fire spread to the next-door neighbour's house. The fire was unlikely, but would certainly cause mischief if it escaped.

Neither must the thing that escapes be dangerous in any intrinsic sense. It is sufficient that it becomes dangerous by the manner of the escape.

> ### *Shiffman v Order of the Hospital of St John of Jerusalem (1936)*
>
> Here, the thing that 'escaped' and caused the damage was a flagpole.

However, the thing must be a source of foreseeable harm if it does escape.

> ### *Hale v Jennings Bros (1938)*
>
> A car from a 'chair-o-plane' ride on a fairground became detached from the main assembly while it was in motion and injured a stallholder as it crashed to the ground. The owner of the ride was liable. Risk of injury was foreseeable if the car came loose.

Strangely enough, even people who 'escape' have been held to be dangerous and a potential mischief under the rule.

> ### *Attorney-General v Corke (1933)*
>
> Here, a landowner allowed gypsies to camp on his land. When they then committed nuisances and trespass against his neighbours the landowner was liable. The gypsies were held to be 'likely to do mischief if they escaped'. One potential problem here is whether or not the landowner would have been in a position to lawfully restrict the gypsies' free movement.

10.2.4 A non-natural use of land

Lord Cairns, in the House of Lords in *Rylands v Fletcher* itself, indicated the requirement of a non-natural use of land. He said:

'if the defendants, not stopping at the natural use of their close, had desired to use it for any purpose which I

may term a non-natural use … and in consequence of doing so … the water came to escape … then it appears to me that which the defendants were doing they were doing at their own peril.'

This concept of non-natural use was developed and explained by Lord Moulton in *Rickards v Lothian* (1913):

'it is not every use of land which brings into play this principle It must be some special use bringing with it increased danger to others, and not merely by the ordinary use of land or such a use as is proper for the general benefit of the community.'

The question of what is a non-natural use of land is, by necessity, a complex concept and one which inevitably changes to take into account technological change and changes in lifestyle. It is inconceivable, for instance, that leaving a car garaged with petrol in the tank could be seen as a non-natural use of land today, though it was seen as such in 1919 at the time of *Musgrove v Pandelis*.

The case law suggests that we must consider that non-natural is something more than artificial and refers to some extraordinary use of land.

In general, as a result things associated with a domestic use of land will not normally be classified as non-natural, even though they may be potentially hazardous.

- So, fire in a domestic context has been held a natural use.

Sochaki v Sas (1947)

There was no liability for a fire that started from a spark from a domestic grate and spread to the claimants premises.

- As has electric wiring.

Collingwood v Home & Colonial Stores (1936)

Defective wiring caused a fire to start that then spread to the claimant's premises. It was impossible to show negligence and the defendants escaped liability.

- A domestic water supply has also been held to be a natural use of land for the purposes of the rule.

Rickards v Lothian (1913)

Here, the defendant was not liable when an unknown person turned on water taps and blocked plugholes on his premises, so that damage was caused in the flat below.

Even owners of commercial premises may be exempt from the rule because the activity leading to the escape is held to be a natural rather than a non-natural use of land.

Peters v The Prince of Wales Theatre (Birmingham) Ltd (1943)

The claimant occupied part of the premises of the theatre. A sprinkler system in the theatre caused flooding and damaged the claimant's stock. There was no liability since the use of land was not non-natural.

Where such facilities are in question it will often be the volume, size or quantity involved that will lead to the thing being classed as a non-natural use of land. In the *Charing Cross Co.* case, for instance, it was the volume of water in the main and the pressure at which it was held that made the use of land non-natural, rather than the storage of water itself. This, as we have already seen, can be viewed as a natural use.

It is also, at times, the context in which the thing is brought on to land and accumulated that leads to the court holding that it is a non-natural use of land.

Mason v Levy Auto Parts of England (1967)

Large quantities of scrap tyres were stored on the defendants' land. These were ignited and the resultant fire spread and caused damage to the claimant's premises. The storage of such large quantities of a combustible material, the casual way in which they were stored and the character of the neighbourhood were all considered by the judge in determining that there was a non-natural use of the land.

On the other hand, the fact that the public may derive a benefit from the particular use of land that is in question may mean that the court holds it to be a natural use of land.

British Celanese v A H Hunt (Capacitors) Ltd (1969)

Here, the defendants stored strips of metal foil, which were used in the process of manufacturing electrical components. Some of these strips of foil blew off the defendants' land and on to an electricity substation causing power failures. The court held that the use of land was natural. This was partly because of the benefit derived from the manufacture by the public, and there was no liability under the rule as a result.

The fact that an activity is associated with war does not mean that it constitutes a non-natural use of land merely because it occurs in peacetime.

Ellison v The Ministry of Defence (1997)

Here, bulk fuel installations on a military airfield were held not to be a non-natural use of land when rainwater that naturally gathered on the airfield ran off, flooding neighbouring land.

However, the courts have been prepared to accept that certain activities may be seen as always leading to a potential level of danger that amounts to a non-natural use of land, regardless of the benefit to the public derived from the activity that has led to the danger.

Cambridge Water Co. v Eastern Counties Leather plc (1994)

Here, the storage of particular chemicals on an industrial site was held to be a classic example of a non-natural use of land. The House of Lords, therefore, rejected the defendants' plea that just because the activity was an important source of local employment this made it a natural use of land.

10.2.5 The thing must actually escape

Blackburn J's original rule in the case of *Rylands v Fletcher* does not appear to contain any specific application of the word 'escape'. It is unlikely, therefore, that it was intended at that point that the requirement should be for the thing to escape on to land in which the claimant held a proprietary interest. If this were the case, then it would support the general idea of a strict liability tort for the control of dangerous activities.

However, the rule was seen as a development of the law of nuisance in which there is a clear requirement for the claimant to have an interest in land. This explains the opinion expressed by Lord MacMillan that there must be such an escape, since the rule derives *'from a conception of mutual duties of adjoining or neighbouring landowners'*.

Read v J Lyons & Co. Ltd (1947)

A munitions inspector was inspecting a munitions factory and was injured, along with a number of employees, one man dying, when certain shells exploded. The House of Lords held that the rule did not apply because there was *'no escape at all of the relevant kind'*. Viscount Simon explained that an *'escape'* in *Rylands v Fletcher* means:

'... an escape from a place where the defendant has occupation or control over land to a place which is outside his occupation or control.'

This is obviously a very restrictive limitation on the operation of the rule. However, this interpretation of the meaning of escape for the purposes of the rule has not always been accepted as an absolute requirement. In *British Celanese v A H Hunt (Capacitors) Ltd* (1969), Lawton J felt that the escape in question should be *'from a set of circumstances over which the defendant has control to a set of circumstances where he does not'*. The test here is far less restrictive and far more appropriate to a tort of strict liability.

Certainly, there are cases that appear to operate according to this reasoning rather than that in *Read v Lyons*.

Hale v Jennings (1938)

Here, both stalls operated on the same piece of land. Neither the 'chair-o-plane' operator nor the other stallholder owned the land.

A similar principle has been seen where both parties are operating on the same stretch of river.

Crown River Cruises Ltd v Kimbolton Fireworks Ltd (1996)

Here, inflammable material from a firework display fell on to barges used as a jetty for pleasure cruisers, causing fire damage.

10.3 Claimants and defendants in *Rylands v Fletcher*

10.3.1 Potential defendants

The question of the identity of potential defendants depends very much on the test of an escape that is accepted and used in the case.

According to Viscount Simon's test in *Read v Lyons*, a defendant to an action in *Rylands v Fletcher* will be either the owner or occupier of land who satisfies the four ingredients of the tort, which must all be present for liability.

On the other hand, according to the test as described by Lawton J in the *British Celanese case*, a potential defendant is one who satisfies the four ingredients of the rule where the escape is from a set of circumstances over which (s)he has control to a set of circumstances over which (s)he does not.

The natural development of the less restrictive rule is to include a claim where the defendant is merely in control of the highway and not the occupier of land.

Rigby v Chief Constable of Northamptonshire (1985)

Here, the defendant was liable for the damage caused by the negligent release of CS gas canisters on the highway.

10.3.2 Potential claimants

The question of who can sue is not necessarily quite so clear cut. In the original case we have already seen that Blackburn J made no suggestion of any requirement for a claimant to have a proprietary interest in land. Nevertheless, Lord MacMillan in *Read v Lyons* suggested that there is such a requirement.

Lawton J in the *British Celanese case* felt that Lord MacMillan's requirement was too restrictive, and his test would necessarily include a wider class of potential claimants. Indeed, in the case it was a third party who had suffered damage as a result of the loss of power when the foil landed on the power station.

The logical development of a less restrictive test here is to allow a claim for accumulations that escape causing damage to the claimant, regardless of where the damage occurs.

Crown River Cruises Ltd v Kimbolton Fireworks Ltd (1996)

Here, the claimant was able to recover in nuisance and negligence despite the fact that the damage caused was to barges moored on the river. However, the opportunity to extend the rule here to cover the escape was rejected.

10.4 Recoverable damage, remedies and defences

10.4.1 Types of recoverable loss and remoteness of damage

If Lord MacMillan's test is accepted as correct, then this has the effect of limiting claims to recovery only for damage to the land owned or occupied by the claimant, and to damage to property found on that land. Lord MacMillan also expressed doubts as to whether a claim for personal injuries was possible under the rule.

On the other hand, if Lawton J's test is preferred, then damages that can be recovered for are much wider, and indeed wide enough to include personal injury claims. Certainly there were cases before *Read v Lyons,* including both *Shiffman* and *Hale v Jennings,* in which the court found no problem in granting damages for personal injury.

Nevertheless, since the modern view following *Cambridge Water* is to accept *Rylands v Fletcher* as a form of nuisance, and since in *Hunter v Canary Wharf Ltd* it was doubted whether personal injury was recoverable in nuisance, then this issue might also be settled in *Rylands v Fletcher.*

It is certainly unlikely that a claim for economic loss will be successful.

Weller v Foot and Mouth Disease Research Unit (1966)

Auctioneers sued for their loss of usual income when there was a ban on the movement of livestock following the escape of a virus from the defendant's premises. In the case there was, in fact, held to be no liability because the claimants had no proprietary interest in land. It is unlikely that they would have succeeded in any case in respect of the type of damages claimed.

The tort is not actionable *per se,* and this means that any claimant must show damage in order to succeed. So there can be no liability for the mere interference with the enjoyment of land.

Eastern & South African Telegraph Co. Ltd v Cape Town Tramways Co. Ltd (1902)

Electric emissions interfered with the transmission of telegraphic messages sent down underground cables. The claimant's action failed because of their 'hypersensitive' use of land. It was also suggested in *obiter* that the damage could not be classified as damage to property.

The rule on remoteness of damage was only recently settled. Blackburn J's original remarks referring to *'the natural consequence of the escape'* suggest that the test of direct consequence in *Re Polemis* is applicable.

However, the House of Lords, in *Cambridge Water,* has now stated that reasonable foreseeability of damage is a prerequisite of liability. In other words, the defendant must have known or ought reasonably to have foreseen that damage of the relevant type might be a consequence of the escape of the thing likely to cause mischief.

10.4.2 Possible defences

Despite the tort being described as strict liability, a number of defences are possible in the event of a claim. Blackburn J identified some of these at the time of the original case; others have developed since.

Volenti non fit injuria (consent)

There will be no liability where the claimant has consented to the thing that is accumulated by the defendant.

Consent is a commonly available defence in the case of multiple occupation of buildings, particularly tall buildings. The claimant will be said to consent when the thing accumulated is for the common benefit of the occupants.

Peters v Prince of Wales Theatre (Birmingham) Ltd (1943)

Here, the claimant's stock was damaged by water from the defendant's sprinkler system. The water supply was nevertheless for the benefit of both, and so there was no liability for the escape.

Common benefit

There will, in any case, be no liability on a defendant when the source of the potential danger is something that is maintained for the benefit of both claimant and defendant.

Dunne v North Western Gas Board (1964)

A gas mains exploded without any negligence on the part of the Gas Board. The court doubted whether the Board had accumulated the gas for their own benefit; it was for the benefit of the consumers and there was no liability.

Act of a stranger

If a stranger over whom the defendant has no control has been the cause of the escape causing the damage, then the defendant may not be liable.

Perry v Kendricks Transport Ltd (1956)

The defendants parked their bus on their parking space, having drained the tank of petrol. When an unknown person removed the petrol cap a child was then injured when another child threw in a match which ignited the fumes in the tank. The Court of Appeal considered that the burden of proof here was on the claimant to show that such an eventuality was foreseeable. There was a valid defence and no liability.

Nevertheless, in other jurisdictions the strict liability of the rule can mean that there is liability regardless of who causes the escape or whether it was foreseeable (*Mehta v Union of India* (1987)).

Act of God

This defence may succeed where there are extreme weather conditions that *'no human foresight can provide against'*. So, the nature of the defence is that it is only possible in the case of unforeseeable weather conditions.

> ### Nicholls v Marsland (1876)
>
> The defendant here made three artificial, ornamental lakes by damming a natural stream on his land. Freak thunderstorms accompanied by torrential rain broke the banks of the artificial lakes that then caused the destruction of bridges on the claimant's land. There was no liability because the weather conditions were so extreme.

Statutory authority

A statute on construction may provide a defence if the escape is a direct result of the carrying out of the duty contained in the statute.

> ### Green v Chelsea Waterworks Co. (1894)
>
> The defendants were obliged by statute to provide a water supply. The court held that from time to time burst pipes were an inevitable consequence of this duty and there could be no liability in the absence of negligence.

In the absence of a duty there may still be liability when the thing escapes.

> ### Charing Cross Electric Supply Co. v Hydraulic Power Co. (The Charing Cross Co. case) (1914)
>
> There was liability here because there was only a power rather than a duty to provide the water supply.

Fault of the claimant

A defendant will not be liable when a claimant is, in fact, responsible for the damage that (s)he suffers.

> ### Eastern & South African Telegraph Co. Ltd v Cape Town Tramways Co. Ltd (1902)
>
> Here, the defendants were not liable because the interference with the telegraphic transmissions was said to be the fault of their excessive sensitivity.

Contributory negligence

Where the claimant is partly responsible then the provisions of the Law Reform (Contributory Negligence) Act 1945 will apply and damages may be reduced according to the amount of the claimant's fault.

10.5 Points for discussion

The rule in *Rylands v Fletcher* has a number of problems associated with it. The modern perception of the rule seems to be that it is a more particular development of the law of nuisance and, therefore, it not only has all the shortcomings of that tort, but also would seem to be far from being strict liability in any straightforward sense. It is certainly unlikely that there is a future possibility of the tort being used as a general means of controlling dangerous activities or things by the use of strict liability. This is a pity since the introduction of the tort shortly after the major period of the industrial revolution gave the common law the opportunity to have an all-embracing tort of strict liability for the control of hazardous activities, substances and other things. This could in turn have been used to make industry more responsible, and one element of tort could have had real deterrent value. The opportunity was wasted and *Rylands v Fletcher* is merely a tort based on property rights.

In other jurisdictions, such as India, the tort has been expanded, but that has not been the case in England. On the contrary, the rule has been constantly limited in its scope by the decisions in the cases.

- Lord Cairns limited it immediately in the actual case in the House of Lords when he imposed the requirement that the thing brought on to land should be a non-natural use of land for there to be liability.
- The tort was further restricted in its development by the requirement of proprietary interest in land established by Lord MacMillan in *Read v Lyons*. This inevitably limits the circumstances in which a claimant can recover for damage caused by dangerous things accumulated on land.
- The *Cambridge Water* case even seems to be taking the tort towards a negligence-style fault liability with the requirement of foreseeability.

The court in *Crown River Cruises Ltd v Kimbolton Fireworks Ltd* expressly rejected suggestions that the tort could or should be developed. The very breadth of the defences that have been made available in the tort seem, in any case, to be at odds with the principle of strict liability.

The tort then seems to be of questionable significance in the modern day. The judges are reluctant to allow claims under the tort to succeed. Most claims that could be brought under the tort could probably just as easily be brought under negligence instead, and indeed the requirement of foreseeability means that a claimant has similar concerns in some aspects.

The tort is rarely used and almost never successfully. Indeed, shortly after the *Cambridge Water* case the Australian High Court in effect abolished the rule, claiming that the rule had been absorbed by the general rules of negligence.

Most areas of activity that could be affected or controlled by the rule are probably dealt with in the modern context by statutory controls. Certainly there are few hazardous activities that are not controlled by some form of statutory regulation.

Blue Circle Industries plc v Ministry of Defence (1998)

Here, the Nuclear Installations Act 1965 was used in respect of contamination caused to land by radioactive materials, even though the actual damage involved was economic.

Clearly one area where the rule could have great potential is in control of pollution and protection of the environment. The first block on this possibility is the fact that the tort is exclusively concerned with property rights, so a general interest in the environment is not within the scope of the tort. While the House of Lords in the *Cambridge Water case* recognised the potential for use of the tort in this area, they also dismissed it as unnecessary in the light of available legislation. Certainly, under pressure of European directives much legislation has been introduced. The Environmental Protection Act 1990 and the Environment Act 1995 are examples. Besides these, there is a mass of health and safety legislation regulating the use of hazardous activities and substances. So even though the tort could be used to great effect in the area, it is unlikely, given the attitude of the judges, that it will.

The judges, since the rule was first devised, appear to have missed a golden opportunity to have a real strict liability tort to deal generally with dangerous activities and substances. They, instead, have developed a tort that is so limited in its application as to be relatively unusable.

The House of Lords has recently had the opportunity to review the law but confirmed the point on foreseeability in *Cambridge Water* (1994) and did not really change anything.

Transco plc v Stockport MBC (2003)

The defendants had built multi-storey flats that were supplied with water via a large pipe from the water mains into tanks in the bottom of the building. These pipes failed and, although there was no negligence involved, escaped over time, causing an embankment to collapse onto the claimant's gas pipe. The claimants then sued for the cost of repairs and making the gas pipe safe. The House of Lords held that the use of the water for domestic supply meant that there was no non-natural use of land and no liability.

Activity

Self-assessment questions

1. What are the key ingredients of the rule in *Rylands v Fletcher*?

2. To what extent is liability under the rule really 'strict liability'?

3. What, exactly, is a 'non-natural' use of land?

4. Which things situated on land that are dangerous will lead to liability if they escape?

5. What must escape for the tort to operate?

6. Does the rule help the victims of damage caused by dangerous activities in general?

7. Who will be liable under the rule?

8. What are the different consequences of the tests in *Read v Lyons* and in the *British Celanese* case?

9. How limiting are the defences to a successful claim under the rule?

10. How are personal injuries covered under *Rylands v Fletcher*?

Key Facts

- The basic rule, according to Blackburn J, is that a person is liable for the damage caused by things bought on to and accumulated on the land, which then escape.
- The tort is seen as strict liability.
- There are four essential ingredients to the tort:
  - bringing on to the land – the thing must not normally be there (*Pontardawe RDC v Moore-Gwyn*)
  - of a thing likely to cause mischief if it escapes (*Hale v Jennings*)
  - which must involve a 'non-natural' use of land – Lord Cairns in *Rylands v Fletcher*
  - the thing must actually escape (*Read v Lyons*).
- Who will be a defendant and who can claim as a claimant will depend on whether the escape has to be from one person's land to another's, or from the defendant's control to a situation outside of his control (*British Celanese v Hunt*).
- The tort is now generally seen as a type of nuisance requiring foreseeability of damage (*Cambridge Water v Eastern Counties Leather*).
- There is a wide range of possible defences, including act of God, act of a stranger, consent, common benefit and statutory authority.

Activity

Consider the following essay title:

Discuss the extent to which the tort of *Rylands v Fletcher* can still be accurately referred to as a tort of strict liability.

Answering the question
There are usually two key elements to answering essays in law:

- Firstly, you are required to reproduce certain factual information on a particular area of law, and this is usually identified for you in the question;

- Secondly, you are required to answer the specific question set, which is usually found in some critical element, i.e. you are likely to see the words 'discuss', or 'analyse', or 'comment on', or 'critically consider', or even 'compare and contrast' if two areas are involved.

Students, for the most part, seem quite capable of doing the first, and also generally seem less skilled at the second. The important points in any case are to ensure that you only deal with relevant legal material in your answer, and that you do answer the question set, rather than one you have made up yourself, or the one that was on last year's paper.

For instance, in the case of the first element, in this essay, you are likely to provide detail on the following:

- definitions of both the tort and the meaning of strict liability in tort

- the many defences available to the tort

- specific references to the recent additional requirement of foreseeability of harm.

Legal Essay Writing

This, then, is a rare opportunity to use nearly all of your available knowledge on a particular tort.

In the case of the second element, the essay asks you to discuss whether *Rylands v Fletcher* can be classed as a strict liability tort. This clearly indicates that you must identify and evaluate all of the restrictions imposed on the tort and the effect they have upon it in the context of strict liability. So you must reach a conclusion based on your discussion. What will not be relevant is to consider *Rylands v Fletcher* in the context of, for example, environmental protection or pollution, although questions sometimes appear on these issues. So, in this essay it is the object of the discussion that you have to be really selective with, rather than the base of knowledge from which it is drawn.

Relevant law
The appropriate law appears to be:

- A brief explanation of the basic principle of fault liability, i.e. that a claimant can succeed in an action without need to prove fault by the defendant, only the fundamentals of the tort, e.g. in the case of liability for dangerous animals under the Animals Act 1971, the fact that the animal is of a species not commonly domesticated in the UK is sufficient for liability, even though the 'keeper' may argue that such a species is commonly accepted as harmless in its country of origin.

- A definition of the major elements of the tort would see that there were three in the original case at the first instance, added to in the case in the House of Lords, and with a fifth major inclusion in the recent case of

Cambridge Water v Eastern Counties Leather. These are:

- a bringing on to and accumulation on the defendant's land (*Charing Cross case*), so that there can be no 'accumulation' if the thing is already naturally there (*Giles v Walker*)

- of a thing likely to cause 'mischief' if it escapes (*Rylands v Fletcher*), and large quantities of water – although the thing need not be inherently dangerous, e.g. a flagpole in *Shiffman v Order of the Hospital of St John of Jerusalem*

- involving a non-natural use of land (the requirement added by Lord Cairns in the case), which is the most troublesome requirement since things become more natural and commonplace over time (*Musgrove v Pandelis* – fire from a car engine), but things stored in large quantities are commonly non-natural (*Mason v Levy Autoparts*), while truly domestic use of even dangerous things are unlikely to lead to liability (*Rickards v Lothian*)

- there must be an actual escape, although there is contrary law on whether this should be over land over which the defendant has control (*Read v Lyons*) or from circumstances over which the defendant has control (*Hale v Jennings*)

- the most recent requirement, foreseeability that the thing will cause damage if it escapes (*Cambridge Water v Eastern Counties Leather*).

- Some detail on the major defences available should also be given:

- *volenti non fit injuria* – consent of the claimant is a possible defence where the claimant derives a benefit from the accumulation (*Peters v Prince of Wales Theatre*)

- common benefit – on a similar basis is an available defence where the thing is specifically accumulated for the benefit of both defendant and claimant (*Dunne v North West Gas Board*)

- act of God is also a possible defence in the case of extreme weather conditions (*Nicholls v Marsland*)

- act of a stranger may also protect the defendant, provided that the defendant had no control over or knowledge of the intrusion (*Perry v Kendricks Transport*)

- statutory authority, as with nuisance, can also excuse a defendant (*Green v Chelsea Waterworks*)

- the defendant will also have a complete defence where the damage was actually caused through the fault of the claimant himself (*Eastern & South African Telegraph v Cape Town Tramways*)

- finally, wherever there is contributory negligence damages may be reduced under the Law Reform (Contributory Negligence) Act 1945.

- Other factors to consider are who the potential claimants and defendants may be according to the very different tests in *Read v Lyons* and *British Celanese v A H Hunt.*

Discussion and evaluation

The commentary in the essay requires you to discuss whether *Rylands v Fletcher* can still be considered a tort of strict liability. Obviously, one of the major factors prompting this particular title is the inclusion of a requirement of foreseeability of damage from the case of *Cambridge Water*. This is not the only feature of the tort that limits its application as strict liability, and all should be discussed. Relevant comments might include:

- that the style of liability apparently envisaged by Blackburn J in the original case was for a general head of liability for accumulations of hazardous things that then did damage

- that the scope of the tort was limited straightaway by Lord Cairns in the House of Lords with the addition of a requirement of non-natural use of land

- the potential of the tort to be a general response to the dangers presented by the Industrial Revolution was immediately wasted, and no general head of claim in respect of hazardous activities, objects or substances has ever developed

- that the requirement in *Read v Lyons* by Lord MacMillan that the escape should be from land to land further reduced the potential

applicability of the tort, although this in itself runs contrary to tests in both *Hale v Jennings* and *British Celanese v A H Hunt*

- that, while defences still can be raised to strict liability torts, there seems to be an unusually wide range of defences available here, limiting the scope of the tort still further

- that the requirement of foreseeability in *Cambridge Water* is probably the final nail in the coffin of the tort – it is hard to see how it differs from negligence, which in any case is probably easier to claim under

- it has been suggested at times that the tort is a very specific type of nuisance, and certainly foreseeability could be an issue, but after *Cambridge Water* a negligence action is still probably more straightforward

- any sensible conclusion would do, but it is probably appropriate to conclude by stating that to all intents and purposes now, the tort has all of the essential ingredients of fault liability and cannot accurately be considered strict liability.

Dilemma Board

In the Dilemma Board below, consider the accuracy of each of the four statements, A, B, C and D, as they apply to the facts in the central scenario. You only need to give the basic principles. The answer is in the Appendix at the end of the book.

Dilemma Board

A.

Precious Pets will be able to sue Toxichem for private nuisance.

B.

Precious Pets will be unable to sue Toxichem in *Rylands v Fletcher* because there is no non-natural use of land.

Toxichem stores large containers of chemicals outside its back door. Some containers rust after rain. Vandals also knock over some of the other containers and unscrew the caps. The chemicals from all the containers then seep out and run down a slope, escaping into the next-door premises, Precious Pets, which breeds and sells dogs, cats, rabbits etc. The chemicals kill all of Precious Pet's stock that is kept outside and is valued at £50,000.

C.

Precious Pets will be unable to sue Toxichem in *Rylands v Fletcher* for the damage caused by chemicals leaking from the rusted containers because the defence of Act of God is available.

D.

Precious Pets will be unable to sue Toxichem in *Rylands v Fletcher* for the damage caused by the containers knocked over by the vandals because the defence of act of a stranger is available.

	Trespass to land	Private nuisance	Public nuisance	*Rylands v Fletcher*
Claimants	A person in possession of land	A person with a proprietary interest in land	A member of a class of Her Majesty's citizens	A person harmed by the escape of the dangerous thing
Defendants	Any person carrying out the trespass	A landowner, or a creating or adopting nuisance	A person creating nuisance	A person in control of land from which thing escapes
Duration of interference	A single trespass is enough	Must be continuous	A single interference is enough	A single escape is enough
Directness	Must be direct	Must be indirect	Could be direct or indirect	Could be direct or indirect
Need to prove fault	Actionable *per se* – so no need to prove fault	Requires unreasonable use of land, which is similar	Fault need not be proved	*Cambridge Water* says says foreseeability is required, so suggests fault
Locality of interference	Not relevant	Relevant unless damage is caused	Could be relevant, e.g. to losing client connection	Could be relevant in deciding what is non-natural
Availability of damages	Any damage related to the trespass, and no need to show damage	Physical harm, personal injury to proprietor, economic loss	Physical harm, personal injury, economic loss	Physical loss and personal injury
Defences	Customary right to enter, common-law right, statutory right, consent, necessity, licence	Statutory authority, prescription, consent, act of stranger, public policy, over-sensitivity of claimant	General defences	Consent, common benefit, act of a stranger or God, statutory authority, contributory negligence
Whether also a crime	Yes, possible under some statutes	No, unless statutory	Yes, can be	No

Figure 6 *Table illustrating the similarities and differences between the torts relating to land*

Chapter 11

Strict Liability: Liability for Animals and Product Liability

11.1 The nature of strict liability

Strict liability occurs in both criminal law and in tort, although it tends to operate differently in each.

In tort, liability is strict where there is no requirement to prove fault on the part of the defendant. The defendant is liable because the wrong has occurred, without reference to any blame on his or her part. This is where it is debatable whether *Rylands v Fletcher* can any longer be considered to be a tort of strict liability, since the requirement of foreseeability of harm was added by *Cambridge Water Co v Eastern Counties Leather plc* (1994).

The fact that liability is strict does not prevent a defendant from raising defences, and there are many individual defences appropriate to the different strict liability torts, e.g. Act of God in relation to *Rylands v Fletcher*; s 5(1) of the Animals Act 1971, where the damage is due wholly to the fault of the person suffering it in relation to liability for animals; and the due diligence defence under s10 of the Consumer Protection Act 1987 in relation to product liability are just some of many defences.

There have been common-law torts of strict liability, but the major areas of strict liability are now contained in statute.

11.2 Animals and the common law

11.2.1 Introduction

Liability for animals goes back to medieval times. Such liability developed for two reasons. Firstly, livestock in particular at that time was a major source of wealth and may have been crucial to survival, so attitudes to straying livestock were different. Secondly, though animals are personal property, they have always been placed in a separate category of civil liability because they are mobile and 'have a will of their own'.

The common law originally provided two basic actions in respect of animals:

- A *scienter* action was an action for knowingly keeping a dangerous animal that escaped and caused damage. The animal could be of a dangerous species or, if not, it might have dangerous characteristics known to its keeper.
- Cattle trespass was an action in respect of cattle or similar animals that strayed and caused damage.

In both actions liability was strict. This was justified on two levels. Firstly, in the case of dangerous animals, it was only fair that the keeper should be expected to be liable for any damage caused. That is the risk of keeping dangerous animals. Secondly, in the case of trespassing livestock, it was sensible to keep the dispute within the community rather than have recourse to law.

Whatever liability formerly existed has now been replaced by the Animals Act 1971, which retains the essentials of both of the above torts. It is still possible to sue under different types of liability where the Act does not, in fact, apply.

Although actions involving animals are rare, that is not to say that the damage caused by animals is also rare. The Pearson Committee in 1978, for instance, found that animals are responsible for up to 50,000 injuries annually. The damage caused by certain breeds of dog has also led to numerous developments in the law.

11.2.2 Common-law actions

Although actions involving animals would most likely be bought under the Animals Act 1971, if the ingredients of a particular tort are met by the situation in question then it is clearly possible to use that tort to seek compensation for the wrong suffered. A variety of actions illustrate this point. Clearly, negligence is one of the more obvious torts that could be used.

Trespass to goods

> *Manton v Brocklebank (1923)*
> A defendant who taught his dog to steal golf balls was liable under this tort.

Trespass to land

> *League Against Cruel Sports Ltd v Scott (1985)*
> A keeper of foxhounds was liable for allowing the hounds to trespass on to the land owned by another person during a hunt.

Private nuisance

> *Rapier v London Tramways Co. (1893)*
> The owner of horses that created 'foul stenches' was liable to neighbours in private nuisance.

Rylands v Fletcher

> *Brady v Warren (1900)*
> The keeper of a captive fox was liable when he allowed it to escape and it caused damage.

Defamation

It has been suggested that if an owner of a parrot or similar creature taught it to repeat defamatory remarks that were then overheard, this could create liability on the owner.

Trespass to the person

It has also been suggested that a party who taught animals to attack another party could be liable for assault and battery.

Negligence

Possibly more importantly than most of these, because it perhaps has more widespread application, an action is possible in negligence for a failure to control an animal where there is a foreseeable risk of it causing harm.

> *Gomberg v Smith (1962)*
> An owner of a dog who failed to control it was liable for the damage caused when the dog bolted across the road on a dangerous bend.

This will be particularly so where the owner knows of the characteristics of the animal that are likely to result in harm.

> ### Birch v Mills (1995)
>
> A farm manager was liable for injuries done by a herd of Charolais cattle in an unfenced field. The cows were known to be frisky and, since they chased dogs, it was likely they would injure anyone walking close by.

Negligence is, in any case, particularly useful and appropriate in dealing with non-dangerous species where, under the Animals Act, liability will only result if the keeper knows of the animal's dangerous characteristic, so that there may often be no statutory cause of action.

> ### Draper v Hodder (1972)
>
> A child was savaged by a pack of Jack Russell Terriers that were rushing from their owner's house next door. They had never acted this way before, so there could be no liability under the Act. However, this breed characteristically attacks in packs, so there was foreseeable risk of harm and negligence.

So a keeper of animals has a duty to guard against foreseeable risks.

> ### Smith v Prendergast (1984)
>
> A scrap yard owner was liable for an attack by a stray Alsatian that had been in his yard for three weeks. While the dog had done nothing vicious up to the point of the attack, the owner of the scrap yard had done nothing to remove it or to control it.

It is also always possible for a party to bring an action in more than one tort.

> ### Pitcher v Martin (1937)
>
> A dog owner was liable in both negligence and public nuisance when his dog tripped and injured a pedestrian while it was chasing a cat.

11.3 The Animals Act 1971

11.3.1 Introduction

In determining when to fix liability, the Act distinguishes between animals of a dangerous species (*ferae naturae*) and species which are domesticated or ordinarily not dangerous (*mansuetae naturae*).

11.3.2 Dangerous species

Under s6(2) of the Act a dangerous species is one:

'a) *which is not commonly domesticated in the British Isles*

b) *Whose fully grown animals have such characteristics that they are likely, unless restrained, to cause severe damage or that any damage they may cause is likely to be severe.*'

What is dangerous, then, is a question of law rather than fact.

> ### Behrens v Bertram Mills Circus Ltd (1957)
>
> When a circus elephant injured the claimant it was irrelevant that the animal was said to be as docile as a domestic cow.

This means that under s6(2) a species may be classed as dangerous even though it is ordinarily classed as domestic in its country of origin.

> ## Tutin v Chipperfield Promotions Ltd (1980)
>
> A camel was classed as dangerous under the Act, although it would ordinarily be a means of transport and beast of burden in its country of origin.

Very few animals that are natives of the British Isles would be likely to satisfy the test in s6(2)(b). Therefore, the provision applies mainly to imported animals.

This subsection also offers alternative tests, likely to cause severe damage, or damage caused is likely to be severe, so it can include animals such as the elephant in *Behrens* which, because of its size, could cause harm.

According to s2(1), the duty in respect of such animals lies on any 'keeper'. 'Keeper' is defined in s6(3) as a person who:

'a) ... owns the animal or has it in his possession; or

b) ... is head of a household of which a member under the age of sixteen owns the animal or has it in his possession.'

So it is possible for there to be more than one keeper at any time, and the Act makes, for example, a parent responsible for animals kept be his/her children. So a claimant may have a choice of people to sue.

Under the Dangerous Wild Animals Act 1976, keepers of dangerous species of animals are required to be licensed by the local authority to keep the animal, and are also required to carry third party insurance.

11.3.3 Non-dangerous species

The duty owed in respect of species that are not classed as dangerous is contained in s2(2) and is much more complex. There are three characteristics identified in the subsection and all must be demonstrated for a successful claim. The keeper will be liable if:

- the damage is of a kind likely to be caused by the animal if unrestrained, or if caused by that type of animal is likely to be severe; and
- the likelihood of the damage being caused or being severe is due to characteristics peculiar to the animal in question – which are either not common to that species or only common to that species at particular times; and
- the particular characteristics of the animal causing the damage were known to the keeper, a servant of the keeper, or a person under sixteen who is the keeper and a member of the keeper's household.

The subsection obviously creates problems for interpretation and the correct approach is to consider each part in turn, according to Start-Smith LJ in *Curtis v Betts* (1990).

S2(2)(a), then, is widely stated. It inevitably points to breeds of dogs that, for instance because of their size, if they should bite or attack people, are likely to cause severe damage even if they are breeds that do not commonly attack.

This might include the bites of particular breeds such as an Alsatian in *Cummings v Grainger* (1977) and a Bull Mastiff in *Curtis v Betts* (1990). It could also include infectious animals.

While the kind of damage caused should be likely, the way in which it is caused is not necessarily important.

> ## Smith v Ainger (1990)
>
> The claimant's leg was broken when the defendant's dog attacked his own dog.

S2(2)(b) identifies the causal link between the damage and the characteristics of the animal causing it. There can be no liability if the damage was not due to the characteristics in question.

Jaundrill v Gillett (1996)

The keeper of horses that had been released on to a highway by a stranger acting in malice was not liable to a motorist who was injured in collision with the horses. The Court of Appeal held that the real reason for the damage was the release of the horses. It was doubted whether horses panicking because they were loose on a road at night amounted to an abnormal characteristic rather than just abnormal circumstances.

The subsection also draws distinctions between permanent and temporary characteristics, and between the animal in question and its breed or species.

In this way, while we would accept that dogs in general do not attack people, there would be liability for a dog that regularly did attack people or for one that attacked people at certain times or in certain circumstances.

An example of the first point could be *Smith v Ainger* (1990), where the dog in question was known to regularly attack other dogs.

Examples of the latter point might include a bitch that was known to attack to protect her litter. It might also include dogs left freely to roam to act as guard dogs in the event of anyone intruding on the premises.

Cummings v Grainger (1977)

An owner of a scrap yard allowed an untrained Alsatian to roam free at night. The dog savaged a woman who entered with her boyfriend who worked there. The circumstance in which the dog would attack was when being used as a guard dog.

The fact that a dog is trained to attack, e.g. by the police, does not necessarily count as an abnormal characteristic. The appropriate characteristic in question is the ability of the dog to be trained and to follow instructions.

Gloster v Chief Constable of Greater Manchester Police (2000)

The dog, a German Shepherd, was trained by police, among other things to attack. The claimant, a police officer, was injured when the dog slipped its lead after its handler fell, having already shouted a warning that the dog would be loosed to chase a car thief. The dog mistakenly bit the claimant police officer. There was no liability, there being no abnormal characteristic.

By s2(2)(c) the knowledge of the animal's characteristics required of the keeper is actual knowledge. It is not sufficient that the keeper ought to have known. If (s)he did not know then there can be no liability under the Act, though there may be liability in negligence if the damage is foreseeable, as we have already seen with the Jack Russells in *Draper v Hodder* (1972).

But s2(2)(c) only requires actual knowledge of the peculiar characteristics. It is not vital to a successful claim that the keeper also knew the precise circumstances in which those characteristics arose causing damage.

Mirvahedy v Henley (2001)

A motorist was injured when his car collided with a horse that had escaped from a field. The horse displayed temporary characteristics because of its fear of being loose on the road. Its owner was still liable despite not knowing of the precise circumstances in which the characteristics surfaced. They would be normal to the breed in specific circumstances and the keeper would know this.

Activity — *Quick Quiz*

In the following instances, suggest whether and why the animal in question would fall under the Act as a dangerous species, or as a non-dangerous species, or not fall under the Act at all.

1. Jeff, aged 15, has a pet hamster that regularly bites his friends when they hold it or stroke it.

2. Jasvinder owns a cat that has just had its first litter of kittens. The cat scratches Raj when she goes to pick up a kitten.

3. Ali owns a 26-foot-long Rock Python that he allows to roam freely in his house.

4. Ernie, a postman, takes his pet Rotweiler with him on his round to exercise it. Ernie's dog bites another dog on the round one day, though it has never fought with or attacked any animal before.

5. Lucretia keeps a herd of goats for milk. One day one of the goats kicks the boy who is delivering the newspaper.

11.3.4 Defences

Available defences are provided by s5 of the Act. Under s5(1), the keeper of the animal is not liable for any damage suffered which is *'due wholly to the fault of the person suffering it'*.

Sylvester v Chapman Ltd (1935)

There was liability on the keeper for injuries sustained by the claimant, who had entered a leopard's pen to recover a lighted cigarette.

By s5(2) there will be no liability in respect of a person who has voluntarily accepted the risk of some harm caused by the animal.

Cummings v Grainger (1977)

Here, the girl entered the scrap yard knowing that the dog was dangerous. In fact, she admitted that she was frightened of the dog.

This may even include situations where the animal is deliberately used against the claimant, e.g. to effect an arrest.

Dhesi v Chief Constable of the West Midlands Police (2000)

Police had tracked the claimant, who was armed with a hockey stick, after a violent confrontation. When the claimant hid in bushes he was repeatedly warned that the dog would be set free. The claimant was bitten when trying to escape the dog, but was unsuccessful in his claim. He had accepted the risk of being injured.

By s5(3) a keeper will not be liable to a trespasser if (s)he can prove either that the animal was not kept for the purposes of protecting people or property, or if it was that it was not unreasonable to do so. In *Cummings v Grainger*, for instance, it was not considered unreasonable to have a guard dog in a scrap yard in the East End of London. This point is in any case qualified by the Guard Dogs Acts 1975 and 1995, which require a guard dog to be under the control of a handler at all times and which impose criminal sanctions for non-compliance.

Contributory negligence is also possible under the Act, as identified in s10, and if a plea is accepted then damages will be reduced accordingly.

Activity   *Quick Quiz*

Consider whether or not the keepers of animals have a defence in the following circumstances:

1. Sarbjit visits Alison's home at Alison's request. Gnasher, a Pit Bull Terrier owned by Denis, Alison's husband, attacks and savages Sarbjit without warning, requiring hospital treatment. Gnasher has frequently attacked visitors, though Denis still allows him to freely roam the house.

2. Gerry keeps poisonous spiders in glass cases. Terry receives a very bad sting when he puts his hand inside the case and strokes one of the spiders.

3. Greta is kicked by a horse when she takes a short cut through a field where the horses are grazing.

4. Matthew is playing games with the mongrel dog belonging to his next-door neighbour, Simon. Matthew runs away from the dog, causing the dog to chase him. He does this on several occasions and, on one occasion, when he tries to turn quickly the dog runs under his leg, tripping Matthew and causing him to sustain a broken leg.

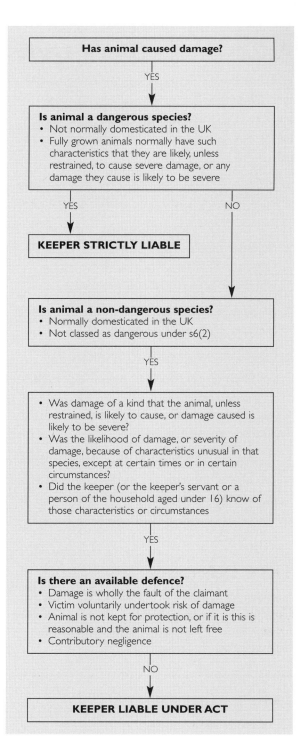

Figure 7 *Flow chart illustrating liability under the Animals Act 1971*

11.3.5 Trespassing livestock

The Act abolishes the former action of 'cattle trespass' and replaces it with a new statutory action under s4. The owner of livestock that strays on to the land in the ownership or possession of another is liable for any damage done by the livestock, or for reasonable expenses incurred in keeping the animal until it can be returned to the owner.

The section specifies physical damage and reasonable expenses, so claims for personal injury would be bought under s2(2).

'Livestock' is defined in s11, the interpretation section. The definition includes cattle, horses, asses, mules, hinnies, sheep, pigs, goats, poultry, deer that are not wild, and pheasants, partridges and grouse in captivity. So this is a wide group of animals.

There are a number of defences available under the Act. Under s5(1) a person is not liable if the damage was wholly the fault of the party suffering it. Again, under s10 damages can be apportioned if a claim of contributory negligence is accepted.

Older defences are also preserved. A person will not be liable where the livestock strayed from the highway and its presence on the highway was lawful, in other words for passage from one place to another. What is considered lawful is a question of fact in each case.

Matthews v Wicks (1987)

Sheep allowed to roam free on the highway damaged the claimant's garden. This was held to be an unlawful use of the highway and so the owner of the sheep was liable. This contrasts with older attitudes that damage from straying livestock was a natural consequence of living next to the highway.

The owner of livestock may still owe a duty of care in negligence so that an action of some sort is still possible.

S5(6) identifies that there is no general duty to fence land to keep livestock in or out. So an owner of livestock will not have a defence merely because it was possible for the other party to avoid the damage by fencing the land. However, if there is an obligation to fence land arising from custom, easements or contract, then there may be a defence if the other party has failed in that duty.

Under s7 there are powers to detain and even sell livestock that has strayed on to land. The section, in effect, replaces the old remedy of 'distress damage feasant'. The person on whose land the livestock has strayed must notify the police within 48 hours. Under s4 they may also detain the animal until compensated for damage, or until expenses of keeping the animal till it is collected are paid. After 14 days the animal may also be sold at public auction and the damages or expenses under s4 recovered, the remainder being passed on to the owner. The person detaining the animal must, of course, properly feed and maintain it.

11.3.6 Liability for injury to livestock caused by dogs

By s3 of the Act the owner of a dog that kills or injures livestock is liable for that damage. There is no requirement to show that the dog has abnormal characteristics, so in this sense livestock is given a greater degree of protection than people are.

The normal defence under s5(1) is available, that the damage was wholly the cause of the owner of the livestock. Contributory negligence can also be pleaded under s10. It may also be a defence under s5(4) that the livestock killed or injured had strayed on to the land of the dog owner, and the dog was therefore entitled to be on the land.

Owners of livestock are entitled to protection from dogs that kill or injure their livestock. So, by s9 it is lawful to kill or injure such dogs to protect livestock in certain circumstances:

- The person harming the dog must be entitled to act for the protection of the livestock.
- The dog must be 'worrying' or 'about to worry' the livestock, or has already done so and has not left the vicinity and there is no way of ascertaining who owns the dog.
- There must be no other way of dealing with the situation.
- The person harming the dog must then report it to the police within 48 hours.

11.3.7 Animals straying on to the highway

Prior to the passing of the Act there was no particular liability for animals that strayed on to the highway. This was, in the past, seen as an inevitable in a rural community.

The Act abolishes any immunity from liability that might have existed formerly in the common law. Under s8 there is now a duty of care and, therefore, liability in negligence.

Liability is, however, limited by s8(2). A person will not be liable merely for placing an animal on unfenced land and allowing it to stray provided that: a) the land is common, or fencing is customarily not required, or the land is a town green or village green; and b) (s)he had a right to place the animal there.

Any duty that exists is inevitably only to do what is reasonable. So it would not be reasonable, for instance, to require someone to fence a moor.

It is easier to prove now whether a person has a right to graze animals freely. The Registration of Commons Act 1971 required that everyone entitled to such use of common land had to register it or lose it.

11.3.8 Remoteness of damage

This issue is not dealt with in the Act, so the ordinary principles of negligence will apply. S2(2), however, states that the keeper is liable for 'any damage'. This suggests the test is one of direct consequences rather than foreseeable damage.

Animals are taken to have several features in common with the tort of *Rylands v Fletcher*, and indeed the damage caused is often due to their 'escape'. The tort was specifically excluded in the foreseeability test in *The Wagon Mound*, which tends to reinforce the point.

Damage caused by non-dangerous species under s2(2) of the Act is limited to such damage as is the result of unusual characteristics known to the keeper.

Activity

Self-assessment questions

1. How limited was the law on animals prior to the Animals Act 1971?

2. When will it be particularly appropriate to bring an action under negligence for damage caused by animals?

3. Why does the law distinguish between dangerous and non-dangerous species?

4. In what ways is the distinction a sensible one?

5. What happens if my Golden Retriever bites someone and has never done so before?

6. Would it be different if my dog was an Alsatian left guarding my property?

7. How would the law deal with an animal that gave somebody a disease?

8. What are the practical differences between the defences available under s5(1), s5(2) and s10 of the Act?

9. What is significant about the level of protection applying to livestock attacked by dogs by comparison with liability generally under the Act?

10. Why has the law on animals straying on to the highway been completely reversed by the Act?

11. How is it generally determined what damage is recoverable under the Act?

12. Why should harm done by animals be said to have several features in common with *Rylands v Fletcher*?

Key Facts

- The common law originally provided strict liability actions for damage caused by dangerous species of animals and for damage caused by straying livestock.
- These have now been replaced by the Animals Act 1971.
- However, it is possible to bring actions under many other torts, e.g. negligence (*Draper v Hodder*).
- Even strange common-law actions are possible, e.g. a parrot being trained to repeat defamatory remarks.
- The Animals Act 1971 draws a distinction between 'dangerous species' and 'non-dangerous' species.
- A dangerous species is one not domesticated in the UK and which is likely to cause severe damage unless restrained – s6(2).

- A keeper of such an animal is liable for all the damage it causes, so liability in this case is strict.
- A keeper of a non-dangerous animal is liable if: damage is likely if the animal is unrestrained, or damage is likely to be severe; damage is because of characteristics not normally associated with the species, or only at specific times or in specific circumstances; the characteristics were known to the keeper.
- It may particularly apply to guard dogs and large dogs (*Cummings v Grainger*).
- A keeper is somebody who is responsible for the animal, or who is head of the household where the actual keeper is a person under the age of 16.
- Defences under s5 include consent, damage caused wholly by the claimant's own fault and contributory negligence.
- S4 of the Act also provides an action for damage caused by straying livestock.
- Under s3 there is also an action for livestock killed by dogs, including the right to kill the dog in some circumstances to protect the livestock.
- By s8 there is a limited duty to prevent livestock from straying on the highway.
- Remoteness of damage is likely to be measured by the *Re Polemis* test of direct consequence loss, rather than by the 'reasonably foreseeable' test of *The Wagon Mound*.

11.4 Liability for defective products and the Consumer Protection Act 1987

11.4.1 Common-law product liability

Product liability at common law is found in the narrow *ratio* of *Donoghue v Stevenson*. A manufacturer owes a duty of care to a consumer or user of his or her products not to harm or injure the consumer.

This basic principle of negligence is qualified by the fact that, for a successful action, the goods must arrive with the ultimate consumer in substantially the same condition as they left the manufacturer.

> ### *Evans v Triplex Glass Co Ltd (1936)*
> Here, the claimant's action against the manufacturer of a windscreen that shattered inexplicably failed. There was too little in the case of showing that the fault was due to a defect in manufacturing.

Besides the duty of care itself, the claimant would in any case have to demonstrate the other essential elements of negligence. These are: a breach of the duty of care; damage caused by the defendant and suffered by the claimant which is not too remote a consequence of the defendant's breach, i.e. it is foreseeable damage.

11.4.2 The Consumer Protection Act 1987

General

The Act was passed to comply with the requirements of EC Directive 85/374. The main purpose of the directive, and hence of the Act, is to insert minimum product safety standards into domestic law. The Act operates mostly through regulatory controls enforceable by criminal law sanctions. However, it also provides for the possibility of civil actions and remedies. So the Act in its civil context is in fact a statutory tort.

In many ways the Act reflects the idea that 'prevention is better than cure'. There are 7,000 deaths each year in the home from accidents so that the Act in both its criminal and civil contexts is clearly necessary.

Potential defendants

By s2(2) the Act can be used against:

a) the producer of the product (the manufacturer)
b) any person … who has held himself out to be the producer of the product (referring to retailers, particularly 'own branders')
c) any person who has imported the product (distributors).

So, the Act has widespread application against those responsible for bringing the consumer into contact with faulty or dangerous goods.

The scope of liability in the Act

Product is defined in broad terms under the Act, so that it includes, in addition to manufactured goods, those that are processed in some way, but not unprocessed agricultural products. In this way the Act could refer to a packet of frozen peas, but not to fresh peas, from a greengrocers.

By s2(3) the defendant is not liable for any damage that is caused wholly or partly by the product.

Recoverable damage is identified in s5 and includes all death and injury caused by the defective product, and also consequential loss where the damage exceeds £275 in value. It will not include property damage that is under that figure, nor recovery for the defective product itself, since that could be sued for more naturally in contract law.

Also, by s5(3), there can be no recovery unless

the product itself was of a type usually supplied for private use and intended for private use.

Defences

There are a number of possible defences under the Act and these are in s4 and s6:

- the product was not supplied in the course of a business
- the defect was caused by complying with a legal requirement
- the defect did not exist at the time the goods were first distributed
- the so-called 'state of the art defence' – that the state of knowledge at the time was such that the defect could not have been readily discovered – is the type of defence that might excuse the use of potentially hazardous substances because, for example, Government safety standards are still being complied with
- where the product is incorporated into another product the producer of the final product is usually liable
- contributory negligence.

Activity

Self-assessment questions

1. What are the significant differences between common law liability and liability under the Consumer Protection Act 1987?

2. How wide is liability under the Act?

3. How fair are the defences in the Act?

Key Facts

- The common law originally provided product liability under the narrow ratio in *Donoghue v Stevenson*.
- Now, strict liability is possible under the Consumer Protection Act 1987.
- Defendants include manufacturers, 'own branders', and importers.
- The Act covers all manufactured and also all processed goods.
- Defences include: compliance with a legal requirement, 'state of the art' defence, not supplied in course of a business, not in existence.

Dilemma Board

In the Dilemma Board below, consider the accuracy of each of the four statements, A, B, C and D, as they apply to the facts in the central scenario. You only need to give the basic principles. The answer is in the Appendix at the end of the book.

Dilemma Board

A.

Dennis will be liable under the Animals Act 1971 for the injury caused to Lena by the cheetah.

B.

Lena will be able to claim successfully under the Animals Act 1971 against Dennis's parents for the injuries caused by the cheetah.

Dennis, aged 12, has a pet cheetah which he keeps in a cage outside the kitchen. He also has a pet Labrador bitch which has just had a litter of puppies. Lena, Dennis's friend, visits him. Dennis warns Lena not to go too close to the cage but she puts her hand in to stroke the cheetah which then scratches her hand. Lena runs, crying, through the kitchen, knocking over one of the puppies, and the Labrador bites Lena's leg severely. It has never behaved violently before.

C.

Lena will not be able to claim under the Animals Act 1971 for the injury caused by the Labrador bite because it is not a dangerous species.

D.

Lena will not be able to claim successfully under the Animals Act 1971 for the injury caused by the Labrador bite because it has never behaved violently before.

Chapter 12

Torts Affecting Civil Liberties: Trespass to the Person

12.1 The origins and character of trespass

Trespass is as old as the English legal system itself. The word 'trespass' most literally comes from the Latin *trans* (meaning 'through') and *passus* (meaning 'a step'). So its most natural connections are with land.

Since Biblical times, however, the term has been used quite generally to indicate an 'interference'. So an action for trespass, traditionally, was an action for infringement of personal rights whether over land, personal property, or personal security and liberty.

It is not difficult to see how and why trespass to the person developed. In medieval times a person might be subject to all sorts of personal interference from footpads, highwaymen, robbers and burglars. There were no sophisticated, separate systems of civil and criminal law, and no organised police force to enforce the law. Victims of wrongs might have little choice other than to bring actions themselves, under writs of trespass, to protect themselves from attack, or to ensure their liberty.

One of the key characteristics of trespass is that it is actionable *per se*. This means that the claimant is not obliged to show that any damage has been caused. So in this case it is sufficient to show that the trespass has taken place.

Traditionally, then, a trespass only occurred if it was the direct consequence of the defendant's positive act. Omissions are not covered by trespass. If an action arose indirectly from the defendant's act then a claimant would need to bring an action 'on the case' and show damage. These days, the appropriate action for the latter would be in negligence.

Trespass to the person can be committed in one of three ways, as shown in Figure 8 on the following page.

Interestingly, all three are also represented in the criminal law. This is possibly inevitable since it is of no great comfort to the injured victim of a serious assault that his or her attacker has been punished under the criminal law when compensation might be needed. The use of the Criminal Injuries Compensation scheme is available in modern times, but an action in tort is still available and is likely to lead to greater levels of compensation if successful.

While the basic elements of all three are similar in both tort and crime, defences might differ in their application. For example, consent is a common defence in the case of sporting injuries in claims in tort, but is unavailable in certain circumstances in crime, particularly in the case of wounding offences.

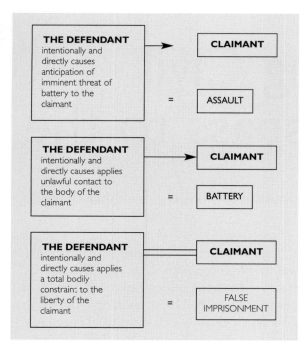

Figure 8 *Diagram illustrating how liability is established in the different types of trespass to the person*

R v Brown and Others (1993)

In this criminal case, the House of Lords prevented sadomasochists from using consent as a defence when they inflicted on each other various harm and wounding in order to heighten their sexual pleasure.

12.2 Assault

It is not uncommon for assault to be mistaken for battery, and indeed in the criminal law the distinctions between the two are much more blurred.

The older view of assault was that it was merely an incomplete battery. Certainly there is no requirement for any physical contact for an assault to have occurred, and the claimant need not have suffered any harm as long as he or she is caused apprehension that some harm will occur.

I de S et Ux v W de S (1348)

W, in attempting to break into I's inn, swung his axe at her and missed. There was still liability for an assault.

The modern view, however, is that the tort requires intention also.

Letang v Cooper (1965)

Here, the claimant was sunbathing on a verge by a car park. The defendant ran over her legs, injuring her. There was direct harm caused by the defendant's negligence, but there was no intention.

So a more accurate definition might now be that:

'a person commits assault where he intentionally and directly causes the claimant to apprehend that he is to be the victim of a battery ...' (Baker).

The intention involved is the intention to create apprehension or fear in the claimant, not what the defendant will actually do. So, in effect, it does not matter whether the defendant will inflict violence or not, or indeed whether there is any contact with the other party at all, provided that there is intent to cause this apprehension in the victim of the assault.

Blake v Barnard (1840)

The defendant pointed a gun at the claimant, causing reasonable apprehension of an imminent battery. The gun was, in fact, unloaded so that, even if he had fired, the defendant could not have harmed the claimant. There was still an actionable assault because the claimant was put in fear.

It is generally accepted, however, that an assault does require some form of active behaviour, so that a passive state is insufficient for an action.

Innes v Wylie (1844)

There was no assault where a policeman merely stood at a door and barred the claimant's entry. Behaviour was passive through obstruction, but there was no indication of any potential harm to the claimant.

Threatening behaviour, then, can amount to an assault, provided that it includes some form of active behaviour.

Read v Coker (1853)

The claimant owed the defendant rent. When the defendant told the claimant to leave the premises the claimant refused. The defendant then ordered some of his employees to see the claimant off the premises. These men then surrounded the claimant, rolled their sleeves up and told him that if he did not leave they would break his neck. There was an assault.

Where there is an attempt to commit a battery but this is thwarted or prevented, then it may still amount to an assault if the party threatened is put in fear of a possible battery.

Stephens v Myers (1830)

At a political meeting the defendant tried to attack the claimant, a speaker. He was prevented from doing so since he was apprehended as he launched himself towards the claimant. There was still an assault present in the attack because initially the claimant could apprehend imminent personal danger.

Nevertheless, it must be possible for the threats to be carried out but for the intervention of others to prevent it, otherwise the claimant would have no reason to fear any possible harm. In both *Stephens v Myers* and *Thomas v NUM* (1985), the defendants were restrained from making any actual attack by the audience in the first and by the police in the second, but there were still actionable assaults.

One clear requirement, then, is that, whatever constitutes the assault, it must cause the claimant fear of impending violence of some kind in order to be actionable.

Smith v Superintendent of Woking (1983)

It was accepted as a criminal assault when Smith entered the grounds of a private house and appeared at the bedroom window of a bedsit, seriously frightening the occupant.

Words

Whether or not words on their own can amount to an assault is more problematic. The traditional view was straightforwardly that they could not.

On the other hand, it is always possible for words alone to show that there is no assault.

Tuberville v Savage (1669)

There was no assault in this case because the words used showed that the claimant should not fear an impending battery. In an argument the defendant did actually handle his sword and said: 'If it were not Assize time I would not take such language from you.' Clearly, the defendant had no intention to harm the claimant at that time, so the claimant could not be put in fear of any personal violence.

However, there are circumstances where little more than a mere threat can be taken to be assault. In *Read v Coker* the men did little more than issue the threat. In the contract case *Barton v Armstrong* (1976) a threat of violence made over the telephone was accepted as leading to a possible cause of action, since it could lead to immediate apprehension that it would be carried out.

In recent criminal law cases, it has been accepted that words alone, and even silence, can amount to an actionable assault.

R v Ireland; R v Burstow (1998)

In these joined appeals, the House of Lords dealt with the issue of silence. The significant point in each case was that the victims had suffered psychological harm and the House of Lords was prepared to accept this as 'actual bodily harm'. Ireland made numerous silent telephone calls. Burstow was, in effect, a 'stalker', who waged a long campaign of making silent telephone calls and sending anonymous letters to a young woman he had briefly gone out with three years previously, as well as some much more extreme behaviour. The House of Lords accepted that a person who uses silence in order to produce apprehension of immediate violence in others is guilty of assault. So there is possibly some room for development on this point in tort as well as criminal law, and it is possible that in certain circumstances words alone can amount to an assault.

12.3 Battery

12.3.1 Definition

Battery, in some ways, should be the most straightforward form of the tort of trespass to the person, since in its purest form it is the unlawful application of force. However, this is not always a satisfactory definition since it ignores those areas where no force, as such, is applied, notably in medicine.

Winfield traditionally argued that technically the *'ordinary collisions of life...'* also amount to batteries. This would create impossible difficulties in a busy, modern, urban environment. For instance, a brief journey on the London Tube in the rush hour would result in countless batteries. Public policy and recent case law suggest that we need to show more than the 'ordinary collisions' to bring an action for battery.

A better definition may be:

'Where the defendant, intending the result, does an act which directly and physically affects the person of the claimant.' (Baker)

The tort certainly requires that there should be a direct and intentional interference with the 'bodily integrity' of the claimant.

Intention

Intention is in some ways a fairly recent development.

Fowler v Lanning (1953)

The defendant had shot the claimant. The claimant, possibly acting under the mistaken belief that battery had traditionally operated as a tort of strict liability, merely referred in his claim to the fact that he had been shot. The appeal judge confirmed that no cause of action had been revealed in the statement of claim, since the claimant was obliged also to demonstrate either intention or negligence on the part of the defendant.

Direct interference

A modern development of the principle has been to replace the traditional distinction between direct and indirect interference with a distinction, instead, between intentional application of force and negligent application.

Letang v Cooper (1965)

A woman was sunbathing in the grounds of a hotel near to where cars were parked. The defendant reversed over her legs, injuring her. While there was no intention to hurt her, there was direct harm caused by the defendant's negligent act. The woman's claim in fact failed because it fell outside the limitation period for negligence. Lord Denning felt that there was no overlap between trespass and negligence, but Lord Diplock felt that there could be.

At times the courts have taken a fairly liberal view of what is and is not direct in order to ensure that a defendant who appears culpable is also liable.

Scott v Shepherd (1773)

Shepherd was found liable for battery when he had thrown a lighted firework into a market. The firework had then been picked up and thrown by two further people before it exploded near to Scott, injuring him.

There are also instances of battery where the application of force can be said to be indirect rather than direct, but where liability was still accepted.

Gibbons v Pepper (1695)

A horse was whipped so that it bolted. It then ran down the claimant. The defendant who had whipped the horse was found liable for the claimant's injuries in battery.

However, where the battery is not direct it can be shown to be negligent.

Nash v Sheen (1953)

A woman went to the hairdressers and asked for a 'permanent wave'. Instead, she was given a 'tone rinse'. This caused her hair to change colour quite unpleasantly, and it also caused a painful rash all over her body. The hairdresser was liable for battery.

In this way it is generally thought that only positive actions can amount to a battery and an omission would presumably not lead to liability.

12.3.2 Hostility

Hostility is another fairly recent requirement of the tort, although it does have some foundation in tradition in the judgment of Holt CJ in *Cole v Turner* (1704): *'The least touching of another in anger is a battery.'*

The issue of hostility has been a recent focus because of some of the difficult circumstances in which a judge may be required to determine whether or not there is a battery.

Wilson v Pringle (1987)

The claimant, a 13-year-old boy, suffered injuries to his hip when a school friend played a practical joke on him. The court, referring to *Cole v Turner*, held that hostility was a necessary element of an actionable battery.

Nevertheless, this position seems to be out of step with the previous presumed position that, subject to the everyday brushes of life, any intentional unwanted contact could amount to a battery. It also seems at odds with certain established practices in specific circumstances.

> ### Collins v Wilcock (1984)
>
> A police oficer was liable for a battery when she took hold of a suspect's arm but did not arrest her. Lord Goff felt that here the appropriate test was whether or not the contact was acceptable within the conduct of ordinary daily life.

12.3.3 Medical treatment and battery

Medical treatment, with a few exceptions, mostly in emergency situations, is dependent on the consent of the patient

The classic definition of patient autonomy comes from an American case. In *Schloendorff v Society of New York Hospitals* (1914) Cardozo J identified it as follows:

'Every human being of adult years and sound mind has a right to determine what shall be done with his own body; a surgeon who performs an operation without the patient's consent commits an assault.'

So, medical treatment that exceeds the consent given by the patient has always been seen as technically at least a battery.

> ### In re F (mental patient: sterilisation) (1990)
>
> A woman in a mental institution, with a mental age of four or five, has become sexually active with another inmate. Since other forms of contraception were considered unacceptable in the circumstances, the doctors applied to the court for a compulsory sterilisation, in the interests of the patient. The treatment was allowed because it was in the patient's best interests. However, Lord Goff confirmed the principle in the last case that, in the case of adult competent patients, medical treatment carried out without justification in the absence of the patient's consent are a battery.

The courts have even accepted that patient autonomy means that a refusal to accept treatment must be honoured by doctors, even though this may ultimately lead to the death of the patient. To treat following such a refusal would be an actionable battery because consent to treatment is absent.

> ### Re T (an adult) (refusal of medical treatment) (1992)
>
> T was injured in a car crash and at one point in her treatment needed a blood transfusion. She was a Jehovah's Witness, and on religious grounds refused the transfusion. The Court of Appeal accepted that in the case the patient was delirious at the time of refusal, and was acting under undue influence of her mother, so that doctors, in giving the transfusion, had acted in her best interests. The court, however, accepted the absolute right of a competent patient to refuse treatment even to the point of death.

Generally, in any case, a patient complaining about medical treatment is more likely to bring an action in negligence according to the principles in *Bolam* rather than to sue in battery.

12.3.4 Defences to assault and battery

There are a number of possible defences to claims of assault and battery and they are interchangeable.

a) *Volenti non fit injuria* – consent

As we have just seen, a doctor will always try to avoid liability by means of consent to treatment, and will always try to gain written consent in advance of any intrusive medical treatment of whatever kind.

Consent will be invalid and treatment may amount to a battery where the patient is not broadly aware of the type of treatment that is to be given.

Chatterton v Gerson (1981)

Here, in an operation for a hernia, the patient's leg was rendered numb following an injection for a trapped nerve. She claimed that she suffered a battery because she had not been informed of the potential consequences of the injection. She failed because that court accepted that she had been informed in broad terms of the purpose of the injection.

However, where the patient has been informed of the existence of the risks of treatment, even without full briefing on the full extent of the possible risk, this will not be a battery either. There is no doctrine of 'informed consent' in English law.

Sidaway v Governors of Bethlem Royal and Maudsley Hospitals (1985)

Here, where Mrs Sidaway was rendered paralysed following the operation, there was no viable claim that she had not consented, having not been fully informed of the potential consequences of the risk. The court accepted that there was no doctrine of informed consent.

Consent is also commonly available as a defence to sporting injuries, but only where the injury occurs within the proper bounds of the sporting activity.

Simms v Leigh Rugby Football Club (1969)

A broken leg resulted from a tackle during a rugby game. Rugby is quite a dangerous contact sport and it was accepted that, as a professional rugby player, the claimant had accepted the normal risks of the activity.

Of course, by definition this means that injuries arising from foul and therefore unlawful play are not consented to and are actionable.

Condon v Basi (1985)

In an amateur game an unlawful challenge did give rise to an action.

b) Necessity

Providing that the trespass is for the prevention of a greater harm, there will be a defence to any action.

Leigh v Gladstone (1909)

Suffragettes in prison were force-fed while on hunger strike. This was allowable because it was to prevent their deaths.

Again, necessity is a defence that doctors will try to use where they have intervened to treat a patient without the patient's consent. There are limited justifications for doing so: the patient is unconscious and in need of emergency treatment, or the patient is in need of urgent treatment and lacks the mental capacity to make a decision. It was on this latter ground that doctors were able, ultimately, to justify their intervention in *Re T*.

In all instances the decision to intervene in the absence of consent must be based on what is in the 'best interests' of the patient (*Airedale NHS Trust v Bland* (1993)). Here, consent was implied when discontinuing feeding and hydration for a patient in an irretrievable permanent vegetative state so that the patient died. In *Ms B v An NHS Trust* (2002) a woman who was completely paralysed and being kept alive on a ventilator successfully argued that the doctors should turn the ventilator off so that she could die. The court accepted that continued treatment was trespass and respected her wishes as she was in sound mind.

c) Self-defence

A person is entitled by law to protect him/herself, another person or even property. However, the defence will only succeed where the force used is reasonable in all the circumstances.

Lane v Holloway (1968)

Neighbours enjoyed a fairly poor relationship. When one came home drunk and rowdy one night, he was told to be quiet by the woman next door. He replied 'Shut up you monkey-faced tart', which led to an altercation between him and the woman's husband. He made a friendly and ineffectual shove at the husband who then beat him in the face so that he required 18 stitches. This attack was out of proportion to the gestures of the drunken man.

This principle may apply even where a person is dealing with a trespasser to his land.

Revill v Newbury (1996)

It was not reasonable force where a person shot a trespasser to his allotment through a hole in his shed.

---

d) Parental chastisement

This, if done reasonably, has traditionally been a good defence. However, it may not have survived the Children Act 1989. It has already been shown to be in conflict with Art 3 of the European Convention on Human Rights (inhuman and degrading treatment) in *A v United Kingdom* (1998). It is also the subject of current debate and clearly has an uncertain future.

e) Inevitable accident

If the alleged battery is beyond the control of the defendant then there will be no liability in trespass.

Stanley v Powell (1891)

A beater was shot during a grouse shoot. It was an inevitable accident because it was shown that the man was not shot directly. The bullet ricocheted off a tree before it hit him.

---

f) Lawful ejectment of a trespasser and lawful arrest

These are, of course, both possible defences to a claim of battery.

They would need to be carried out lawfully. In the case of lawful ejectment of a trespasser, only reasonable force could be used, as has been seen already in *Revill v Newbury*.

For lawful arrest to provide a defence the arrest must be carried out lawfully. Only a police officer could arrest on suspicion that an offence had been committed, was being committed, or was likely to be committed. Besides this, the standard rules of the Police and Criminal Evidence Act 1984 would apply. A citizen's arrest is based on actual knowledge that the offence has been carried out or is being carried out. This is more restrictive and there is a clear danger for people such as store detectives and security guards.

g) Gaining attention

Since, in general, the ordinary touches of life give no rise to an action, touching to gain a person's attention is another possible defence. Again it would have to be done without unreasonable use of force.

Activity

Self-assessment questions

1. What does it mean that trespass to the person is actionable *per se*?

2. What are the major differences between assault and battery?

3. What, traditionally, were the effects of words where an assault is claimed?

4. How has the criminal law possibly changed or developed this?

5. What sort of behaviour is required for an assault?

6. Where battery is alleged, what is likely to happen where the contact is indirectly caused?

7. To what extent is hostility a necessary ingredient of a battery?

8. Why is battery so appropriate in the case of medical treatment?

9. To what must a claimant have consented to give rise to a successful defence in assault or battery?

10. How is the defence of consent applied in sporting activities?

11. How is consent measured in relation to medical treatment?

12. What, exactly, are the 'ordinary collisions of life'?

12.4 False imprisonment

12.4.1 The elements of the tort

The tort is committed where the defendant intentionally imposes a total restraint on the liberty and free movement of the claimant. The term 'false' is actually quite misleading, since in this context it means wrongful or unlawful.

In modern circumstances it is most usually associated with wrongful arrests and detention by the police, or by people such as store detectives and security guards.

There is no requirement for actual imprisonment either. However, there must be total bodily restraint of whatever type.

Bird v Jones (1845)

Bird wished to cross Hammersmith Bridge. The footpath was closed and cordoned off for people to watch a regatta and he was invited to return the way he had come. Since there was a way of him getting away there was no unlawful restraint and no actionable trespass.

In this way an action will fail wherever there is a reasonable means of escape which is open to the claimant to use.

Wright v Wilson (1699)

Here, escape from the alleged tortfeasor was available, though it meant trespassing on someone else's land. It was held that that was sufficient to prevent liability.

The restraint must be direct. Nevertheless, if it is not an action in negligence may still be available.

> ## Sayers v Harlow Urban District Council (1958)
>
> Mrs Sayers became locked in the lavatory because the lock on the door jammed. This was negligence on the council's part rather than false imprisonment.

It has been suggested *in obiter* in *Murray v Minister of Defence* (1988) that there may be a false imprisonment even though the claimant is unconscious at the time. It is certainly the case that a false imprisonment can occur without the claimant being aware of it.

> ## Meering v Graham White Aviation (1919)
>
> The claimant was being questioned in relation to thefts from his employer. Unknown to him, two men were posted at the door to prevent him from leaving. This was a false imprisonment.

It is not a false imprisonment merely because, in the circumstances, the claimant is obliged to pay for his release, providing there has already been a voluntary agreement to that effect.

> ## Robinson v Balmain New Ferry Co. (1910)
>
> The claimant had entered an enclosed wharf from which the ferry sailed. He was obliged to pay a penny to enter and a penny to exit at the other side. When he missed the ferry he changed his mind and wished to exit. The gate manager would not allow him to without paying a penny, which he refused to do. This was not a false imprisonment.

In a similar way, there is no false imprisonment where an employer has a legitimate expectation that his employee will stay till the end of a shift and will not provide the worker with the means of leaving earlier.

> ## Herd v Weardale Steel, Coal and Coke Co. (1915)
>
> Miners, already down a mine but towards the start of their shift, decided that what they were being asked to do was too dangerous and asked to be returned in the cages to the surface. There was no false imprisonment when the employer refused, since the men had already contracted to stay down the mine for a specific time and the employer was not obliged to use the lift until that time came.

It will be a false imprisonment to detain a person wrongly who has committed only a civil offence.

> ## Sunbolf v Alford (1838)
>
> It was false imprisonment where a landlord wrongly detained his lodger for not paying the rent.

It will also be a false imprisonment to detain a prisoner past the proper date for his release (*Cowell v Corrective Services Commissioner* (1989)).

12.4.2 Defences

a) Consent

This is again available. It may apply, for instance, where a lawyer is locked in the cell with his client for confidential consultation.

b) Mistaken arrest

This is only available as a defence to the police. It can also only apply where the officer has acted reasonably in the circumstances.

c) Lawful arrest

Powers of arrest differ between the police and the public generally, the latter being known as 'citizen's arrest'. This is important to store detectives who have no special powers of arrest. The police can generally arrest on suspicion, where the public can arrest only where they are sure that an arrestable offence has been or is being committed.

The arrest, in any case, must be effected with reasonable force.

Treadaway v Chief Constable of West Midlands (1994)

Medical evidence supported the claimant's allegation that while police were interviewing him they placed a bag over his head and threatened to suffocate him.

Hsu v Commissioner of Police of the Metropolis (1996)

A hairdresser refused to allow police with a warrant to enter his house. He was grabbed, punched, kicked and verbally abused, and later found to have blood in his urine. This would not be reasonable force.

The person being detained must also be informed of the reason for their arrest (*Christie v Leachinsky* (1947)).

In a citizens' arrest the person detained must be transported to the police or the police fetched in a reasonable time.

Tims v John Lewis & Co. Ltd (1951)

Here, an employee of a store locked up suspected shoplifters for an unreasonable time.

What is an unreasonable period of detention can be a very short time.

White v W P Brown (1983)

There was a false imprisonment when a lady was locked in a cubicle for 15 minutes by a store detective who suspected her of shoplifting.

In all cases, an arrest must then conform to the rules laid down in the Police and Criminal Evidence Act 1984.

d) Lawful detention under the Mental Health Act 1983

This Act allows appropriate authorities to take a person into a mental hospital, and even to treat them despite the absence of any consent on the patient's part. The power is only exercised subject to stringent conditions and certification as to the patient's mental condition.

Activity

Self-assessment questions

1. What degree of restraint is necessary for a false imprisonment?

2. Of what must store detectives and security guards beware in relation to accusations of trespass to the person?

3. What, exactly, amounts to a lawful arrest?

4. What happens if a claimant had the opportunity to 'escape' from the defendant?

5. Does the claimant need to be aware that he is held for there to be liability?

6. What does the 'false' in 'false imprisonment' mean?

12.5 Intentional indirect harm and protection from harassment

In some past cases it was necessary to establish a novel cause of liability where trespass was apparently unavailable. Now, these cases would probably be covered by negligence.

This occurred in giving limited protection to trespassers, who were traditionally beyond protection.

Bird v Holbreck (1828)

A trespasser succeeded in an action against an occupier of land who had set a spring-gun which caused him injury.

It also provided a means of action before nervous shock was accepted in negligence.

Wilkinson v Downton (1897)

The claimant suffered shock when the defendant told her, as a joke, that her husband had been seriously injured in an accident. There was no direct interference to allow the action in trespass, but there was indirect but intentional harm.

Although the principle would seem to have limited application, it has subsequently been followed in at least one case, although the courts have not taken up a general tort based on intention.

Janvier v Sweeney (1919)

Here, the claimant was able to recover for the shock caused to her when the defendant told her a false story that she was wanted by police for corresponding with a German spy.

More recently, the courts in a nuisance claim accepted the logic of these two cases to allow an injunction to restrain nuisance phone calls in *Khorasandjian v Bush* (1993). There was no actual psychological injury involved in the case, but the court allowed the injunction to prevent any risk of harm to the claimant.

However, the House of Lords, in *Hunter v Canary Wharf Ltd* (1997), later overruled this decision. They did so on the basis that the claimant in *Khorasandjian* was daughter of the tenant and had no proprietary interest in land to justify a nuisance claim.

More recently, the House of Lords has had to consider whether the tort in *Wilkinson v Downton* (1897) still exists.

Wainright v Home Office (2004)

A mother and her son (who suffered from cerebral palsy and arrested development) visited her other son in prison. The prisoner was suspected of supplying drugs, so the governor had instructed that his visitors should be strip-searched and denied their visiting rights if they refused. This was unknown to the mother and son. They were taken to separate rooms and examined naked, including examination of their sexual organs and anuses. They claimed under *Wilkinson v Downton* but the Court of Appeal doubted that the tort still existed. The House of Lords, however, accepted the continued existence of the tort in *Wilkinson v Downton* but held that there could be no liability for distress which fell short of a recognised psychiatric injury and that, on the facts of the case, the intention essential for proving the tort could not be proved.

Even more recently, there has been a successful claim in *Wilkinson v Downton* in *C v D* (2006). Here, claims for abuse, including videoing the claimant in the school showers, could not be brought under trespass to the person but could succeed as intentional indirect harm.

There is still protection to be found in statutory form through the Protection from Harassment Act 1997. S3 of the Act gives a claimant a civil claim to an injunction or to damages. According to s1(1) there must be more than one act of harassment, since the section refers to '*a course of conduct which amounts to harassment and which* [the alleged harasser] *knows or ought to know amounts to harassment*'. S7(2) indicates that the conduct can include causing the claimant alarm or distress, and by s7(4) this is possible by words alone.

There is now also case law on the Act.

Green v DB Group Services (UK) Ltd (2006)

A company secretary was subjected to constant abuse by a group of female staff, was constantly undermined by a male colleague and despite reporting it to her manager and seeking help was given no support from her company. She suffered depression as a result and on returning to work suffered a relapse and was unable to return again. She was awarded £800,000 for the mental illness resulting from the bullying for both negligence and breach of the 1997 Act.

Following *Majrowski v Guy's and St Thomas' NHS Trust* (2006) it is now accepted that employers can be vicariously liable under s3.

The Act has clearly lessened the importance of the rule in *Wilkinson v Downton*. Nevertheless, the tort may still have a place for development to cover individual instances of harassment which would not fit into the 'course of conduct' required for the Act to have effect.

Activity

Self-assessment questions

1. In what ways is the principle in *Wilkinson v Downton* inconsistent with trespass to the person generally?

2. Has the principle really been developed?

3. How will the Protection from Harassment Act 1997 affect the use of the case?

4. How does the Act protect people differently from trespass to the person?

Activity

Multiple choice questions

Say which of the following situations raises a possible claim of assault.

1. Nigel points a gun at his friend Nawab. Nawab knows that the gun is not loaded.

2. Nigel argues with Claire and tells her that he hates her.

3. Nigel waves his fist at Gustav and says that if he was not so easy-going he would thump Gustav in the face.

4. Nigel is badly tackled in a football match by Kevin. He runs towards Kevin, fists raised, but is stopped by the referee.

Say which of the following situations raises a possible claim of battery.

1. Joanne, a black belt, is kicked in the face during a karate contest.

2. Joanne, who is pregnant, is rushed into hospital unconscious after a car crash and doctors perform a Caesarean section delivery to save the baby.

3. Joanne goes into hospital for a routine exploratory operation. While she is under anaesthetic doctors discover that she has an infected womb. Though she is in no danger because of this, the doctor still performs a hysterectomy.

4. Joanne is bumped into by several people as she is trying to get off a busy Tube train.

Say which of the following situations raises a possible claim of false imprisonment.

1. Sukvinder wishes to go down High Street, but she is prevented by police from going down it because there is a demonstration coming the other way.

2. Sukvinder is arrested for stealing goods by store detectives after leaving a store, informed of the arrest and taken straight to the police station.

3. Nigel holds Sukvinder tightly around the waist and will not let her go till she gives him a kiss.

4. Nigel locks Sukvinder in his ground-floor front room. There are no locks on the windows.

- Trespass involves a direct interference with the claimant's person.
- It is actionable *per se* so there is no need to show damage.
- There are three types: assault, battery and false imprisonment.
- An assault occurs where a person intentionally and directly causes another to fear that he is to be the victim of physical violence (*Smith v Superintendent of Woking*).
- No actual contact is required, but there must be actions; words on their own are insufficient (*Read v Coker*).
- There must be active behaviour (*Innes v Wylie*).
- A prevented battery may be an assault (*Stephens v Myers*).
- Consent, self-defence and necessity are all possible defences.
- A battery is the unlawful application of force to a person.
- Intention is a fairly recent requirement (*Fowler v Lanning*).
- The force must be directly applied – compare *Nash v Sheen* with *Scott v Shepherd*.
- It can also occur through negligence (*Letang v Cooper*).
- There is conflict over whether or not hostility is a requirement – compare *Wilson v Pringle* with *Collins v Wilcock*.
- Battery is important in medical treatment – medical treatment in the absence of consent is generally a battery, except where there is some justification for not obtaining consent (*Re F*).
- Defences include: consent, provided the actual risk is consented to (*Simms v Leigh RFC*); necessity, e.g. to protect life (*Leigh v Gladstone*); self-defence, but only where reasonable force is used (*Lane v Holloway*).
- False imprisonment involves total restriction of movement (*Bird v Jones*):
  - it can occur even where the claimant is unaware of the restraint (*Meering v Graham White Aviation*)
  - however, it is possible that the claimant is required to pay for his freedom (*Robinson v Balmain New Ferry Co.*)
  - it is possible that the claimant can be legitimately restrained, e.g. by his employer (*Herd v Weardale Steel, Coal & Coke Co.*)
  - defences include: consent; mistaken arrest (in the case of police officers); and lawful arrest, where the proper requirements of arrest are adhered to.
- Traditionally, it was not possible to bring actions for harm that was intentional but indirectly caused.
- However, such an action was made possible where an action in trespass would have proved impossible by the cases of *Wilkinson v Downton* and *Janvier v Sweeney*.
- Since the Protection from Harassment Act 1997, it is now possible for a claimant to get an injunction and damages where there is a 'course of conduct' amounting to harassment.

Dilemma Board

In the Dilemma Board below, consider the accuracy of each of the four statements, A, B, C and D, as they apply to the facts in the central scenario. You only need to give the basic principles. The answer is in the Appendix at the end of the book.

Dilemma Board

A.

Richard cannot be found liable for an assault on Gayle.

B.

Richard will be liable for a battery on Gayle.

Gayle has told her husband, Richard, that she is leaving him because of his violent rages. As she is going, Richard asks Gayle for a farewell kiss. Gayle reluctantly agrees. Richard holds Gayle tightly round the waist, kisses her but does not release her. Gayle asks Richard to let her go but Richard replies 'You know I will never let you leave me Gayle'.

C.

Richard may be found liable for false imprisonment.

D.

Richard will be found liable under the tort in *Wilkinson v Downton* (1897).

Chapter 13

Torts Affecting Civil Liberties: Defamation

13.1 The categories of defamation

Defamation is a tort with the specific purpose of protecting a person's reputation. Traditionally it could be made in one of two ways, although the distinctions are now perhaps less important than in previous times.

The two specific types are:

- **slander**, originally said to be the spoken word, but more accurately described as being a transitory form
- **libel,** originally recognised as written words, or more accurately described as being in a permanent form.

Modern technology has made this distinction somewhat outdated and most other jurisdictions have now abolished it. This was, indeed, recommended by the Faulkes Committee, though not taken up in the Defamation Act 1996.

The important modern distinction, then, is probably simply between a transitory and a permanent form of masking the defamatory statement. Even so, the difference is not always easy to see, though there are some accepted categories relating to one or the other.

Youssoupoff v MGM Pictures Ltd (1934)

The suggestion in a picture about the Tsars was that Rasputin had seduced the Princess Youssoupoff, one of the Russian Royal family. She sued successfully for libel for the damage to her reputation

- A written defamation, for instance, has long been accepted as libel.
- Film has also been accepted as libel and does seem to represent a permanent form.
- Defamatory statements made on radio or TV will be libel as a result of the Defamation Act 1952 and the Broadcasting Act 1990.
- Defamation made in a live play may be libel as a result of the Theatres Act 1968.
- An effigy made in wax or other substance can be a libel.

Monson v Tussauds Ltd (1894)

A man accused of murder had actually been released on a 'not proven' verdict. A wax effigy of him at the entrance to the Chamber of Horrors was held to be a libel. The clear implication of being in the chamber of horrors was that he was, in fact, a killer.

- Spoken words, and even gestures, are very easily distinguishable as slander because of their transitory nature.
- Areas that present more difficulties are things like tape recordings of live performances.

Traditionally, there were two reasons why it was important to distinguish libel from slander.

- Firstly, libel could be a crime as well as a tort.

> ### R v Lemon and Gay News (1979)
>
> This case involved a successful prosecution for blasphemous libel for a poem likely to shock Christians because it portrayed Christ as a homosexual.

- Secondly, libel is actionable *per se*, that is, actual damage need not be proved, whereas in slander damage must be shown except in four situations:
    - where a criminal offence is alleged to have been committed by the person slandered
    - where the person slandered is accused of having a contagious or socially undesirable disease
    - where a woman is accused of being 'unchaste' – this comes from the Slander of Women Act 1891, and was clearly important in times when such an accusation might damage a woman's marriage prospects
    - where the accusation is that a person is unfit for any office, trade, profession or calling, or indeed any employment where the claimant could be harmed as a result of the slander.

13.2 Essential elements of the tort

13.2.1 The definition of 'defamation'

Winfield has described defamation as the '. . . *publishing of a defamatory statement which refers to the claimant and which is made without lawful justification'.* Each of these elements will need to be proved in any successful claim:

- a publication
- of a defamatory statement
- referring to the claimant.

Finally, the inclusion of lawful justification is a reference to defences, so a final qualification is the absence of an appropriate defence. In any case, besides these the statement must obviously be false.

Each element of the definition can then be considered in turn.

13.2.2 Publication

Publication involves repeating the defamatory statement to at least one person. This will inevitably not include the person defamed, since damage can only be done to his/her reputation if someone else hears the statement. In this way, a letter written to the claimant containing the defamation will not be a publication where the claimant then shows it to other people.

It may well be a publication, however, where the defamation is made in a postcard because we can assume that people other than the claimant might read it. A letter addressed wrongly and then opened could be a publication.

It could also be a publication where the defendant knows that a person other than the claimant will open the letter.

> ### Pullman v Hill (1891)
>
> Here, it was a publication where the defendant was aware that the secretary would open the mail.

For liability, the third person, for obvious reasons, would not normally include a spouse.

> ### Theaker v Richardson (1962)
>
> A member of a local council wrote to another member calling her a *'lying, low down brothel keeping whore and thief'.* When the claimant's husband opened and read it there was a publication. It was reasonable to assume he might open it, thinking it was an election address.

Nevertheless, it will not be a publication when a third party not authorised to do so opens a sealed letter addressed to the claimant. This is because there could be no expectation on the defendant's part that the letter would be seen by that party.

Huth v Huth (1915)

Here, the letter was sent in a sealed envelope to the claimant but the claimant's butler opened the letter and so there was no publication.

Graffiti can amount to a publication and the owners of premises are liable if they fail to remove it.

Byrne v Deane (1937)

Police had removed an illegal gambling machine from a golf club. A poem had then appeared on a notice board that remarked 'he who gave the game away may he byrne in hell'. The claimant was clearly concerned that because of the spelling the poem was an accusation that he was the one who reported the illegal machine. There was a publication here, even though for other reasons there could be no liability.

It is important to remember that each separate repeat of the defamatory statement could be a separate publication. In this way, a publisher could be liable under many different actions or indeed there could be many different defendants including, for instance, authors, printers, publishers and those who repeat the defamation in another context, such as reviewers and their publishers, and even booksellers and distributors.

Vizetelly v Mudie's Select Library Ltd (1900)

A mobile library was liable for defamation for failing to prevent circulation of a defamatory book after receiving a warning about its content. The court accepted, however, that there could be a defence available of innocent dissemination in such circumstances if the defendants could show:

- they were unaware that the book contained defamatory material at the time they distributed it
- there was nothing suspicious to alert them to the presence of the defamatory material
- there was no negligence on their part.

It has, however, been held possible for a party to be liable for repetition of a defamatory statement that is reasonably foreseeable.

Slipper v BBC (1991)

The defendants were liable here not just for their original statements, but for repeats of the defamatory statement made in reviews of the film in which they were made, and which was seen as a foreseeable consequence.

Repetitions of defamatory comments through processes such as internal mail represent a less certain possibility, and in any case may be protected by privilege.

13.2.3 The defamatory statement

Defamatory statement is another term requiring exact definition. This has been supplied and explained as meaning:

'a statement which tends to lower the claimant in the minds of right-thinking members of society generally, and *in particular to cause him to be regarded with feelings of hatred, contempt, ridicule, fear and disesteem ...'.* (Lord Atkin in *Sim v Stretch* (1936)).

What amounts to a defamatory remark, then, depends entirely on the context in which the words appear, but can inevitably include vulgar and unjustified abuse.

Cornwell v Daily Mail (1989)

The newspaper unfairly accused an actress of *'having a big bum ... and the kind of stage presence that blocks lavatories'.* This was defamatory.

It might also include derogatory remarks of any kind.

Roach v News Group Newspapers (1992)

An actor was accused of being as boring as the character he portrayed in *Coronation Street.* This was classed as defamatory in the case.

It can also include references to a person's moral character.

Charleston v News Group Newspapers (1995)

The heads of two of the stars of an Australian soap were superimposed on the near-naked bodies of a couple engaged in a sexual act, with the caption *'Strewth! What's Harold up to with our Madge?'* The picture was potentially defamatory. However, the action did not succeed because an article about the picture being reproduced from a computer game where it was used without the stars' knowledge or consent accompanied the picture.

It will not, of course, be defamatory where the accusation is one implying decency or honesty, even if it is untrue.

Byrne v Dean (1937)

Here, Byrne's action could not succeed because the inference in the poem was that he had done his duty as a law-abiding citizen.

Neither will a statement be defamatory where, however untrue, it only produces feelings of sympathy rather than feelings of scorn or ridicule.

Grappelli v Derek Block Holdings Ltd (1981)

Here, an article suggested that a famous Jazz violinist was ill and unlikely to tour again. It was not defamatory because it would not harm his reputation.

Nor does it really matter how hurtful the remark is. It is purely the fact that it will lower the reputation of the claimant that makes it defamatory.

Berkoff v Burchill (1996)

Julie Burchill, a journalist, described an actor, Berkoff, as 'hideously ugly'. Lord Justice Millet accepted the actor's claim that the words would expose him to ridicule and were therefore defamatory.

Statements, while they may not be defamatory on their own, can easily become so because of their juxtaposition to other things.

Monson v Tussauds Ltd (1894)

The effigy on its own did not amount to defamation, but indicating its connection with other tableaux in the Chamber of Horrors did.

Innuendo

Where the statement contains a hidden or implied meaning then this may also make the statement defamatory.

Cassidy v Daily Mirror Newspapers Ltd (1929)

Mrs Cassidy sued successfully when a picture was taken of her husband at the races accompanied by a young woman described in the caption as his fiancée. The implication was that Mr and Mrs Cassidy were not married, which was a slur on her character and defamatory.

This is otherwise known as defamation by innuendo and it may operate even though no positive statement is made.

Tolley v Fry & Sons Ltd (1931)

A caricature of a famous amateur golfer of the time appeared in an advertising poster for Fry's chocolate bars, with a bar of chocolate sticking out of his back pocket. He was disturbed that his amateur status was compromised as a result, since by implication people would think that he had been paid.

However, such cases may require the introduction of further evidence to show how, exactly, the statement is defamatory.

Allsop v Church of England Newspaper Ltd (1972)

A broadcaster was referred to as having a '... *preoccupation with the bent*'. Since the word 'bent' had a number of different slang meanings as well as its normal meanings it was ambiguous in the context. The claimant was therefore required to show which meaning was being applied.

13.2.4 Referring to the claimant

A claimant must be able to show that the defamatory statement referred to him/her. This proves simple enough when the claimant is actually named in the statement. This is not vital, however, providing people will know that the statement is referring to the claimant.

It could be proved, for instance, even where an entirely fictitious name is used.

Hulton & Co. v Jones (1910)

A humorous article about the London to Dieppe motor rally suggested that the people entering the rally were really only interested in chasing French girls. A central character in the article was called Artemus Jones who was described as a churchwarden from Peckham. An actual Artemus Jones, who was a barrister from Wales, sued successfully. Even though any defamation was entirely unintentional, his friends might easily believe that the article referred to him.

A claim is even possible, then, when there are two people with the same name, and people may be unclear which one is being referred to.

Newstead v London Express Newspapers Ltd (1940)

Two men were both named Harold Newstead, were both aged 30, and both lived in Camberwell. When the conviction of one for bigamy was reported, the other was able to claim defamation because there was nothing to say which of them the report referred to.

So it is not important that the claimant is named in the statement, because often there will be some words in the statement which will make the claimant recognisable to people who know him or her.

Morgan v Odhams Press Ltd (1971)

A newspaper article alleged that a girl who was probably going to be an important witness in a trial of a dog-doping gang had been kidnapped, though there were no names given of the kidnappers. The girl had actually been staying with the claimant, who was able to show that people who knew him would assume, in the circumstances, that the article was referring to him.

So in the same way a visual image, such as a cartoon or a caricature, can also refer to the claimant.

Tolley v Fry & Sons Ltd (1931)

The caricature of the golfer was still easily identifiable as Tolley and so it was defamatory.

Defamation of a class

Generally, a vague reference to people in general, or to a class which is too large for the claimant to

be recognised, will not be actionable. For instance, the assertion that all law lecturers are boring could not be defamatory.

Knupffer v London Express Newspapers Ltd (1944)

An article about the Young Russian Party described them as unpatriotic. Knupffer was head of the British branch of the party. It had only 24 members. His claim failed, however, because the party was international, so an individual could not easily be identified.

A claim in respect of defamation of a class is possible, however, provided that an individual claimant can still show that (s)he is individually identifiable.

Le Fanu v Malcolmson (1848)

Articles were published about cruelty to the workforce in Irish factories. The claimant's factory was described perfectly in the article, so it was possible to say that the article referred to him.

Activity

Self-assessment questions

1. Why is it necessary to have a law protecting reputation?

2. How does such a law affect basic principles, such as freedom of speech?

3. What are the main differences between libel and slander?

4. What are the main elements that must be proved to show defamation?

5. What is a 'publication' and what is not?

6. Why was the BBC liable in *Slipper v BBC*?

7. Why did Byrne fail in his action against Deane?

8. What, exactly, is meant by 'innuendo'?

9. In what circumstances can a class of people be defamed?

5. A student e-mails most of his fellow students, complaining that I caught another student cheating in an exam and reported her. This is, in fact, not true. The student was caught cheating, but not by me.

Activity *Quick Quiz*

In the following situations, if there is no truth in the statement being made, consider whether or not I could succeed in a claim of defamation.

1. An existing student has told a group of new students over lunch that I never attend my classes.

2. In a letter addressed to me, a student accuses me of being a liar and a cheat and, when marking assignments, of failing any student that I do not like. My wife actually opens the letter and reads it.

3. An article in a local newspaper refers to 'appallingly low standards of teaching at the School of Legal Studies' and 'a college staffed by a bunch of amateurs without a qualification between them'.

4. For a joke, an ex-student of mine persuades a number of his friends whom I also taught that I have been unwell and that they should send me 'get well soon' cards.

13.3 Defences and remedies

There were originally four basic common-law defences to defamation, but these have been added to over the years by different statutes. The defences are generally quite complex and often only apply to specific situations, but they are an important part of the law of defamation.

13.3.1 Justification

Justification basically refers to the fact that the statement is true. The basic principle is that the truth can never be defamatory, no matter how hurtful.

However, the defence is not straightforward since the burden of proof is on the defendant to show that the allegation was true.

Archer v The Star (1987)

In an action that has been subsequently discredited by the imprisonment of the claimant, the allegation was that the claimant politician had visited a prostitute. The prostitute gave much of the evidence and was treated by the court as an incredible witness. She was also compared to the politician's wife, who was described as of high social standing and elegant, so the allegations appeared to lack credibility and, at the time, the defendant newspaper and the defence witnesses were unable to convince the court of the truth of the allegations.

Proof of the truth of the allegation can also prove difficult where the claims are of a general rather than a specific nature.

Bookbinder v Tebbitt (1989)

The defendant, during an election campaign, referred to the policies of a local council as '*a damn fool idea*'. The policy in question was overprinting stationery with '*Support Nuclear Free Zones*'. The court would not allow the defendant to introduce evidence of the council's overspending, so the words in context were incapable of supporting the allegation made by the defendant.

By s5 Defamation Act 1952, where there are many allegations the action should not fail '*... by reason only that the truth of every charge is not proved*'.

Justification can also sometimes be used in respect of spent convictions, provided that there is no malice shown in revealing them.

13.3.2 Fair comment

Fair comment is sometimes known as the 'critics defence' because it is designed to protect the rights of the press, in particular to state valid opinions.

On this basis the defence can only succeed where to state such opinions is in the public interest because they can be seen as a matter of public concern.

London Artists Ltd v Littler (1969)

When actors resigned, the director wrote to each of them accusing them of plotting against him, and he sent a copy of his letters to the press. The case was a matter of public concern because the public has a general interest in art and entertainment.

Of course, the incorporation of the European Convention on Human Rights may have an impact on what is considered to be in the public interest, because of the need also to recognise the right to privacy contained in Art 8 of the Convention.

For the opinion to be fair comment, it must be based on an appraisal of true facts in existence at the time that the statement is made.

Kemsley v Foot (1952)

A former leader of the Labour Party, while a junior MP, wrote an article, in response to an article, attacking it as: '*one of the foulest pieces of journalism perpetuated in this country for many a long year*'. The article itself appeared under the headline '*Lower than Kemsley*'. This was reference to another newspaper concerning their conduct, so the defence could apply.

What is 'fair' comment is measured according to an objective test, so that there is no particular need for the author of the comment to prove an honest belief in it.

Telnikoff v Matusevitch (1992)

The claimant wrote an article in the *Telegraph* criticising the BBC Russian Service for over-recruiting employees from ethnic minority groups. The defendant then replied, accusing the claimant of racism. The House of Lords felt that the defendant had to show that he was commenting, since many people might not have seen the original article and would not necessarily know to what he was referring.

The defence can always be defeated where there is shown to be malice.

> ## Thomas v Bradbury, Agnew & Co. Ltd (1906)
>
> A review in *Punch* was not only critical of the claimant's book, but made many personal slurs against the claimant also. The fact that there was malice was also then demonstrated by the defendant's conduct in court.

13.3.3 Absolute privilege

Defamation, as we have seen, has to be concerned with balancing the right to protect reputation with the right to freedom of speech and expression.

In certain circumstances, the law recognises that the freedom to speak out without any fear of repercussions is vital to maintaining a free society. In many of these circumstances a defence of privilege has been applied.

In some instances, privilege will be absolute so that there is no right to challenge the making of the statement at all. These situations include:

- statements made on the floor of either House of Parliament – this right is guaranteed by the Bill of Rights 1688, though it is now possible to waive the right under the Defamation Act 1996 s13. This right of waiver has been strongly criticised because it allows MPs to hide behind privilege, but then to abandon it when it suits them in order to pursue defamation actions. Although the House of Lords has suggested that the privilege was that of Parliament, not of the individual MP (*Hamilton v Al Fayed* (2000))
- official reports of parliamentary proceedings (*Hansard*) – this is by virtue of the Parliamentary Papers Act 1840
- judicial proceedings – the right here covers judge, jury, counsel, solicitors, parties and witnesses, but it will not include the public (*Mahon and another v Rahn* (2000))

- *'fair, accurate and contemporaneous'* reports of judicial proceedings – this is by Law of Libel Amendment Act 1888 and the Defamation Act 1952
- communications between lawyer and client
- communications between officers of state.

13.3.4 Qualified privilege

There are also a number of situations where the communication rather than the occasion itself may be covered by privilege. In this case the privilege is qualified so that showing malice can cause the defence to fail.

> ## Angel v Bushel Ltd (1968)
>
> The defendant engaged in a business venture with the claimant, who had been introduced to him by a mutual friend. When the venture failed the defendant wrote to the friend in a fit of anger, saying that the claimant was *'not conversant with normal business ethics'*. This was malice.

However, actual malice must be shown.

> ## Horrocks v Lowe (1974)
>
> Both parties were members of a local council. The defendant called the claimant's actions into question, calling them *'brinkmanship, megalomania or childish petulance'*. He then tried to claim qualified privilege when the claimant sued. The claimant tried to defeat this defence by arguing malice, but failed because the court accepted that the defendant believed the statements.

The defence can be claimed in a number of situations including:

- comments made in the course of exercising a duty, e.g. a reference. The reference made about an employee to a potential future employer is confidential. Traditionally, where the reference was defamatory, the employee would have to prove malice first to even see the document, making actions virtually impossible. Now, since *Spring v Guardian Assurance*, the claimant may bring an action for negligence, making action easier

- comments made in the protection of an interest, e.g. memos in business
- fair and accurate reporting of parliamentary proceedings

Reynolds v Times Newspapers (1998) CA and (1999) HL

The claimant had been leader of the Irish Parliament and had done much to promote the Northern Ireland peace process. A political crisis arose, at which point he resigned his position and withdrew his party from the governing coalition. The *Sunday Times* then published an article which the claimant believed indicated that he had misled the Irish Parliament and had withheld information on the crisis from them. He brought his action when the newspaper failed to print an apology. The newspaper sought to rely on qualified privilege. The Court of Appeal held that qualified privilege can be argued by the press when: (i) the paper has a moral, social or legal duty to inform the public of the matter in question; (ii) and the public has a corresponding interest in receiving the information; (iii) and the nature, status and source of the material and the circumstances of the publication are such as to warrant the protection of privilege.

On appeal, the House of Lords decided that there was no general category of qualified privilege for political information. Despite arguments based on Article 10 of the European Convention on Human Rights, the standard test of duty to disseminate and duty to receive should be applied. They held that ten matters were critical:

- the seriousness of the allegation
- whether or not it is of public concern
- the source of information
- steps taken to verify it
- the status of information
- the urgency of the issue
- whether comment is sought from the claimant
- whether the claimant's comments were included in the article
- the tone of the article
- circumstances and timing of publication.

Since the article here was highly critical and the defendants had not sought Reynolds' side of the story, they had no privilege.

In *Jameel and Others v Wall Street Journal* (2006) it was held that the defence should be treated as a question of law and not as a matter of fact to be decided in each case.

- fair and accurate reporting of judicial proceedings – which, since the Defamation Act 1996, would include all court and other proceedings in, for example, Commonwealth or other courts
- a complex list of situations identified in the Schedule to the Defamation Act 1996:
  - those privileged without explanation and identified in Part 1 (these might include fair and accurate reporting of public proceedings in Commonwealth parliaments, or of courts in any part of the world, or of public inquiries anywhere)
  - those privileged subject to an explanation and identified in Part 2 (these might include fair and accurate copies of EU documents, or of reports of UK companies, or reports of trade associations, or of any association formed for the purpose of promoting sport, art, science, religion, or learning in general).

13.3.5 Unintentional defamation and innocent dissemination

The general rule has always been that a person can be liable for defamation even if he or she is actually unaware of the defamation; every publication is still defamation. This is plainly unfair on many parties and the law has long had exceptions to this basic rule where the defamation has been made innocently.

1. Innocent publication under the common law

The leading case is *Vizetelly v Mudie's Select Library Ltd* (1900), which provided that there would be a defence of innocent publication if the defendant could show: (i) publication was done innocent of the defamation; (ii) there was nothing suspicious to alert the defendant to the defamation; (iii) the publication was made without any negligence.

2. Innocent publication under the Defamation Act 1996

- The defence in *Vizetelly* has probably now been subsumed in s1 Defamation Act 1996, which is similar but wider than the common law test.
- Under s1(1) a defendant has a defence if (s)he can show that (s)he was not the *'author, editor or publisher'* of the matter complained of; took reasonable care in relation to its publication; and had no reason to believe that his/her actions had contributed to the defamation.

3. Unintentional defamation

- This defence was originally available under s4 Defamation Act 1952, and was available where the defendant was unaware of the defamatory nature of the remarks made.
- Provisions here were clearly designed to prevent situations such as those in *Hulton* and in *Cassidy*.

- The basics of the defence were that: (i) the statement must have been made innocently; (ii) the defendant could avoid an action by offering amends and a suitable apology, and a payment into court; (iii) if this was not accepted then a defence was still available if the publication was innocent, the offer of amends had been made promptly, and there was no malice.
- This defence was criticised by the Faulkes Committee, and now a rebuttable presumption of innocent publication and an offer of amends is available under ss2–4 Defamation Act 1996. To succeed the defendant must offer to publish a suitable correction and apology, in appropriate form, and must offer compensation and costs. A claimant can actually refuse such an offer, but it would count against him or her in an action.

13.3.6 Consent

A claimant's apparent consent to publication may defeat a claim of defamation. This may be because the claimant has actually passed the material to the defendant. It may also occur where it can be shown that the claimant in effect invited publication.

Moore v News of the World (1972)

The newspaper actually failed in their use of this defence here, when they reproduced a private account of Dorothy Squires' private life with Roger Moore. She believed that she was being interviewed about her comeback and was not prepared for personal details such as were published. Otherwise the defence may have been available.

Activity

Self-assessment questions

1. How does the defence of 'justification' differ from that of 'fair comment'?

2. What are the differences between 'absolute privilege' and 'qualified privilege'?

3. What is so significant about the case of *Reynolds v Times Newspapers*?

4. What features are common to areas covered by absolute privilege?

5. Why is fair comment so significant to freedom of speech?

6. What is different about innocent publication under common law and under statute?

7. How does a defendant make an 'offer of amends' to avoid liability?

2. Jeffrey, a well-known public figure, was so outraged when he read a letter to him from Paul, accusing him of perjuring himself in a court case, that he gave the letter to Ian, the editor of a newspaper. Ian then published a report on the letter and Jeffrey's reaction to it.

3. During a debate in the House of Commons one MP, Reggie, accuses Ronnie, an MP from another party, of taking bribes from a large company. In fact, Ronnie has never had anything to do with that company.

4. Maurice has always disliked his employee, Archie. When Archie applies for a job with another firm, Maurice writes as part of the reference he sends 'A competent worker, on the occasions that he attends', even though Archie's attendance record is perfect.

Activity   *Quick Quiz*

Consider whether or not there might be a defence to a claim of defamation in the following situations, and identify which defence is appropriate.

1. An MP, Michael, has been interviewed by police in relation to a party at which drug taking and other illegal activities occurred, and at which one party goer died from an overdose. A newspaper prints a report on this.

13.4 Remedies

There are two basic remedies available in defamation actions.

13.4.1 Injunctions

Interim injunctions are often awarded in advance of any action in order to prevent publication or broadcast of the alleged defamation. However, these are criticised and accused of being 'gagging orders'.

In any case, injunctions are of limited use because claimants are very often unaware of the defamation until it has been published and done the damage.

13.4.2 Damages

In defamation actions damages are of three types:

- nominal cases – where the case is proven but there is little if any damage suffered
- contemptuous damages – where, though the claimant wins it is felt that there is no real justification for the action having been brought, as in *Dering v Uris* (1964), where damages of only 1/2d were granted
- exemplary damages – used to punish the defendant and express disapproval, so damages are often high.

There are constant criticisms in defamation actions, both of the fact that it is the jury that awards damages and that their awards are too high and are out of proportion with, for instance, personal injury awards. Lord Aldington received £1.5 million, and Jason Donovan came close to putting the magazine *Face* out of business when awarded £100,000.

Nowadays, it is possible for excessive sums to be reduced by the Court of Appeal, as when damages of £650,000 awarded to Sonia Sutcliffe, the Yorkshire Ripper's wife, against *Private Eye* were reduced to a more acceptable £60,000.

13.5 Points for discussion

13.5.1 Protection of reputation, freedom of speech and rights of privacy

Defamation is the main area of law used to protect reputation. It is clearly an important right that all people, particularly those in the public eye, should be able to use the law to protect their reputation from unwarranted attack.

However, as with many other areas of tort, nuisance being an obvious example, this is an area of the law where a balance needs to be struck between this right and the right of others.

This particularly applies to the right of the press to enjoy freedom of speech, and to be able to comment freely on issues of public importance, however damaging to another person.

Obviously, one of the key issues here is that the comments complained of, in order that the right to make them can be protected, should be the truth, or at least a fair statement of opinion. It is important that the truth, however damaging, should never be suppressed in a free society.

The common criticism of English defamation law is that it often does just that. In the recent defamation action by McDonald's (popularised as the 'McLibel case') against two environmental campaigners, many of their allegations against the fast food chain were accepted by the court as having foundation in fact, including that the company paid low wages to its employees in England, reared some of its animals in cruel conditions, and exploited children in its target advertising. Nevertheless, the case demonstrated how easy it is for a wealthy party or corporate body to 'protect reputation' possibly at the expense of the public's right to know matters of concern. The two environmental campaigners made a successful application to the European Court of Human Rights in *Steel and Morris v UK* (2005). The court held that the trial had infringed their human rights under Art 6 and Art 10, as the nature of English law meant that they had to run their own defence against a large corporate body.

The current law is out of line with both US law, in the form of the 1st amendment to the constitution, and with the European Convention on Human Rights which, at Art 10, states:

'Everyone has the right to freedom of expression. This right shall include freedom to hold opinions and to receive information and ideas without interference by public authority and regardless of frontiers.'

The passing of the Human Rights Act 1998, which came into force in 2000, does not significantly alter the position on freedom of speech since the Act does not fully incorporate the provisions of the Convention. What it does do is to provide that all primary and secondary legislation must be interpreted, as far as possible, in line with the Articles of the Convention. It also provides that no public authority shall act in any way that is incompatible with the basic rights identified in the Convention.

On this basis, although the Act will certainly change the law of torts, actions before the European Court of Human Rights are still a possibility, particularly in this area. Significantly, the courts had already previously accepted Article 10 in *Rantzen v Mirror Group Newspapers* (1996), in which the House of Lords said that the right of freedom of speech in Article 10 must underlie common-law principles.

The danger of the libel laws in the UK as they currently stand is said to be that they discourage people from making comment on matters of public concern and *'may prevent the publication of matters which it is very desirable to make public'*.

The other area of human rights law that is significant to the tort of defamation is the right to privacy, which is guaranteed under Art 8 of the Convention.

The House of Lords in *Wainright v Home Office* (2004) declared that there was no right of privacy in English law. The European Court of Human Rights in *Wainright v UK* held that there were breaches of Art 8 and of Art 13. In *Campbell v MGN* (2004) and *Douglas v Hello* (2003) English courts concluded that while there were no rights to privacy, the claimants did have rights of confidentiality.

Quite clearly, exercising rights of freedom of speech can actually have harmful consequences for privacy. Difficult questions then arise as to how to balance these different rights.

13.5.2 Criticisms of the administration of defamation law

One of the first and most obvious criticisms of defamation law is that it is really only available to the rich, or to corporate or public bodies.

There is no public financial support available. As a result, most defamation actions seem to be between famous personalities and the press. Apart from the obvious cynical view that 'any publicity is good publicity', and therefore that a defamation action may be as useful in publicity terms to a public figure as advertising, it is also evident that there are many people who suffer slurs on their character but are prevented from clearing their reputation because of the cost and restrictions on finance.

Certainly bringing defamation actions is expensive, and costs are prohibitive. This was shown in *Taylforth v Metropolitan Police Commissioner and the Sun Newspaper* (1994) where a 'soap' actress's unsuccessful action left her with costs of half a million pounds.

Juries are commonly used in defamation actions. This is justifiable since they are being asked to consider whether the defamatory remark would lower the estimation of the claimant in the minds of right thinking people. Nevertheless, juries have come under attack, most commonly for their inconsistencies and more significantly for the level of damages they are prone to award.

The award of £1.5 million granted by the jury in *Lord Aldington v Tolstoy and Watts* (1989) was undoubtedly excessive and was criticised by the European Court of Human Rights for being *'not necessary in a free society'*. Since the award of damages in personal injury cases is so carefully restrained, it seems illogical that the award of damages in respect of protection of reputation should be left in the hands of an amateur body such as the jury.

There is now provision, under s8 Courts and Legal Services Act 1990, for the Court of Appeal to reduce excessive awards of damages made by the jury, and this has been used.

A different type of problem in relation to defamation actions is the number and complexity of defences available. This can make matters very difficult for particular types of claimant. In the case of employees suffering a damaging and inaccurate reference, traditionally any attempt to seek redress would be defeated by a claim of qualified privilege unless they were able to show malice. The development of a claim in negligence under the principle in *Spring v Guardian Assurance plc* (1994) has gone some way to modify this position.

One final criticism is that a significant class of people is denied the protection of the defamation laws, and these are the dead. It is possible to make any comment once a person is dead, which seems unfair since they are not able to defend their reputation.

13.5.3 Reform of defamation law

Defamation law has been criticised over many years. The Faulkes Committee in 1975 looked into possible reforms of the system and made many recommendations. Included in these were:

- ending the unnecessary and cumbersome distinction between libel and slander
- altering the defence of justification to a simple defence of truth
- improving the defence of fair comment so that it will only fail if the comment does not represent a truly held opinion
- altering the defence of qualified privilege so that it will fail when the maker of the statement merely takes advantage of their privileged position, as well as when malice is present
- simplifying the procedural requirements for unintentional defamation
- prohibiting punitive awards of damages
- reforming the law on defaming the dead
- reducing the limitation period

- making legal aid available
- making judges responsible for awarding damages.

These recommendations have subsequently been added to, with recommendations for generally much more simplified procedures. In fact, there has been reform through the Defamation Act 1996. However, this is partial rather than sweeping reform, making fairly minor changes.

The Act has created a new 'fast-track' system for claims of under £10,000 in order to dispose of less significant cases more quickly. It has also created a new 'offer of amends' defence for newspapers to plead in the case of unintentional defamation. In certain cases judges will be able to hear a case without a jury, and the limitation period has been lowered.

Activity

Self-assessment questions

1. To what extent has the Defamation Act 1996 altered the law on defamation and met criticisms of the law?

2. What are the roles of judge and jury in defamation actions?

3. What criticisms can be made of the role of juries in defamation actions?

4. Which is actually the more effective remedy in a defamation action, an injunction or damages?

5. What is the significance of the Human Rights Act 1998 and of the European Convention on Human Rights to the law of defamation?

6. How has the case of *Spring v Guardian Assurance* made the law much fairer?

- Defamation is a tort protecting a person's reputation from false allegations.
- It is of two types: libel (a permanent form) and slander (a transitory form).
- Libel can be a crime as well as a tort (*R v Lemon*).
- Libel is actionable *per se* (without proof of damage), but slander is not, except where contagious disease, commission of a criminal offence, unchastity in women, or professional unfitness is alleged.
- Defamation is defined as a publication of a falsely made defamatory statement referring to the claimant, and with no lawful justification.
- Publication must be to a third party, so it will not be a publication where only the claimant is addressed, or where the defamation is contained in a sealed letter (*Huth v Huth*).
- A defamatory remark is one that lowers the estimation of the claimant in the minds of right-thinking people, or would cause them to shun or avoid him/her (*Sim v Stretch*).
- Implying decency or honesty cannot be defamatory (*Byrne v Dean*).
- Defamation can be by innuendo (*Tolley v Fry*).
- The claimant must show that the statement referred to him/her personally, which could occur where two people have the same name (*Newstead v London Express Newspapers*), or even where a fictional name is used (*Hulton & Co. v Jones*).

- However, a class defamation can only result in action where the claimant can show that (s)he is identifiable as a member of the class (*Le Fanu v Malcolmson*).
- There are many defences available including:
  - justification, which is basically where the allegation is true (*Bookbinder v Tebbitt*)
  - fair comment, where the press is entitled to express honest opinions on matters of public interest (*London Artists v Littler*)
  - absolute privilege, for instance in respect of proceedings in parliament or in the courts
  - qualified privilege, which concerns confidential communications, generally between privileged parties
  - unintentional defamation and innocent dissemination, where the party accused of publishing the defamation has done so in all innocence, ignorant of the fact of the defamation.
- Remedies include both damages and injunctions.
- There are numerous criticisms of defamation law, including:
  - it is out of step with freedom of speech it is basically for the rich, i.e. lack of legal aid
  - juries award excessive damages.

Chapter 14

Vicarious Liability

14.1 The character and purpose of vicarious liability

Vicarious liability is not an individual tort in the same way as other torts that we have looked at, such as negligence or nuisance. It is a means of imposing liability for a tort on to a party other than the tortfeaser, the party causing the tort.

It was, in fact, originally based on the 'fiction' that an employer has control over his or her employees, and therefore should be liable for torts committed by the employee. This was possibly less of a fiction when the 'master and servant' laws still reflected the true imbalance in the employment relationship.

In a less sophisticated society, with fewer diverse types of work, control was indeed possible. In domestic service, for instance, the master could dictate exactly the method of the work done by the servant. Modern forms of employment make control less evident. For instance, the actual work done by a surgeon can hardly be said to be under the control of a hospital administrator with no medical expertise.

Nevertheless, the origins of the liability are important because it is rare that vicarious liability will exist outside of the employment relationship.

The rule has been criticised for being harsh and 'rough justice', since an apparently innocent party is being fixed with liability for something which (s)he has not done. On this level, imposing liability by this method is a direct contradiction of the principle requiring fault to be proved to establish liability.

There are a number of justifications for the practice, many of which have to do with ensuring that the victim of a wrong has the means of gaining compensation for the damage or injury suffered.

- Traditionally, as we have seen, an employer may have had a greater degree of control over the activities of employees. Indeed, it may well be that an employee has carried out the tort on the employer's behalf, so it is only fair that the employer should bear the cost.
- The employer, in any case, is responsible for hiring and firing and disciplining staff. The employer may have been careless in selecting staff, and if employees are either careless or prone to causing harm and the employer is aware of this, then (s)he has the means of doing something about it. The internal disciplinary systems allow the employer to ensure that lapses are not repeated, ultimately to the extent of dismissing staff. The employer is also responsible for ensuring that all employees are effectively trained so that work is done safely.
- The major concern of an injured party is where compensation is likely to come from. In this respect the employer will usually be better able to stand the loss than the employee will. In any case, the employer is obliged to take out public liability insurance and can also pass on loss in prices.
- This is itself a justification for vicarious liability, since it is also a means of deterring tortious activities.
- In certain instances, imposing vicarious liability makes the conduct of the case easier for the injured party in terms of identifying specific negligence. This is particularly so in the case of medical negligence.

Proving vicarious liability first depends on satisfying a number of other basic tests:

- Was the person alleged to have committed the tort an employee? There is only very limited liability for the torts of independent contractors.
- Did that party commit the alleged tort 'during the course of his or her employment'? An employer is generally not liable for torts that occur away from work or while the employee is *'on a frolic on his own'*.
- Was the act or omission complained of a tort? Again, an employer will not generally incur liability for other wrongs, such as crimes carried out by the employee.

14.2 Tests of employment status

14.2.1 Introduction

It is not always possible to determine at first sight whether, in fact, a person is employed under a contract of service. It will often be in the interest of an 'employer' to deny that the relationship is one of employment. Definitions such as that contained in the Employment Rights Act 1996, that the employer is a person employed under a contract of employment, are no real help in determining a person's employment status. It has been suggested in *WHPT Housing Association Ltd v Secretary of State for Social Services* (1981) that the distinction lies in the fact that the employee provides himself to serve, while the self-employed person only offers his services. This is no greater help in determining whether or not a person is employed.

There is, in any case, inconsistency in the methods of testing employee status according to who it is that is doing the testing. For instance, the only concern of the tax authorities in testing employee status is in determining a liability for payment of tax, not for any other purpose. So the fact that a person is paying Schedule D tax is not necessarily definitive of their status as self-employed. Again, industrial safety inspectors may have less concern with the status of an injured party and more with the regulations that have been breached.

Besides this, a number of different types of working relationship defy easy definition. 'Lump' labour was common in the past. Casual and temporary employment is possibly even more prevalent in recent times.

Over the years the courts have devised a number of methods of testing employee status. They all have shortcomings. Some are less useful in a modern society than others.

14.2.2 The 'control' test

The oldest of these is the 'control' test. This test derived from the days of the 'master and servant' laws as we have already seen. In *Yewens v Noakes* (1880), the test was whether the master had the right to control what was done and the way in which it was done. According to McArdie J, in *Performing Right Society v Mitchell and Booker* (1924), the test concerns '... *the nature and degree of detailed control.'*

Lord Thankerton, in *Short v J W Henderson Ltd* (1946), identified many key features that would show that the master had control over the servant. These included the power to select the servant, the right to control the method of working, the right to suspend and dismiss, and the payment of wages.

Such a test is virtually impossible to apply accurately in modern circumstances. Nevertheless, there are circumstances in which a test of control is still useful, in the case of borrowed workers.

> ### Mersey Docks & Harbour Board v Coggins and Griffiths (Liverpool) Ltd (1947)
>
> Here, the test was applied when a crane driver negligently damaged goods in the course of his work. The Harbour Board hired him out to stevedores to act as their servant. The Harbour Board was still liable for his negligence, however, since he would not accept control from the stevedores.

whatever factors may be indicative of employment or self-employment. In particular, three conditions should be met before an employment relationship is identified:

- the employee agrees to provide work or skill in return for a wage
- the employee expressly or impliedly accepts that the work will be subject to the control of the employer
- all other considerations in the contract are consistent with there being a contract of employment rather than any other relationship between the parties.

14.2.3 The 'integration' or 'organisation' test

Lord Denning, in *Stevenson Jordan and Harrison Ltd v McDonald and Evans* (1969), established this test. The basis of the test is that someone whose work is fully integrated into the business will be an employee, whereas, if a person's work is only accessory to the business, then that person is not an employee.

According to this test the master of a ship, a chauffeur and a reporter on the staff of a newspaper are all employees, where the pilot bringing a ship into port, a taxi driver and a freelance writer are not.

The test can work well in some circumstances, but there are still defects. Part-time examiners may be classed as employed for the purposes of deducting tax, but it is unlikely that the exam board would be happy to pay redundancy when their services were no longer needed.

14.2.4 The 'economic reality' or 'multiple' test

The courts in recent times have, at last, recognised that a single test of employment is not satisfactory and may produce confusing results. The answer under this test is to consider

> ### Ready Mixed Concrete (South East) Ltd v Minister of Pensions and National Insurance (1968)
>
> The case involved the question of who was liable for National Insurance contributions, the company or one of its drivers. Drivers drove vehicles in the company colours and logo, but which they bought on hire-purchase agreements from the company. They were also obliged to maintain the vehicles according to set standards in the contract. They were only allowed to use the lorries on company business. Their hours, however, were flexible and their pay was subject to an annual minimum rate according to the concrete hauled. They were also allowed to hire drivers in their place. McKenna J developed the above test in determining their lack of employment status.

The test has subsequently been modified so that all factors in the relationship should be considered and weighed according to their significance. Such factors might include:

- the ownership of tools, plant or equipment – clearly an employee is less likely to own the plant and equipment with which he works

- the method of payment – again, a self-employed person is likely to take a price for a whole job, where an employee will usually receive regular payments for a defined pay period
- tax and National Insurance contributions – an employee usually has Class 1 National Insurance contributions and tax deducted by the employer out of wages under the PAYE scheme under Schedule E. A self-employed person will usually pay tax annually under Schedule D and will make National Insurance contributions by buying Class 2 stamps
- self-description – a person may describe himself as one or the other and this will usually, but not always, be an accurate description
- level of independence – probably one of the acid tests of status as self-employed is the extra degree of independence in being able to take work from whatever source, and turn work down

All of these are useful in identifying the status of the worker, but none are an absolute test or are definitive on their own.

14.2.5 Irregular situations

Certain types of work have proved more likely to cause problems in the past than others. Not every working relationship is clear cut, and judges have been called on to make decisions, sometimes based on the factors we have already considered. Often their answer will depend on the purpose of the case, so that the court might seek to bring a person within industrial safety law although they appear to be self-employed.

Casual workers

Such workers have traditionally been viewed as independent contractors rather than as employed. This may be of particular significance since modern employment practices tend towards less secure, less permanent work.

O'Kelly v Trust House Forte plc (1983)

Here, it was important for wine butlers, employed casually at the Grosvenor House Hotel, to show that they were employees in order that they could claim for dismissal. They had no other source of income and there were a number of factors consistent with employment. However, the tribunal took the view that, since the employer had no obligation to provide work and since they could, if they wished, work elsewhere then there was no mutuality of obligations and they were not employed.

The House of Lords has also confirmed this lack of mutual obligation test of employment status more recently.

Carmichael v National Power plc (1998)

The case involved a tour guide at Sellafield. She was given work as required and paid for the work done, and tax and NI were also deducted. But the House of Lords decided that there was no obligation to provide work and no obligation on her part to accept any that was offered, although the Court of Appeal had reached an entirely different result.

Agency staff

Many large companies now hire staff through employment agencies. On past cases they have not always been seen as employees of the agency.

Wickens v Champion Employment (1984)

Here, it was held that the agency workers were not employees since the agency was under no obligation to find them work and there was no continuity and care in the contractual relationship consistent with employment.

Workers' co-operatives

Again, it is uncertain whether such workers would be employees or not. Usually we would expect them to be so. However, there are instances where such workers have been classed as self-employed.

Addison v London Philharmonic Orchestra Ltd (1981)

The orchestra operated as a co-operative. The musicians could do other work on their own account. It was held that they were subjecting themselves to discipline rather than control as employees.

Outworkers

People who work from home, usually women with young children, are a very disadvantaged sector of the workforce. They tend to work for little pay and have few rights. There is obviously little control over the hours that they work. Nevertheless, working in areas such as the garment industry, they normally fall into a general framework of organisation. They were, in the past, always considered to be independent contractors. Some recent cases have suggested otherwise.

Nethermere (St Neots) Ltd v Taverna & Gardiner (1984)

Here, workers in the garment industry were held to be employees because it was felt that they were doing the same work as employees in the factory, only at home.

Trainees

Apprenticeships were traditionally subject to their own rules, but there are few of these now. In the case of trainees, the major purpose in their relationship with the 'employer' is to learn the trade rather than to actually provide work. Therefore, they have usually not been classed as employees.

Wiltshire Police Authority v Wynn (1980)

A female cadet tried to claim unfair dismissal, which required proving first that she was an employee. Although she had been placed on various attachments, was paid a wage, could do no other work, and had set hours, she was only undergoing training with a view to becoming a police officer and was not yet employed.

Labour-only sub-contractors ('the lump')

Such workers are common in the construction industry, where they will do work for a lump sum. There are advantages to both sides in not making tax and National Insurance contributions. These workers are classed as self-employed.

Crown servants

People working for the crown were traditionally viewed as not being under a contract of employment. This meant that they had very restricted rights. The trend in modern times has been to move away from this position.

Office holders

An office is basically a position that exists independently of the person currently holding it. So the general category might include ministers of the church and justices of the peace. The picture on these is confused, but it has been held that there is no vicarious liability by the church.

Directors

A director may or may not also be an employee of the company.

Hospital workers

Obviously, vicarious liability for the work of people in health care can be critical. Nevertheless, the traditional view in *Hillyer v Governor of St Bartholomews Hospital* (1909) was that a hospital should not be vicariously liable for the work of doctors. This was justified on the grounds that hospitals generally lacked adequate finance before the creation of the National Health Service. The more recent view, expressed in *Cassidy v Ministry of Health* (1951) is that hospitals and health services should be responsible for the work done in them.

Activity　　*Quick Quiz*

Consider whether the following would be classed as employees using the tests above.

1. Sandra, a machinist, works from home, stitching shirts from pieces of cloth pre-cut and delivered by her employer, Tej, who also deducts National Insurance payments from her pay, but leaves her to settle her own tax. Tej owns the sewing machine that Sandra uses.

2. Eric, a plasterer, travels round building sites and works for cash payments. Neither he nor builders that he works for pay tax or NI for him. He uses his own tools.

3. Coco, a circus clown, also sells tickets before performances and helps to pack up the big top when the circus goes on to the next town. He also drives one of the lorries that transports the circus. The circus owner says that Coco is self-employed.

4. Alistair is a consultant orthopedic specialist. He is paid a full-time salary by an NHS Trust, but spends three days per week seeing private patients.

14.3 Torts in or not in the course of employment

14.3.1 Introduction

We have already discussed whether or not it is fair to impose liability on an employee for torts committed by his/her employee. Since it is a potentially unjust situation, it is strictly limited and the employer will only be liable for those torts committed while the employee is *'in the course of the employment'*.

What is and is not in the course of employment is a question of fact for the court to determine in each case. It is often difficult to see any consistency in the judgments. It seems inevitable that judges will decide cases on policy grounds and this may explain some of the apparent inconsistency.

Regardless of the reasoning applied in them, there are two lines of cases:

- those where there is vicarious liability because

the employee is said to be acting in the course of the employment
- those where there is no vicarious liability because the employee is said not to be in the course of employment.

14.3.2 Torts committed in the course of employment

It is very hard to find a general test for what is in the course of employment. However, courts have appeared to favour a test suggested by Salmond, that the employer will be liable in two instances:

- for a wrongful act that has been authorised by the employer
- for an act that, while authorised, was carried out in an unauthorised way.

Authorised acts

An employer, then, will inevitably be liable for acts that (s)he has expressly authorised, and since an employee is only obliged to obey all reasonable and lawful acts, (s)he could refuse to carry out tortious acts that the employer instructed him/her to.

The more difficult aspect of this rule is whether the employer can be said to have authorised a tortious act by implication and should therefore be liable. At least one case has suggested that this is possible.

Poland v Parr (1927)

The employee assaulted a boy who was stealing from his employer's lorry. The employer was held to be vicariously liable since the employee was only protecting the employer's property.

Authorised acts carried out in an unauthorised manner

An employer can be liable for such acts in a variety of ways:

- where something has been expressly prohibited by the employer

Limpus v London General Omnibus Company (1862)

Bus drivers had been specifically instructed not to race. When they did and the claimant was injured the employer was vicariously liable. The drivers were authorised to drive the buses, but not in the manner they did.

- where the employee is doing the work negligently

Century Insurance Co. Ltd v Northern Ireland Transport Board (1942)

A driver of a petrol tanker was delivering to a petrol station. He carelessly threw down a lighted match, causing an explosion. The employer was still liable since the driver was in the course of employment, and merely doing his work negligently.

- where the employee gives unauthorised lifts contrary to instructions

Rose v Plenty (1976)

Here, a milkman continued to use a child helper despite express instructions not to allow people to ride on the milk floats. When the boy was injured, partly through the milkman's negligence, his employers were liable. The milkman was carrying out his work in an unauthorised manner. Lord Denning suggested that the employers were liable because they were benefiting from the work undertaken by the boy.

- where the employee exceeds the proper boundaries of the job

> ### *Bayley v Manchester, Sheffield and Lincolnshire Railway Co. (1873)*
>
> Part of a porter's work was to ensure that passengers got on to the correct train. Here, the porter pulled the claimant from the train in order to do so, and the employers were vicariously liable for the assault.

14.3.3 Torts not in the course of employment

The area is confusing because many cases where the employer has been found not to be liable appear to cover the same areas as those that do fall within the course of employment. Usually there is some extra element, but it is still confusing. In general, though, an employer will not be liable when the employee's tortious act fell outside of the course of employment or where the employee was *'on a frolic on his own'*. These include:

- expressly prohibited acts

> ### *Beard v London General Omnibus Co. (1900)*
>
> Here, a bus conductor drove the bus, despite express orders to the contrary, and injured the claimant. The employers were not vicariously liable. The conductor was not carrying out his own work, but doing something outside of the scope of his own employment.

- where the employee is *'on a frolic of his own'* – an employer will not be responsible for acts that occur outside of the normal working day, such

as travelling into work. The same will apply where the employee does something outside of the scope of the work.

> ### *Hilton v Thomas Burton (Rhodes) Ltd (1961)*
>
> Workmen took an unauthorised break and left their place of work. On returning, one employee, who was driving the works van, crashed the van and killed somebody. The employer was not liable since the workmen were *'on a frolic'*.

- giving unauthorised lifts

> ### *Twine v Beans Express (1946)*
>
> A hitchhiker was injured through the negligence of a driver who had been forbidden to give lifts. The employers were not liable. This contrasts with the same situation in *Rose v Plenty* because here the employer was gaining no benefit from the prohibited lift.

- acts exceeding the proper boundaries of the work

> ### *Makanjuola v Metropolitan Police Commissioner (1992)*
>
> The claimant was persuaded into allowing a police officer to have sex with her in return for not reporting her to immigration authorities. There was no liability on the employer. The officer was not doing anything that could be described as falling within his work.

Some situations still defy easy analysis. As we have seen, an employer will generally not be responsible for the employee while the employee is travelling to and from work. In some situations, however, this may not be the case. This, for instance might include where the employee works from home and travelling is part of the work.

Smith v Stages (1989)

The employer was liable here because the employees were paid both travelling expenses and travelling time.

Activity   **Problem Solving**

Consider whether the employer would be liable in the following circumstances.

1. Roger is employed by 'Eazi-build', a DIY warehouse. While driving to work one morning his negligence causes a car crash in which Parminder is injured and her car is damaged beyond repair.

2. Simon is a travelling salesman for 'Eazi-build', who works from home. While driving to his first call he negligently collides with a car driven by Oona, injuring her and damaging her car.

3. Taru is a delivery driver for 'Eazi-build'. One day, after completing his last morning delivery, instead of returning to work as he should he goes to the *Red Lion* for a few beers. On driving back to work he negligently runs over a pedestrian, Nellie, killing her.

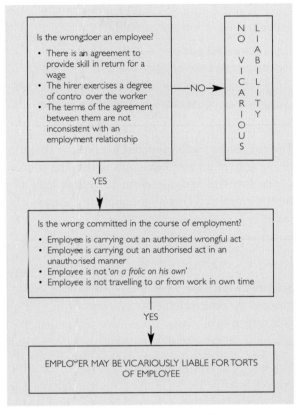

Figure 9 *Flow chart illustrating the process of testing vicarious liability*

14.4 Liability in other circumstances

14.4.1 Liability for the crimes of employees

An employer will not usually be liable for the crimes of an employee that also amount to torts, so there can be civil liability.

Warren v Henleys (1948)

Here, a petrol pump attendant assaulted a customer who he believed was intending not to pay. The court was not prepared to hold that the assault took place in the course of employment.

The courts are more prepared to consider that the dishonesty of an employee falls within the course of employment and, therefore, to impose liability on the employer. This might apply in the case of fraud.

Lloyd v Grace Smith & Co. (1912)

Solicitors were liable when their conveyancing clerk fraudulently incuced a client to convey the property to him.

However, the courts will generally not make an employer liable for an employee's fraudulent activities where they occurred partly in and partly outside the course of the employment.

Credit Lyonnais Bank Nederland NV v Export Credits Guarantee Department (1999)

Here, two parties were involved in a fraud on the bank but some of the activities fell outside their employment.

Vicarious liability can also apply in the case of thefts by the employee.

Morris v Martin & Sons (1966)

The employer was liable when the employee working in his dry-cleaning business stole a customer's fur coat.

One area that has caused difficulty for the courts in recent years is where public bodies are accused of being responsible for abuses carried out by their employees.

On the basis of implied duties owed by employers to their employees, employers have been held liable in cases of sexual harassment by other of their employees (*Bracebridge Engineering v Darby* (1990)), and also in the case of racial harassment (*Jones v Tower Boot Co Ltd* (1997)).

However, the difficulty of identifying abuse as an *'unauthorised mode of carrying out an authorised act'* has led the Court of Appeal to rejecting claims of vicarious liability for sexual abuse.

Trotman v North Yorkshire County Council (1999)

Here, the claimant was a pupil at a special school. He alleged vicarious liability against the local authority after being sexually abused by his deputy headmaster while on a trip with the school. The teacher was sharing the boy's bedroom for nocturnal supervision because of the boy's fits. Butler Sloss LJ found it difficult to reconcile the case with either the harassment cases based on an employer's implied duties to the employee or with the cases based on fraud. The general feeling of the court was that the more extreme the act of the employee, the less likely that the employer would be held vicariously liable for it.

More recently, the House of Lords has developed a newer test based on inherent risk to cover such situations and enable liability more easily to be imposed.

Lister v Hesley Hall Ltd (2001)

The case is a major development in vicarious liability. Three claimants were sexually abused over a period of time by the warden of the school for children with emotional difficulties where they were all resident. The warden was then convicted of criminal charges. The claim against the school was on the basis that it had actual or constructive knowledge of the abuse and had failed to prevent it. The trial judge, despite being bound by *Trotman*, allowed the claim on the basis of breach of a duty to the claimants. The Court of Appeal reversed this on the ground that the wrongful behaviour cou d not be considered to be 'in the course of employment', according to established definitions. In the House of Lords the judges rejected the test in *Trotman* and held that the key test was whether there was sufficient connection between the employment and the torts carried out by the employee. Here, the employee's torts were carried out on the school's premises and at times when the employee should have been caring for the claimants. The House of Lords was satisfied that there was an inherent risk of abuse which the employer should have guarded against, and that vicarious liability was appropriate, despite appreciating the applicability of the 'floodgates' argument to the case.

The reasoning in *Lister* has subsequently been approved and applied.

Mattis v Pollock (2003)

A bouncer employed by a nightclub got involved in a fight with customers and the claimant intervened. The bouncer then left the club, went home, returned with a knife and, intent on revenge, stabbed the claimant outside the club. The Court of Appeal held that what the bouncer did was so closely connected to what his employer expected of him that the employer should be held vicar ously liable. The bouncer was supposed to manhandle and intimidate customers.

14.4.2 Liability for the acts of independent contractors

An employer will not usually be liable for the tortious acts of independent contractors who he has hired. The reason is the lack of control that the employer is able to exercise.

Nevertheless, there are some very limited circumstances in which an employer has been shown to be liable for the acts of independent contractors.

- If the contractor has been hired for the purpose of carrying out the tort, then the employer may be liable, as he would be for his employees.

Ellis v Sheffield Gas Consumers Co. (1853)

The defendants, without authority, hired contractors to dig a hole. When the contractors failed to properly fi l the hole and the claimant was injured the defendants were vicariously liable.

- Where the employers are under a non-delegable duty of care imposed by statute they are liable. This might, for instance, apply where there is an obligation not only to provide, but also to ensure that industrial safety equipment is used.
- Where a similar non-delegable duty of care is owed in common law the employer is liable.

Honeywill & Stein v Larkin Bros Ltd (1934)

Employers were liable for a breach of the implied duty to provide competent staff and a safe system of work when a freelance photographer set fire to a cinema when using magnesium flares for lighting.

14.4.3 The employer's indemnity

Where the employer is vicariously liable then both (s)he and the employee are joint tortfeasers. The consequence of this is that the claimant could actually sue either. One further consequence is that the employer who is sued may then sue the employee for an indemnity.

> ### Lister v Romford Ice & Cold Storage Ltd (1957)
>
> A lorry driver knocked over his father who, at the time, was his driver's mate. The father then claimed compensation from the employers. The employer's insurers, on paying out, then exercised their rights of subrogation under the insurance contract and sued the driver. The House of Lords accepted that this was possible.

The case has been strongly criticised, not least because it destroys the purpose of imposing vicarious liability. As a result, insurers do not generally exercise their rights under the principle.

14.4.4 Vicarious liability for loaned cars

Another area that creates problems apart from travelling to and from work is the practice of lending vehicles. The case law again seems confusing. The defining difference appears to be whether or not the vehicle is being used for a purpose in which the owner has an interest.

> ### Britt v Galmoye (1928)
>
> Here, there was no liability on an employer when the car was lent to the employee for the employee's own personal use.

The result will be different where the owner has requested that the other party should borrow the car to carry out the purposes of the owner.

> ### Ormrod v Crosville Motor Services Ltd (1953)
>
> The owner asked the other party to take the car to Monte Carlo where the owner would later join him, so the owner was liable.

However, in some instances it appears that the logic of the decision is merely that the judges wished there to be liability.

> ### Morgans v Launchbury (1973)
>
> A wife allowed her husband to use her car to go out drinking, on the promise that he would not drive while drunk. In the event, he allowed another drunk and uninsured driver to drive him home. When there was an accident vicarious liability was imposed on the wife in order that a claim could be made against her insurance.

14.4.5 Recent developments

There have been two important recent developments in vicarious liability.

First, in *Viasystems (Tyneside) Ltd v Thermal Transfer (Northern) Ltd, S & P Darwell Ltd and CAT Metalwork Services* (2005), the Court of Appeal declared that there could be dual vicarious liability by two defendants in the same claim.

Second, the House of Lords has declared that there can be vicarious liability for the acts of employees under s3 of the Protection from Harassment Act 1997.

Majrowski v Guy's and St Thomas' NHS Trust (2006)

The claimant was bullied and harassed by his departmental manager because of his homosexuality which, after investigation, was accepted by the Trust. The claimant succeeded in an action against the Trust under s3.

Activity

Self-assessment questions

1. What justifications are there for making an employer liable for the torts of his/her employee?

2. In what ways can vicarious liability be said to be unfair?

3. What will a claimant need to show in order to establish liability on the part of the employer?

4. To what extent is it easy to demonstrate that a person is an employee?

5. Why is the 'control test' an ineffective test on its own?

6. How does the 'economic reality' test operate?

7. What factors are useful indicators of whether a person is employed or self-employed?

8. Is an employer liable for acts done in protection of his property?

9. Explain what is meant by an authorised act done in an unauthorised manner.

10. Why, exactly, was the dairy liable in *Rose v Plenty*?

11. What, exactly, is a '*frolic on his own*'?

12. Why were *Limpus* and *Beard* decided differently?

13. In what circumstances is an employer liable for the crimes of his/her employee?

14. Why is *Lister v Hesley Hall* such an important case?

15. Why is the principle in *Lister v Romford* criticised, and why is it not followed?

16. What consistency, if any, is there between *Morgans v Launchbury* and other cases on vicarious liability?

Key Facts

- Vicarious liability is where one person is held liable for the torts of another.
- This is usually where an employer is liable for the tortious acts of an employee.
- For the employer to be liable: (i) the tortfeaser must be an employee; (ii) the tort must take place during the course of employment.
- Various tests have been developed to determine whether or not someone is an employee rather than an independent contractor (self-employed). These include the 'control' test, the 'indicia' test, and the 'organisation' (or integration) test.

- The most modern test is the 'economic reality' test from *Ready Mixed Concrete v Minister of Pensions and National Insurance*. All factors should be considered and their importance weighed.
- A number of types of work defy easy description.
- 'Course of employment' can include:
  - authorised acts (*Poland v Parr*)
  - acts done in an unauthorised manner (*Limpus v London General Omnibus Co*)
  - negligently carried-out work (*Century Insurance v Northern Ireland Transport*)
  - exceeding the proper bounds of the work (*Bayley v Manchester, Sheffield and Lincolnshire Railway*).
- However, there is no liability for:
  - being '*on a frolic on his own*' (*Hilton v Thomas Burton*)
  - things outside of the scope of employment (*Twine v Beans Express*).
- An employer is not usually liable for an employee's crimes.
- This will apply to fraud (*Lloyd v Grace Smith*)
- and also to crimes generally (*Warren v Henleys*)
- but now a distinction is made where the criminal act of the employee is an inherent risk that the employer should guard against (*Lister v Hesley Hall*).
- An employer is not usually liable for torts of independent contractors (*Ellis v Sheffield Gas Consumers*).
- It is rare but possible to recover the loss from the employee (*Lister v Romford Ice*).
- In some cases it is possible for owners to be liable for torts committed in cars that they have lent to the tortfeasor (*Morgans v Launchbury*).

Activity

Answering problem questions

There are always four essential ingredients to answering problem questions.

- Firstly, you must be able to identify the key facts in the problem, the ones on which any resolution of the problem will depend.
- Secondly, you will need to identify which is the appropriate law that applies to the particular situation in the problem.
- The third task is to apply the law to the facts.
- Finally, you will need to reach conclusions of some sort. If the question asks you to advise, then that is what you need to do. On the other hand, if the problem says 'Discuss the legal consequences of ...', then you know that you can be less positive in your conclusions.

Problem
Barry recently secured work as a delivery driver for 'Dodgy Transport', driving a 15-hundredweight Luton-bodied Transit van, the only qualification being production of a valid driving licence. Barry has a clean licence, but expressed concern at the time of his interview as he was used to driving only motor bikes. He signed a document called a 'document of service' in which it was written that he must work such hours as the firm require, wear their uniform at all times while at work, and that he accepts work from no other delivery business, except as authorised by 'Dodgy' officials. 'Dodgy' owns the van that Barry drives and they pay him a gross amount, leaving him to settle his own tax and National Insurance

contributions. In his first week Barry was delivering to 'Rocky Co.', a very good customer of 'Dodgy'. Alex, the manager of Rocky, asked Barry if he would take a parcel in need of urgent delivery to 'Steady Co.', a customer of 'Rocky' that is five miles away and in the opposite direction to Dodgy's premises. Despite being unable to contact Dodgy on his mobile phone, Barry takes the parcel. When he arrives at Steady's offices Barry has to reverse into their loading bay and negligently runs over the warehouseman, Stan.

Advise Dodgy whether they will be liable for the injuries caused by Barry's negligence

. . . .

The facts
It is important to have a clear idea of what the principal facts are, particularly as here, where there are two significant aspects to the question: whether or not Barry is an employee and, if so, whether the tort occurred in the course of his employment. The main facts seem to be as follows:

1. 'Dodgy' have hired Barry as a delivery driver on presentation of a clean driving licence and despite the fact that he has expressed more confidence with motor bikes.

2. Barry has signed a 'contract of service' including terms that he works whatever hours 'Dodgy' require, that he wears a uniform at all times at work, and that he accepts no work other than that authorised by 'Dodgy'.

3. 'Dodgy' own the van Barry drives, but Barry is bound to pay his own tax and NI.

4. Barry, without authorisation from Dodgy, agrees to carry a parcel for one of Dodgy's customers to another firm.

5. While taking this parcel Barry negligently injures an employee of the firm, Stan.

The appropriate law
It is very important when answering problem questions that you use only the law that is relevant to the precise facts, if for no other reason that you are not getting any marks for using law that is irrelevant, so you are wasting valuable writing time. By looking at the various facts we can say that the following law may be relevant in our problem here:

1. The area involved is most likely vicarious liability.

2. This is where an employer is fixed with liability for the wrongful acts or omissions of his employees that occur in the course of their employment.

3. There are three basic requirements for liability:
   - the act complained of is a tort
   - the tortfeasor is an employee, not self-employed
   - the tort occurs in the course of employment.

4. There are various tests of employment status, including:
   - the 'control' test
   - the 'organisation'/'integration' test.

5. But the most favoured now is the 'economic reality' (or 'multiple') test from the *Ready Mixed Concrete* case, where the worker

agrees to submit to the control of the hirer, there is an agreement to provide work for a wage, and there is nothing inconsistent with employment.

6. Many factors can be taken into account, e.g. payment of tax & NI; ownership of tools; method of payment; level of independence; self-description, etc., but none on its own is definitive.

7. What is or is not in the course of employment is a question of fact in each case:
   * employees will be liable for tortious acts directed or authorised by employers (*Poland v Parr*)
   * and for expressly prohibited acts where they are still done as part of the employment (*Limpus v London General Omnibus*)
   * and for authorised acts done in an unauthorised manner (*Century Insurance v Northern Ireland Transport Board*)
     * but an employee will not be liable for acts that are done outside of the employee's actual employment (*Beard v London General Omnibus*)
     * nor for acts that occur where the employee is '*on a frolic on his own*' (*Hilton v Thomas Burton*).

Applying the law to the facts
Sometimes vicarious liability problems focus more on the tortious acts and include a number. Here, there is equal emphasis on exploring whether or not Barry is an employee, so application must reflect that.

* Factors indicating employment include:
  * service contract (rather than 'contract for services')
  * lack of independence (not allowed to take other work)
  * provision of van
  * hours of work requirement
  * uniform.
* Factors indicating self-employment include:
  * responsibility for payment of tax and NI.

Course of employment/outside of employment:
* Barry was doing his job when he went to 'Rocky'.
* Agreeing to carry Rocky's parcel to 'Steady' is an unauthorised act according to his 'contract of service' and is also an expressly prohibited act.
* The question is whether he is still doing his job or is '*on a frolic*'.
* *Limpus* and *Beard* can be compared.
* The running over of Stan is stated as negligence in the problem, so it is a tortious act.

Conclusions
* We have shown how the law applies both to establishing Barry's employment status or otherwise, and to whether his act is or is not in the course of employment.
* On the balance of facts given, Barry appears to be an employee.
* When Barry delivers to 'Steady' he is still acting as a delivery driver, but is doing an unauthorised act
* It is likely that 'Dodgy' will be liable to Stan.

Dilemma Board

In the Dilemma Board below, consider the accuracy of each of the four statements, A, B, C and D, as they apply to the facts in the central scenario. You only need to give the basic principles. The answer is in the Appendix at the end of the book.

Dilemma Board

A.
Wrotborough Residential Special School will be vicariously liable for Gary's actions only if it can be shown that he is employed by Wrotborough.

B.
Wrotborough Residential Special School will not be vicariously liable for Gary's actions because they were not authorised actions.

Gary is employed as a caretaker by Wrotborough Residential Special School. Gary is bound by his contract to stay overnight at the school at least twice a week, on a rota with other staff. A number of the pupils have complained that they have been sexually abused by Gary on the occasions when he has been on night duty.

C.
Wrotborough Residential Special School will not be vicariously liable for Gary's actions because Gary was 'on a frolic on his own'.

D.
Wrotborough Residential Special School will not be vicariously liable for Gary's actions because they are criminal and not tortious.

Chapter 15

Defences and Remedies

15.1 General defences

15.1.1 Introduction

Defences in tort can be both general and specific. We have already seen a number of specific defences that apply only in the case of specific torts. Good examples of these include absolute privilege in defamation, and 20 years' prescription in nuisance.

Other defences can be applied in numerous situations and are therefore known as general defences. Again, we have already considered a number of these defences, such as *volenti non fit injuria*, which is particularly appropriate in trespass to the person, and *novus actus interveniens*, which is particularly appropriate in negligence. The following includes a number of defences, some that have already appeared earlier in the book and some that have not.

Most of these provide a complete defence, in which case the defendant is relieved of liability. Some, however, will produce only partial relief and may, for instance, act to reduce the damages payable.

15.1.2 *Volenti non fit injuria*

Volenti as a defence concerns a voluntary assumption of the risk of harm by the claimant. Simply translated it means that no injury is done to one who consents to the risk. It is a complete defence and means that, if successfully used, the claimant will receive no damages.

The rule will not apply merely because the claimant has knowledge of the existence of the risk. On the contrary, the claimant must have a full understanding of the nature of the actual risk for the defence to succeed.

Stermer v Lawson (1977)

Consent was argued when the claimant had borrowed the defendant's motorbike. The defence failed because the claimant had not been properly shown how to use the motorbike and did not, therefore, appreciate the risks.

Neither will the defence work where the claimant has no choice but to accept the risk. An assumption of risk must be freely taken and the claimant must actually voluntarily undertake the risk of harm.

Smith v Baker (1891)

A worker was injured when a crane moved rocks over his head and some fell on him. The defence of consent failed. The workman had already done all that he could in complaining about the risks involved in the work taking place above his head. He had no choice but to continue work and did not give his consent to the danger.

Clearly, though, consent is a defence that can naturally arise in certain types of employment because of the character of the work. However, the more obvious the risk in the industry the less likely it is that the defence will succeed.

Gledhill v Liverpool Abattoir (1957)

A worker in an abattoir was injured when a pig fell on him. This was accepted as a well-known risk of the work.

Where a person has a duty to act and is then injured because of the defendant's negligence, *volenti* will not be available as a defence. The duty means that the claimant had no choice but act. This would be particularly appropriate in rescue cases.

Haynes v Harwood (1935)

Here, when the defendant failed to adequately tether his horse, the policeman who was injured trying to restrain the animal was not acting voluntarily. He was acting under a duty to protect the public.

Volenti as a defence is appropriate in cases involving negligence, but consent to physical injury is also particularly appropriate in the tort of trespass to the person.

In this context, then, consent is also a defence that is commonly applied in a sporting context, particularly in the case of contact sports. It will succeed where the injuries sustained fall within the normal activities of the sport.

Simms v Leigh Rugby Football Club (1969)

A rugby player was injured when he was tackled and thrown against a wall. Because the tackle was within the rules of the sport there was consent.

But consent cannot be used as a defence where the injuries are a result of conduct that falls outside of what can be legitimately expected in the sport.

Condon v Basi (1985)

A footballer in an amateur match was held liable for breaking another player's leg in a foul tackle. The injured player had not consented to foul play.

We have already seen, also, that the defence of consent is of critical importance to medical treatment where it can apply to a claim of battery or medical negligence.

Sidaway v Governors of Bethlem Royal and Maudsley Hospitals (1985)

Here, the doctor in question was required to seek the claimant's consent to an operation. However, the House of Lords was not prepared to accept the existence of a doctrine of 'informed consent' in English law. As a result, there was no liability when the doctor had warned of the likelihood of the risk but not the possible consequences.

An interesting question is whether a person who is a known suicide risk in the care of authorities that are aware of this has behaved voluntarily when actually committing suicide. In *Reeves v Metropolitan Police Commissioner* (1999) *volenti* was said not to apply because of the duty owed by the police to protect the claimant from himself.

Activity

Self-assessment questions

1. What, specifically, must the injured party have consented to for the defence of *volenti non fit injuria* to apply?

2. Is the test an objective test or a subjective test?

3. What are the most common contexts in which the defence of consent operates?

4. When will a person who plays sport be said to have consented to the risk of harm?

5. What level of information must be given to a patient by a doctor in order for consent to treatment to be real?

6. What effect does a dangerous type of employment have on the application of the defence?

7. Why could the defence not apply in *Haynes v Harwood*?

15.1.3 Inevitable accident

One strange defence available in tort is inevitable accident. The basic proposition is that there will be no liability for a loss or injury arising from a pure accident. In negligence, for instance, this will indicate that the defendant has not fallen below the appropriate standard of care.

The appropriate test for the defendant to establish the defence is that the event leading to the loss or injury was beyond his/her control.

Stanley v Powell (1891)

The defendant 'accidentally' shot a beater while shooting pheasants. He was able to claim inevitable accident successfully because he showed that the injury was as a result of the pellet ricocheting off trees at unusual angles.

In a fault-based system of tort, the real consequence of applying such a defence is that the defendant cannot be liable because there is no fault. So, in essence there is not really a defence as such, but no actual tort.

15.1.4 Act of God

This defence, in reality, refers to extreme and unusual weather conditions. As a result of this the events leading to the loss or damage are said to be beyond the defendant's control.

For the defence to succeed, therefore, the weather must be both extreme and unforeseeable.

Nicholls v Marsland (1876)

Here, exceptionally heavy rainfall caused artificial lakes to burst their banks, flooding neighbouring land.

15.1.5 Self-defence

The basic principle here is that everybody is entitled to defend himself in law against possible harm from others. However, the defence can only then be claimed where reasonable force has been used.

Revill v Newbury (1996)

An allotment holder fed up with trespasses on his allotment lay in wait in his shed and then fired through a hole in the door at a trespasser. This was out of proportion in the circumstances and the defence was unavailable.

15.1.6 Statutory authority

Many torts in modern circumstances arise from activities that are authorised by Parliament.

Indeed, very often actions under various Acts can be more appropriate than an action in tort.

Where the activity is authorised by statute this can then provide a defence.

> ## Vaughan v Taff Vale Railway Co. (1860)
>
> Claimants were denied an injunction when sparks from railway engines ignited embankments. The railway was authorised by statute.

Besides statutory authority, as has been seen in nuisance, local authority permission can also operate successfully as a defence.

The extent to which such defences are possible in modern society may be used to question the effectiveness of controls of pollution and the degree to which effective protection of the environment is possible.

15.1.7 Illegality (ex turpi causa non oritur actio)

A defendant will generally not be liable where the claimant sustains injury or loss while taking part in an illegal activity. The defence will operate, then, when both claimant and defendant are jointly involved in an illegal activity and the activity has a causal link to the damage.

> ## Ashton v Turner (1981)
>
> Here, both parties were in a car escaping from a crime. When the car crashed and the claimant was injured the defence prevented him from suing the driver for negligence. His injury resulted from participating in crime.

However, the defence was unsuccessfully raised in *Revill v Newbury*, because it is accepted that trespassers have limited rights of protection. The case caused controversy.

15.1.8 Necessity

This defence operates because the defendant's actions are said to be justified in that they were aimed at trying to avoid a greater harm than the one caused.

> ## Watt v Hertfordshire County Council (1954)
>
> The employers were not liable for the injury sustained by the fireman. The failure to properly secure the jack was because of the importance of reaching the scene of the accident and releasing the trapped woman.

Traditionally, acting to save the claimant's life fell naturally within the scope of the defence.

> ## Leigh v Gladstone (1909)
>
> Force-feeding of suffragettes on hunger strike while in prison was not a trespass to the person. It was necessary to save their lives.

This simple rule may be more complex now that the courts are prepared to take a different view to a patient's right to accept or refuse treatment.

> ## F v West Berkshire Health Authority (1989)
>
> The case involved the sterilisation of a mental patient who was becoming sexually active and was incapable of consenting to the treatment. The court determined that in emergency situations a doctor might plead necessity if the treatment is in the best interests of the patient. If the patient is in a position to give consent, however, then the consent must be gained.

Activity

Self-assessment questions

1. What is the difference between an 'inevitable accident' and an 'act of God'?

2. What is the key feature of a successful claim of self-defence'?

3. Why is statutory authority a defence in tort?

4. Why does the law accept a defence of *ex turpi causa non oritur actio*?

5. When would a defence of necessity succeed?

6. How would the defence of necessity work in a medical context?

7. How does the defence of 'necessity' interfere with civil liberties?

15.1.9 Contributory negligence

Contributory negligence was originally a complete defence and if successfully claimed the result would be that no damages at all were payable (*Butterfield v Forester* (1809)). This inevitably caused problems for many claimants, particularly in the nineteenth century for those claiming for injuries sustained while at work.

The Law Reform (Contributory Negligence) Act 1945 now governs the area. The effect of the Act is that a claimant can make a successful claim despite having contributed to the loss or injury suffered. Damages will then be reduced proportionately, according to the degree that the claimant contributed to his/her own harm.

It should be remembered that the defence can only be applied and damages apportioned where both the defendant and the claimant are each partly to blame for the damage suffered by the claimant.

Sayers v Harlow Urban District Council (1958)

The council's negligent maintenance of the premises caused the claimant to become locked in a public lavatory. Her damages were then reduced by 25% when she tried to climb out and stood on the toilet roll holder, which collapsed.

On this basis, 100% reduction in damages has even been held to be possible, although this possibility has also caused some controversy.

Jayes v IMI (Kynoch) Ltd (1985)

The claimant lost a finger at work while cleaning a machine with the guard off. The employers were liable under statutory provisions for a failure to ensure that the guard was in place, but 100% contributory negligence was held on the part of the claimant who admitted his fault in taking the guard off.

An obvious requirement is that the harm suffered must have been foreseeable to the claimant. As Lord Denning said in (*Jones v Livox Quarries Ltd* (1952)):

'A person is guilty of contributory negligence if he ought reasonably to have foreseen that, if he did not act as a reasonable, prudent man, he might be hurt himself; and

in his reckonings he must take into account the possibility of others being careless.'

The defence is now commonplace in some everyday situations.

Stinton v Stinton (1993)

Damages were reduced by one-third for accepting a lift from a drunk driver.

So there is an obvious defence where claimants ignore rules set in place for their own safety.

O'Connell v Jackson (1972)

Damages were reduced for a motorcyclist involved in a crash who had not worn a crash helmet and who sustained worse injuries as a result.

Clearly, contributory negligence is a common feature of motoring accidents.

Froom v Butcher (1976)

Damages were reduced for a claimant injured in a car crash who had not been wearing a seat belt and had thus suffered greater injuries than he might.

The defence does not require that the claimant owed duty of care, merely that he or she failed to take the appropriate care in the circumstances. It is, of course, always necessary to show causation, i.e. that the claimant's acts or omissions helped to cause the loss or injuries that he or she sustained, despite the defendant's liability.

Woods v Davidson (1930)

The defendant negligently ran over the claimant who was drunk at the time. The claim of contributory negligence failed since it was shown that the fact that the claimant was drunk was irrelevant in the circumstances, and the claimant would have been run over even if sober.

A modern context for this is smoking.

Badger v Ministry of Defence (2005)

The claimant died of lung cancer at age 63. The defendant admitted a breach of statutory duty by exposing the claimant to asbestos dust but argued that damages should be reduced because if the claimant had not smoked cigarettes he would also have been unlikely to die of lung cancer at such a young age. Because the claimant had been aware of the dangers since 1971, the court reduced damages by 20%.

Activity

1. In what ways is contributory negligence not a full defence?

2. So how does a successful defence of contributory negligence affect the claim?

3. What was unfair about the defence of contributory negligence before the 1945 Act was passed?

4. What, exactly, must be shown about the claimant when the defence is used?

Self-assessment questions

5. How is contributory negligence appropriate as a defence in the case of road traffic accidents?

6. How can a 100% reduction in damages for contributory negligence be possible?

7. What is the relationship between the defences of *volenti non fit injuria* and contributory negligence?

Activity

Suggest what defence may be argued in each of the following situations and explain whether or not it is likely to succeed.

1. Darren is being sued for negligence when his car collided with another vehicle. Darren claims that hurricane-force winds caused him to lose control of the vehicle.

2. Jed is being sued for breaking Raj's collarbone during a kick boxing contest.

3. A young boy was stealing apples from a tree in Eric's garden. Eric threw a stone at the boy, hitting him in the eye and blinding him.

4. Chan smashes down the door to Ali's house to rescue Ali because the building is on fire.

5. Mario was playing darts in the pub. One of his darts hit the wire on the dartboard,

Quick Quiz

bounced out on to the floor, and then bounced off the floor, hitting a table leg before embedding itself in Sarah's leg.

6. Manjit accepts a lift from Steven, who already has a car full of passengers. Manjit sits in the open boot of the car, and is injured when another car fails to stop when the traffic lights change and hits Steven's car from behind.

7. Elspeth's prize roses wilt and die after smut from a nearby power station falls on them.

8. Angus and Ronaldo stole a jet ski that was moored in a marina, and Angus was badly injured when, through Ronaldo's negligent handling of the machine, the jet ski crashed into a passing yacht.

Key Facts

- There are many defences available only to specific torts, but there are defences that are also generally available.
- Consent is otherwise known as *volenti non fit injuria*.
- The actual risk must be consented to, not just risk in general (*Smith v Baker*).
  - Consent is particularly appropriate to sport, where the incident falls within the rules of the game (*Simms v Leigh RFC*)
  - and medicine, where doctors generally require consent before engaging in intrusive medicine (*Sidaway v Bethlem Royal & Maudsley Hospitals*).
- Inevitable accident can be claimed where the 'accident' and the damage suffered was

beyond the control of the defendant (*Stanley v Powell*).
- Act of God can be claimed only where the damage arises from weather conditions that are so extreme as to be unforeseeable (*Nicholls v Marsland*).
- Self-defence can be claimed where reasonable force is used (*Revill v Newbury*).
- A statutory authority to commit the tort may cause an action to fail (*Vaughan v Taff Vale Railway*).
- A claimant might lose a claim because the damage resulted from his/her own illegal act (*Ashton v Turner*).
- Necessity can be a successful defence where the defendant has caused the damage acting

> - to prevent greater harm (*Watt v Hertfordshire CC*).
> - Following the Law Reform (Contributory Negligence) Act 1945, damages may be reduced where the claimant has helped cause his/her own damage (*Sayers v Harlow UDC*).
>
> - Damages can be reduced by 100% (*Jayes v IMI (Kynoch)*).
> - It must be shown that the claimant failed to take proper care of him/herself, which caused extra harm (*Woods v Davidson*).

15.2 Assessing damages in tort

15.2.1 Tort damages

Damages is a sum of money paid by the defendant to the claimant once liability is established in compensation for the harm suffered by the claimant. The purpose of awarding damages in tort, however, is altogether different since, in the case of damage to property, or personal injury, or damage to reputation, a sum of compensation is an entirely artificial remedy.

The purpose of damages in tort, then, is, as far as is possible to do so, to put the claimant in the position (s)he would have been in had the tort never occurred. Inevitably there is a large measure of speculation involved in awarding damages in tort, since it involves predicting what would have happened if the tort had not occurred. It is a false remedy because a sum of money will not always repair the harm done to the claimant, and there is always the danger of overcompensating or undercompensating the victim of the tort.

15.2.2 The effect of speculation

In tort, damages are to put the claimant in the position (s)he would have been in had the tort not occurred. On this basis, in tort damages are frequently of a speculative nature, in other words an attempt to assess what the claimant's position would have been if (s)he had not been wronged by the defendant. This is known as general damages, and a major feature of tort claims, for instance in personal injury, is in calculating future losses.

15.2.3 Special damages and general damages in tort – calculating future loss

As we have already seen, damages in tort are to place the victim of the wrong as far as possible as (s)he would have been in had that person not been wronged. In this way there are generally two types of damages: special damages, which account for losses already incurred up to the date of the claim; and future damages or general damages, which concern how the claimant's future would have been but for the tort.

In the case of economic losses and property damage, these can easily be compensated for as special damages and quantified before trial of the action. There is usually little problem in calculating such loss.

Damages in respect of property damage or loss are calculated according to:

- loss of the property and its value at the time of the tort
- any costs of transporting replacements
- loss of reasonably foreseeable consequential losses associated with or caused by the damage to property
- loss of use until the property is replaced
- reduction in value if the property is to be retained and any costs of repair.

15.2.4 Non-compensatory damages

In some cases in tort damages are awarded even though there is no quantifiable loss.

These could be in the form of nominal damages, where the tort has been proved but there is no actual loss. An obvious example is in a trespass to land action.

Although rare in England and Wales, exemplary damages are also possible. Certainly large awards of damages by juries in defamation actions would be seen as a punishment rather than representing any loss. Exemplary damages are common in other jurisdictions, such as the USA.

In England and Wales the leading case on the issue is *Rookes v Barnard* (1964), which involved a dismissal for a refusal to be a member of a trade union in a 'closed shop' situation. Such damages are only awarded where:

- government employees have acted in an oppressive, unconstitutional or arbitrary manner, as in *Thompson* v *Commissioner of Police for the Metropolis* (1998) where the court identified that in cases involving misconduct by police amounting to oppressive or arbitrary behaviour, punitive damages could be awarded
- the defendant's conduct was calculated to profit from the tort, as in some defamation actions
- where statute expressly allows for such a provision as in the Copyright Act 1965.

15.2.5 Damages in personal injury claims

Here damages are divided into two types.

a) Special damages

These account for any quantifiable loss up to the date of trial. Such loss might include damage to any property, cost of medical care, any special equipment or similar requirements, e.g. modifying an existing residence to allow for effective wheelchair use, laundry, loss of earnings and all other pre-trial losses.

The principle of mitigation, of course, still applies, and thus the court will only allow recovery for losses that it considers are reasonable in the circumstances. On which basis it is possible that private medical care may not be allowed.

b) General or future damages

These obviously include pecuniary or purely financial losses, such as loss of future earnings, and of course future medical costs or the cost of special care or other facilities.

They also include non-pecuniary losses that will be assessed as pain, suffering and loss of amenities. Such damages are clearly very difficult to quantify, but judges are guided by set sums for each type of injury. Clearly such calculations are entirely arbitrary. They can also show up various anomalies. For instance, a claimant who has been in a coma will get no award for pain or suffering, though a claim for loss of amenities is still possible.

Future earnings are calculated by multiplying what is known as a 'multiplicand' (what the court decides is the claimant's actual net loss after taking account of factors such as payment of benefits) by a 'multiplier' (a number of years based on the claimant's age – but since judgment comes as a lump sum which can be invested and accrue interest, the maximum multiplier is actually set quite low in real terms).

The disadvantages to the claimant of being given damages as a lump sum were explored in *Wells v Wells* (1998). Here, it was accepted that a claimant might use the money unwisely and lose the benefits. Also, a single sum takes no account of a possible deterioration in the claimant's condition.

Deductions from the multiplicand are possible to take account of, for example, private insurance payments, disability pensions and other payments made to the claimant. Deductions can also be made from the multiplier, e.g. where a known illness would have in any case caused early retirement.

In cases where it is hard to assess the full extent of the injury caused, it is possible to seek a split trial with an award of interim damage. Alternatively, where the claimant's condition is likely to deteriorate over time it is possible to seek provisional damages, allowing the claimant to establish liability but to return to court as the need for a greater level of damages arises with the deteriorating condition.

One final point: as is the case with all damages, interest is payable.

15.2.6 The effect of death on tort claims

A distinct possibility in a tort claim is that the claimant will have died as a result of the defendant's wrongful act or omission. Traditionally, a person's tort action died with him, which was clearly very unfair. Now it is the case that a person's action against the defendant survives his/her death.

On death there are two possible actions. Firstly, an action is possible under the Law Reform (Miscellaneous Provisions) Act 1934. This is an action brought by the personal representatives of the deceased in the deceased's name. So any damages awarded will go into the estate of the deceased to be distributed to any beneficiaries along with his/her other assets. The action shares many of the characteristics with the action for personal injury from which it has developed.

The second action is on behalf of the dependants of the deceased under the Fatal Accidents Act 1976. It is available to only a very small class of close relatives. As well as losses that have followed death, it also includes an arbitrarily set, fixed sum for bereavement.

Activity

Self-assessment questions

1. What is the major purpose of awarding damages in tort?

2. What are exemplary damages and what are the justifications for using them?

3. What is the difference between general damages and special damages?

4. When a person has died, what is the difference between a claim under the Law Reform (Miscellaneous Provisions) Act 1934 and an action under the Fatal Accidents Act 1976?

5. When is it fair to say that damages are an inadequate remedy in tort?

Key Facts

- Tort damages are intended to put the claimant financially in the position that he or she would have been in had the tort not occurred.
- Damages can be special (which cover losses up to the date of trial), or general (which cover future loss such as loss, of income).
- Some damages are not intended to compensate, e.g. nominal damages (such as in the case of trespass), or exemplary damages (e.g. where government agents act oppressively).
- Future loss in personal injury damages is based or multiplying a multiplier by a multiplicand.
- There are two possible actions on death: in the deceased's name: for representatives of the deceased (under LR(MP) A 1934, or for the benefit of dependants (under FAA 1976).

15.3 Limitation periods in tort

15.3.1 The purpose of limitation

All actions in tort are subject to limitation periods out of which an action cannot be brought. There are many reasons why a claimant should be limited in the time that (s)he can wait before bringing an action for the damage suffered. Even in equity the maxim 'delay defeats equity' operates to prevent a claimant who delays too long in bringing a claim from succeeding.

Firstly, if there is a valid case to be fought then the claimant is to be encouraged to bring the action as soon as possible. If the evidence for the claim can be gathered there is no purpose in delaying.

Secondly, there is the difficulty of actually preserving evidence intact if a claim is delayed for too long. Certainly the scene will be disturbed over time, forensic evidence may deteriorate, but also the memory of witnesses may fade.

Finally, it is only fair on a defendant to bring the claim as early as possible if it is indeed actionable. Although many claims are settled out of insurance, a defendant may be harmed by the uncertainty of his/her budget when contemplating the possible costs of a successful action against him/her. This may, in turn, prevent the potential defendant from planning effectively for the future.

15.3.2 Basic limitation periods

Most tort actions have the same basic limitation period of six years from the date when the action accrues. This is contained in s2 Limitation Act 1980: 'An action founded on tort shall not be brought after the expiration of six years from the date on which the action accrued.'

There are also a number of different periods applying in more particular instances, for instance in the case of libel and slander, in respect of defective products under the Consumer Protection Act 1987, and in respect of latent damage to property under the Latent Damage Act 1986.

15.3.3 Limitation periods for death and personal injury

Perhaps the most significant variation to the basic period is in claims for personal injury and death. This is not only because the period itself is different, but also because the method of calculating it is different. Furthermore, there is a means for disapplying the limitation period.

The period for personal injuries is identified in s11(4) Limitation Act 1980 as: 'three years from – (a) the date on which the action accrued; or (b) the date of knowledge (if later) of the person injured.' In the case of death by, s12, the same period applies. If the death occurs within three years of accrual of the action then the personal representatives have a fresh limitation period which runs from the date of death or the date of their knowledge.

The date of knowledge is a significant factor in personal injury claims. It is defined in s14 and refers to the date on which the claimant first knew that the injury was significant, knew that it was attributable in whole or in part to the defendant's act or omission, knew the identity of the defendant, and knew of facts supporting a claim of vicarious liability. A 'significant injury' is one where the claimant considers it sufficiently serious to justify beginning proceedings against a defendant not disputing the claim and who could pay the compensation. Knowledge refers to fact rather than law, and knowledge that the claimant might discover on his/her own or with the help of experts.

The power of the court to disapply the limitation period under s33 is another important feature of personal injury claims. The court will only exercise this discretion where 'it would be *equitable to do so'*. In doing so it will consider a number of factors:

- the length of the delay and the claimant's reason for delaying
- the effect of delay on the cogency of the evidence
- the defendant's actions after the cause of action arose, including any response to reasonable requests for information by the claimant
- the duration of any disability of the claimant arising after the accrual of the action
- the extent to which the claimant acted promptly once aware of the possibility of bringing the action
- steps taken by a claimant to obtain expert advice and the nature of any advice given.

Activity

Self-assessment questions

1. What is the purpose of imposing limitation periods?

2. Why is the period treated in a more flexible way in personal injury?

3. What, exactly, is the 'date of knowledge'?

Key Facts

- By s2 Limitation Act 1980 the basic limitation period in tort is six years.
- Specific other periods apply in the case of certain statutory torts.
- In personal injury it is three years from date of accrual or date of knowledge.
- By s33 the court can disapply the limit where it is *'equitable to do so'*.

15.4 Other remedies in tort

15.4.1 Equitable remedies in tort

Equitable remedies are available in tort, although much less so than in contract law, with which equity is much more closely associated. The whole purpose of equitable remedies is that they should operate where an award of damages is an inadequate remedy and justice is not served.

On that basis, the most common equitable remedy in tort is the injunction. Equitable remedies are at the discretion of the court, unlike an award of damages, which is an automatic consequence of liability being established. Because the remedies are discretionary they are awarded subject to compliance with the various 'maxims of equity', such as *'he who comes to equity must come with clean hands'*, (meaning that the person asking for the injunction must have behaved properly himself).

15.4.2 Injunctions in tort

Probably the most common remedy in tort, after damages, is an injunction. An injunction will clearly be sought in order to try to put a stop to the tort.

In this way it may be an appropriate remedy in torts such as private nuisance, where a householder wants to end the indirect interference, or in the economic torts where, for instance, an employer is seeking to end disruption in an industrial dispute. Interestingly, in the nuisance case *Miller v Jackson* the claimant lost the case and had no remedy because Lord Denning considered that, in seeking an injunction, he had gone for the wrong remedy. To allow it would have been, in effect, to close the cricket ground down.

Injunctions can be classified according to what they try to achieve

- The most common form of injunction granted is a **prohibitory injunction**, where the defendant is ordered to cease doing whatever amounts to the tortious action. This would clearly be useful in relation to trespass and nuisance, and also in the case of torts protecting reputation such as defamation.
- **Mandatory injunctions**, those ordering the defendant to carry out a particular act, are granted less frequently because it is hard for courts to oversee them.
- On occasions, a court may grant a *quia timet* **injunction**. This has the effect of restraining conduct that is likely to cause severe damage to the party who is seeking the injunction, but before any damage has actually occurred. In this way, in torts that are not actionable *per se*, such an injunction would be available, in effect, before any cause of action has arisen, so that the likelihood of substantial damage without the injunction being granted must be demonstrated to the court's satisfaction.

Injunctions can also be classified according to the point at which relief is to be achieved, so they can be:

- **perpetual** (formerly known as final) – these injunctions contain all of the relief required in the order itself
- **interim** (formerly known as interlocutory prior to the Woolf reforms) – these injunctions are

an interim measure sought in advance of the actual trial of the issue, so they could be used to prevent continued publication of an alleged libel pending a trial for damages.

Activity

Self-assessment questions

1. Why would a party seek an equitable remedy rather than damages?

2. In what torts would injunctions most commonly be sought?

3. Would it be possible to have an injunction and damages?

4. What is the significance of a *quia timet* injunction?

Key Facts

- Injunctions are a discretionary remedy awarded subject to equitable maxims.
- Injunctions are usually prohibitory rather than mandatory.
- They can be mandatory, brought as an interim measure in advance of trial.
- Relief can be 'perpetual' or 'interim'.

Chapter 16

The Synoptic Element

16.1 The nature and purpose of synoptic assessment

The synoptic element was an inclusion to all A Levels insisted upon by the Dearing Report, which preceded Curriculum 2000.

The general principle behind it is that candidates should be assessed in a form that demonstrates both a good overall understanding of the different components of their course, i.e. the legal system as well as the substantive area studied, and also of the ways in which the individual components connect or affect each other. So it is a general overview of the course.

Candidates choosing tort as an option on A2 would be expected to show an understanding of the way the law of tort operates within the legal system. The individual examination boards chose different styles of papers for the synoptic element, mirroring the different emphases in their individual specifications.

AQA chose a model of synoptic assessment mirroring interest previously shown in abstract conceptual aspects of law, such as justice, principles of fault, morality, etc. illustrated by use of tort examples (or other substantive law areas chosen as a course of study in Units 4 and 5).

OCR chose a narrower focus, basing their synoptic assessment on a previously selected theme for both legal system and substantive law elements. The theme for legal system is common for all substantive law options. A specific theme for each option is then illustrative of the central legal system theme. Building on the style of the existing Sources of Law paper, candidates also have the support of pre-released resource materials in the exam.

WJEC chose a modular structure based on style of assessment rather than on content. For the synoptic element, a model of assessment based on a single compulsory synoptic question drawn from the AS content and an option content was chosen.

16.2 The OCR synoptic element

OCR Law examiners who prepared the draft specification for Curriculum 2000 chose to base the synoptic element, termed the Special Study, on a theme and on use of pre-released source materials, building on use of source materials in Sources of Law.

Each theme lasts for two years or four papers.

The overarching theme linking all of the options is 'the role of judges, precedent, the application of statutory materials and the development of law'. Candidates, as well as answering on a specific theme within their chosen option, should also answer in the context of the overarching theme. From January 2008 to January 2009 inclusive, the theme for the Law of Torts option is nervous shock (psychiatric damage).

Centres are provided with booklets of source materials which candidates can familiarise themselves with during the course of their A2 year. Teachers will also be able to use the materials and the past papers to prepare candidates for the style of exam.

Candidates cannot take their original copy into the exam, but have the benefit of a clean copy of these materials in the exam room at the time of sitting the paper.

These materials are available from OCR and are usually on its website also. They include extracts from judgments of leading cases, extracts from articles in legal journals, and extracts from better quality text books. The questions are designed to draw on material found in these sources.

Each paper has three questions, and these are of distinct types.

Question 1

This is always a question about a case that appears in the source materials, eg in the sample materials available from OCR the case for Question 1 is *Page v Smith* and candidates are asked to discuss how far the case represents a development of the law on nervous shock.

With the new theme of nervous shock, the materials include reference to cases such as *Bourhill v Young, McLoughlin v O'Brian, Dulieu v White, Hambrook v Stokes, Alcock v Chief Constable of South Yorkshire, Chadwick v British Railways Board, White v Chief Constable of South Yorkshire*, and *Page v Smith*. Inevitably on any paper Question 1 will be taken from one of these cases.

Questions will ask candidates to discuss the case in the light of the overarching theme. So they may demand an understanding of how the case changed or developed the law, whether the case has restricted the law, whether the case remedies or produces injustice, etc.

Question 2

This is always the major discussion question about the substantive law theme. In the sample materials produced by OCR, Question 2 focuses on a quote from the source materials of Lord Wilberforce in *McLoughlin v O'Brien* that there is a 'real need' to have limitations on who can claim as a secondary victim. The task for the candidate is to consider whether the development of rules on secondary victims has actually responded to a real need.

It is easy to see areas of discussion that could be asked for in relation to nervous shock. There is the scepticism surrounding psychiatric illness and injury, the uncertain development of liability in the area, and the very different treatment of primary victims and secondary victims.

Question 3

This always involves pure application of the area of law in the theme. Question 3 comes in the form of three small scenarios, so they are more focused than normal problem questions on the option papers. There are significantly more AO2 marks than AO1 marks so candidates need to show good understanding of the law and good application skills. In the sample materials available from OCR the primary victim is badly injured when a crane falls on him. Candidates are then asked about two work colleagues, one who sees the accident from a window and suffers post-traumatic stress disorder, and the other who acts as an amateur rescuer and who is at risk from the crane breaking up further and suffers severe depression. Finally, candidates are asked about the primary victim's wife who sees him brought into the hospital and who suffers grief.

These three types of questions have specific demands in what is required in the exam.

Question 1

- This always requires a response to a case actually to be found in the materials.
- So merely reciting the facts of the case is insufficient – it requires some critical awareness of the significance of the case to the theme.
- Candidates should remember to identify the significant features of the case in the context of the development of law. In the context of nervous shock this may be restrictions on secondary victims or the more liberal attitude towards primary victims or the restrictive view taken on what amounts to a recognised psychiatric injury.

Question 2

- This always requires a discussion about the substantive area, but candidates should not forget the overall theme of precedent and the development of law.
- Again, the source material will be relevant and should be used.
- The question may ask, for example, for a criticism of how the law has developed.
- Or it may refer to a quote from a source from either an author or a judge in an extract from a judgment and then require comment on the quote.

Question 3

- This always calls for pure application of law to be found in the source materials.

- Again, it is the understanding of the principles through application that is important rather than regurgitating facts.
- Candidates have already scored high marks on this question by employing the skills learnt on the Sources of Law paper.

Candidates taking the paper should also remember two significant skills:

- Weighting – the weighting of AO1 marks to AO2 marks is 30:60 so candidates will not be able to gain marks for very narrative answers – they must evaluate or apply the law to get good marks.
- Time management – candidates have approximately 15 minutes to spend on Question 1 and 37½ minutes each for Question 2 and Question 3

16.3 The AQA synoptic element

For the synoptic unit, candidates sitting AQA Unit 6: Concepts of Law are expected to use material in illustration of their answers from anywhere in the other five units.

In order to demonstrate a synthesis of their understanding of legal processes and institutions as well as the substantive areas of law studied, candidates are asked to answer questions on a number of conceptual areas.

These concepts of law are:

- the law and morals
- the law and justice
- the balancing of conflicting interests
- the principle of fault
- judicial creativity.

Not all of these broad headings lend themselves obviously to areas of interest in tort, but certain significant examples do.

- Tort may involve moral judgments, e.g. when it comes to determining what medical treatment is in the 'best interests' of a mentally incapacitated patient.
- Tort inevitably seeks justice for the victim by the provision of compensation.
- Certain areas of tort are all about the competing interests of the claimant and the defendant, e.g. torts to do with land, torts to do with expression.
- Fault is an ever-present concept in tort, particularly with any tort based on breach of a duty of care.
- Judges say that they merely declare the law and do not make it. However, the part played by 'policy' in the development of many torts seems to suggest that judges can be quite creative.

In answering questions on these concepts candidates will need to demonstrate understanding of the concepts themselves.

In the case of law and morality

- Questions here will involve exploring the distinction between the two, e.g. that morals depend on voluntary codes, while legal rules are enforceable in the courts; that morality can have a social context and develops over time, where legal rules can be introduced instantly, without reference to popular views; that things included in a moral code do not always appear in legal rules; and that some things that are accepted in law may still offend some people's sense of morality, e.g. withdrawal of life-saving treatment.
- It will inevitably involve exploring the Hart/Devlin debate, i.e. between the views that morality is a private concept and the law should not intervene in a person's private morality, and the view that judges have an inherent right to protect the public from moral lapses.
- Some context will be introduced to illustrate where morality is a critical issue in law. It is possible in tort where many contradictions can be seen, e.g. sanctity of life used as a justification for a Caesarean delivery against the patient's wishes in *Re S*, though the same argument was used to deny action for 'wrongful life' in *McKay v Essex AHA*.

In the case of law and justice

- Questions will involve some discussion of individual theories of justice and explanations of the theories of natural lawyers, positivists, the utilitarian theories of Bentham and John Stuart Mill, as well as Marxist theorists could all be explored.
- Problems that surface here obviously include that setting the needs of society as a whole against those of the individual may lead to injustice.
- The possibility of unjust laws can also be considered, e.g. the apparent protection given to bodies such as public authorities in negligence actions, use of policy in determining liability.
- Ways of achieving justice should also be considered, e.g. the rule on remoteness of damage.

In the case of balancing conflicting interests

- Again, questions here will focus on the extent to which individual rights can be protected against competing interests
- In tort there are numerous examples of judges having to decide between competing interests, e.g. private nuisance, which is all about balancing the right to use land freely against the rights of neighbours to enjoy their own land without interference; defamation has to

deal with the competing rights of protecting reputation and freedom of speech; medical negligence claims often concern balancing the doctor's duty to treat with any right of 'patient autonomy'.

- Freedoms could be discussed, all of which are subjected to controls, e.g. freedom of movement and lawful arrest, or detention under Mental Health Act 1983; freedom of expression and defamation.

In the case of the principle of liability based on fault

- Questions here demand understanding of fault, i.e. that liability should depend on culpability and responsibility.
- Fault is a key requirement of all torts based on breach of a duty of care.
- Obvious criticisms of fault liability can be raised, e.g. that it denies some people the possibility of a claim, and comparisons can be made with 'no-fault' systems, e.g. New Zealand.

- Ways of mitigating the harshness of fault liability, e.g. *res ipsa loquitur*, and strict liability torts could be considered.

In the case of judicial creativity

- Questions will inevitably involve an explanation of the restrictions on judicial creativity, i.e. Parliamentary supremacy, judges adhere to a declaratory theory of law, and a rigid doctrine of precedent.
- Means of avoiding this would also be considered, e.g. any flexibility within the doctrine of precedent, including the Practice Statement 1966, the impact that judges can have on legislation through statutory interpretation, and processes like judicial review.
- In illustration, tort is an area that has been traditionally developed by common law, e.g. negligence, nervous shock, etc.

Questions

Example Question 1

'Fault is, and should be, an essential element in liability.' Discuss the meaning of 'fault' and explain your reasons for agreeing or disagreeing with the views expressed above. Relate your answer to liability in civil law, or in criminal law, or in both.

Example Question 2

Discuss the relationship between law and morals. Consider how far the law seeks to uphold and promote moral values.

[Both June 2002]

Appendix

Answers to Dilemma Boards

Answers to Dilemma Board on Negligence

In the case of A:

- Road users owe a duty of care to all other road users, including passengers (*Nettleship v Weston*).
- Motorists owe the standard of care appropriate to a reasonable motorist (measured objectively).
- Here by driving at 90 mph and on the wrong side of the road some harm is foreseeable and indeed highly likely, and Ralph could have taken precautions to avoid harm by driving safely.
- Therefore the statement is inaccurate – Ralph does owe a duty and has breached it.

In the case of B:

- If a *novus actus interveniens* by a third party does break the chain of causation then this will relieve a defendant of liability.
- However, the causal chain is only broken where the intervening act is in fact the operating cause of the harm suffered (*Knightley v Johns*).
- Here, the accident was foreseeable irrespective of Susie drinking over the limit.
- So the defence is unlikely to succeed.

In the case of C:

- Ralph owes Theo a duty of care which he has breached by driving unreasonably and this has caused foreseeable damage.
- The defence of *volenti non fit injuria* is not available under the Road Traffic Acts 1988, s149 to such claims because of compulsory insurance.
- Therefore Ralph will be unable to raise the defence successfully.

In the case of D:

- Again, all elements of negligence are satisfied on the facts so a claim is possible.
- Under the Law Reform (Contributory Negligence) Act 1945 damages can be reduced for contributory negligence to the extent that the claimant is responsible for the harm suffered.
- The defence depends on proving first that the claimant failed to take care of his own safety, and second that this failure contributed to causing the harm suffered.
- Here, Theo has failed to take care of his own safety by accepting a lift with Susie who has drunk too much, but that it is harder to prove that this actually caused the injury to her.

Answers to Dilemma Board on Negligent Misstatement

In the case of A:

- Liability under *Donoghue v Stevenson* is based on foreseeability and legal proximity.
- Liability for negligent misstatement requires extra controls which must be satisfied.
- Therefore the statement is inaccurate.

In the case of B:

- There is generally no liability for pure economic loss.
- The law distinguishes between pure economic loss caused by a negligent act and economic loss caused by a negligent misstatement.
- The facts indicate that the loss here is as a result of a negligently prepared report.
- Therefore the statement is not accurate.

In the case of C:

- Liability for economic loss caused by a negligent misstatement requires that the claimant proves a special relationship, advice given by a professional in the area, reasonable reliance on the advice, the defendant knew of the reliance, and accepted responsibility for the advice.
- Here, all five seem to apply.
- Building society surveyors have been held to be in a special relationship even where the report is produced for the mortgagee.
- Therefore the statement appears to be inaccurate.

In the case of D:

- Liability for economic loss caused by a negligent misstatement requires that the claimant proves a special relationship, advice given by a professional in the area, reasonable reliance on the advice, the defendant knew of the reliance, and accepted responsibility for the advice.
- Here all five seem to apply.
- Gillian has been hired specifically for the type of advice given.
- She should therefore have known that Fiona would rely on it.
- If she is taking a fee for the advice then she would be accepting responsibility for the accuracy of the report.
- Therefore the statement appears to be inaccurate.

Answers to Dilemma Board on Nervous Shock

In the case of A:

- A primary victim in nervous shock is one present at the scene of the single traumatic event and either physically injured also or at risk of foreseeable injury.
- There is no danger to Charlie from the collapsed machine.
- Therefore Charlie has no possible claim as a primary victim.
- Charlie would only have a claim as a secondary victim if he satisfies the criteria in *Alcock* and if he suffers a recognised psychiatric injury.

In the case of B:

- Charlie may be classed as a secondary victim as he satisfies the *Alcock* criteria.
- He has a presumed close tie of love and affection with Brett, his son, he is present at the scene and witnesses Brett's injuries with his own unaided senses.
- While grief alone is not a recognised psychiatric injury, when linked to severe depression it can be (*Vernon v Bosley*).

- Therefore the statement is inaccurate, Charlie may have a successful claim.

In the case of C:

- Traditionally, rescuers were able to recover for nervous shock, being presumed primary victims (*Chadwick v British Transport Commission*).
- However, following *White*, a rescuer must now prove that he is a genuine primary victim or a genuine secondary victim.
- A genuine primary victim is one at risk of foreseeable injury.
- Here, Dalvinder is a rescuer but is in no danger from the machine.
- Therefore he would be unable to claim as a primary victim and the statement is incorrect.
- Although otherwise Dalvinder's claim would be sustainable as he did suffer a recognised psychiatric injury.

In the case of D:

- A person claiming as a secondary victim must satisfy the *Alcock* criteria, close tie of love and affection with the primary victim, present at the scene or its immediate aftermath, and witnessing the traumatic event with own unaided senses.
- Here, Dalvinder might show the last two but would have to prove a close tie with Brett which seems unlikely on the facts.
- So would seem unlikely.
- Although he does suffer an recognised psychiatric injury.

Answers to Dilemma Board on Omissions

In the case of A:
- An action for negligence is possible where the defendant owes a duty to a claimant, breaches that duty and the breach of duty causes foreseeable harm.
- Liability can result from either a negligent act or a negligent omission.
- Omissions lead to liability only where there is a duty to act: because there is a contractual duty; because there is a special relationship between defendant and claimant, eg doctor and patient; because the damage was caused by a third party who is under the defendant's control; because the damage is caused by the state of land or other things under the control of the defendant.
- Here, Stan is contracted to decorate for Raj and is contractually bound to lock the door when he leaves.
- The £20,000 loss therefore is caused by Stan's failure to act.

In the case of B:

- An action for negligence is possible where the defendant owes a duty to a claimant, breaches that duty and the breach of duty causes foreseeable harm.
- Stan has a duty to act and his omission to act has caused foreseeable loss.
- Stan could only avoid liability by claiming that in leaving to go to the hospital and failing to lock the door he was responding to a greater emergency, the injury to his arm (*Watt v Herts CC*) and so did not breach his duty.
- But it is unlikely that this argument will succeed.

In the case of C:

- An action for negligence is possible where the defendant owes a duty to a claimant, breaches that duty and the breach of duty causes foreseeable harm.
- Liability can result from either a negligent act or a negligent omission.
- Omissions only lead to liability where there is a duty to act: because there is a contractual duty; because there is a special relationship between defendant and claimant, eg doctor and patient; because the damage was caused by a third party who is under the defendant's control; because the damage is caused by the state of land or other things under the control of the defendant.
- Here, there was a special relationship between Stan and Dr Blunder and an assumption of responsibility for Stan's care.
- Dr Blunder owed Stan a duty to examine thoroughly to identify the extent of Stan's injuries.
- The facts show that the disability would not have occurred but for the failure to diagnose the problem.
- Dr Blunder failed to do so and so can be liable for his negligent omission.

In the case of D:

- An action for negligence is possible where the defendant owes a duty to a claimant, breaches that duty and the breach of duty causes foreseeable harm.
- Liability can result from either a negligent act or a negligent omission.
- Here, the permanent disability is caused by the failure to diagnose and to treat.
- Dr Blunder is not responsible for Stan's original injury but he is responsible for worsening Stan's condition through his failure to act.

Answers to Dilemma Board on Occupiers' Liability

In the case of A:

- Hector becomes a trespasser when he exceeds his permission as a lawful visitor by entering a prohibited area so the 1984 Act will be appropriate.
- For liability under the 1984 Act all three aspects of s1(3) must be satisfied: there is an obvious danger, a trespass is foreseeable and the risk could have reasonably been guarded against.
- Here, the pool is empty and in darkness and the pool has been emptied, visitors are still able to enter the pool as without the door being locked a trespass can be anticipated, and the damage could have been avoided by locking the door.
- It is unlikely that under s1(5) the warning: 'Dangerous when unattended' is sufficient to alert the trespasser to the specific danger and so the warning sign may not be sufficient to save Feelbetta from liability.

In the case of B:

- Hector has become a trespasser by exceeding his permission, so the 1984 Act is appropriate.
- All three parts of s1(3) are also satisfied, as in A.
- Therefore there can be liability under s1(4) for personal injury.
- Under s1(6) Feelbetta may claim the defence of *Volenti* successfully only if it can show that Gordon freely accepted the risk by entering a prohibited area and ignoring the warning (*Tomlinson v Congleton BC*).

In the case of C:

- The OLA 1957 applies only to lawful visitors by s2(1) and Hector has entered lawfully as a licensee.

- Hector has exceeded his permission under s2(1), however, and becomes a trespasser when he entered a prohibited place (*The Calgarth*).
- Therefore no claim can be made under the 1957 Act.

In the case of D:

- Hector has become a trespasser by exceeding his permission, so the 1984 Act is appropriate.
- All three parts of s1(3) are also satisfied, as in A.
- However, under s1(4) damages can only be awarded for personal injury, not for property damage, so the claim for the Armani swimwear would fail.

Answers to Dilemma Board on Trespass to Land

In the case of A:

- Trespass to land is defined as intentional and direct entry onto land in another person's possession.
- This can also include remaining after permission has been withdrawn, or placing things on the land and even the merest contact can amount to a trespass.
- Consent is a defence to trespass to land.
- However, here, permission was only given for Karl to walk on Jacques' back garden, not to leave the building materials on his land or for the scaffolding to overhang his land, and indeed this has been expressly refused.
- So the statement is inaccurate, and Jacques could claim in trespass to land

In the case of B:

- Trespass to land is defined as intentional and direct entry onto land in another person's possession.
- The tort is actionable *per se*, that is damage does not have to be proved.
- So the statement is inaccurate, Jacques could take action even without the damage to the plants.

In the case of C:

- Trespass to land is defined as intentional and direct entry onto land in another person's possession.
- For the purpose of the tort land includes the land itself and anything on the land such as buildings, the subsoil below the land and the airspace above the land up to a reasonable height and subject to the Civil Aviation Act 1982.
- In case law this has included temporary intrusions of the airspace by cranes and signs overhanging the land.
- So the statement is inaccurate and Jacques has an action.

In the case of C:

- Trespass to land is defined as intentional and direct entry onto land in another person's possession.
- A claimant does have to show an interest in the land.
- But the claimant does not have to own the land and can merely have a superior right of possession of the land to the defendant.
- So the statement is not absolutely accurate.

Answers to Dilemma Board on Nuisance

In the case of A:

- Public nuisance requires that a substantial class of Her Majesty's citizens are affected but the claimant suffers special damage over and above other citizens.
- Usually the tort is associated with the highway – either obstructions to the highway, projections over the highway, or the condition of the highway.
- Brenda's situation does not involve the highway and there is not a large group of citizens affected.
- So the statement is inaccurate.

In the case of B:

- Private nuisance requires an indirect interference which is continuous and involves unreasonable use of land.
- The noise and vibrations are indirect and continuous.
- It is more arguable whether they involve an unreasonable use of land.
- However, Brenda will probably lose her right to claim because she has shown malice by retaliating.
- So the statement is probably inaccurate.

In the case of C:

- Private nuisance requires an indirect interference which is continuous and involves unreasonable use of land.
- The noise and vibrations are indirect and continuous.
- If the interference also involves an unreasonable use of land, Brenda may be able to claim.
- Albert would not be able to use the defence of prescription – this requires 20 years'

continuous use without complaint and Albert has only just moved next door – so the statement is inaccurate.

In the case of D:

- Private nuisance requires an indirect interference which is continuous and involves unreasonable use of land.
- Where damage is caused there is less need to show that use of land is unreasonable.
- However, claims for personal injury are not possible.
- Nor can claims be made by a person without a proprietary interest in the property affected.
- Candice is a child so the statement is inaccurate.

Answers to Dilemma Board on *Rylands v Fletcher*

In the case of A:

- A private nuisance is an indirect interference with a person's use or enjoyment of his land which involves an unreasonable use of land and is a continuous state of affairs.
- The situation here involves neighbours but is a one-off escape and therefore a successful claim in nuisance is unlikely.
- Although an event of very short duration was accepted in *Crown River Cruisers v Kimbolton Fireworks*.

In the case of B:

- An action in *Rylands v Fletcher* requires an accumulation of something likely to do mischief if it escapes which amounts to a non-natural use of land and does escape, causing foreseeable damage.
- Here, there is an accumulation and an escape of something likely to cause foreseeable harm.

- According to *Cambridge Water v Eastern Counties Leather*, storage of chemicals always constitutes a non-natural use of land.
- So Toxichem cannot avoid liability on this point.

In the case of C:

- There is a bringing onto land and accumulation of a thing likely to do mischief if it escapes, non-natural use of land, and an escape causing foreseeable damage.
- Act of God is a defence to a claim in *Rylands v Fletcher* but Act of God requires extreme and unforeseeable weather conditions to succeed as a defence.
- Here, there is only rainfall and, besides, Toxichem need not have stored the containers where they could rust.
- Therefore a defence of Act of God is unlikely to succeed.

In the case of D:

- There is a bringing onto land and accumulation of a thing likely to do mischief if it escapes, non-natural use of land, and an escape causing foreseeable damage.
- Act of a stranger is a defence to a claim in *Rylands v Fletcher* where the presence of the stranger is not foreseeable and the occupier does not have control over the stranger and does not adopt the act leading to the damage.
- The defence may succeed on the facts given but only in respect of damage caused by the chemicals leaked by the vandals' actions and this may be hard to quantify.

Answers to Dilemma Board on Animals

In the case of A:

- The cheetah is a dangerous species under s6(2) – not commonly domesticated in UK and damage caused likely to be severe.
- And liability is strict under s2(2).
- But under s6(3) either the owner of the animal or the head of a household in which a person under 16 is the owner will be liable.
- So Dennis's parents rather than Dennis would be liable for any injury caused.

In the case of B:

- The cheetah is a dangerous species under s6(2) – not commonly domesticated in UK and damage caused likely to be severe.
- And liability is strict under s2(2).
- And Dennis is under 16 so his parents would be liable for the injury to Lena.
- But there are defences under s5(1) where the damage was due entirely to the fault of the victim (*Sylvester v Chapman*), under s5(2) *volenti* (*Cummings v Grainger*) and under s10 for contributory negligence.
- As Lena was warned against going too near to the cage but nevertheless put her hand in one of these defences is likely to apply and her claim will not succeed.

In the case of C:

- The Labrador would be classed as a non-dangerous species under the Act.
- But under s2(2) liability is possible for such animals if: (a) the damage is of a kind the animal is likely to cause unless restrained or if caused by the animal is likely to be severe; and (b) the likelihood or severity of damage is due

to abnormal characteristics of the individual animal or species or of species at specific times; and (c) the keeper knows of the characteristics.

- So the statement is not accurate.

In the case of D:

- The Labrador would be classed as a non-dangerous species under the Act.
- Applying s2(2): (a) Labradors are quite large dogs so the damage is likely to be severe; (b) bitches are likely to protect their litters so this is a characteristic normally found in particular circumstances; but (c) it is arguable whether Dennis's parents would foresee that the Labrador would bite since it has never behaved violently before.
- Therefore liability is unlikely, although *Mirvahedy v Henley* seems to have created a form of strict liability for non-dangerous animals.

Answers to Dilemma Board on Trespass to the Person

In the case of A:

- Assault is defined as causing a person to apprehend imminent battery.
- The defendant must intend that the victim believes the threat will be carried out but need not intend to carry out the threat.
- Traditionally, words alone could not amount to assault (some accompanying threatening action was needed) – but in criminal law this is now possible.
- Here, the words may amount to a threat and are accompanied by physical actions – Richard holding Gayle firmly round the waist.
- Liability for assault is possible.

In the case of B:

- Battery is defined as direct and intentional application of unwanted force.
- The least touching may also be battery but not the normal brushes of life.
- It is arguable whether hostility is also a requirement.
- Consent is a defence to battery.
- Gayle has consented to the initial touching but not to the continued holding.
- But it is arguable whether a battery has occurred.

In the case of C:

- False imprisonment is defined as direct and intentional bodily restraint.
- The restraint must be total with no reasonable/safe means of escape.
- The only defences are all based on lawful justification for the restraint.
- There is no lawful justification here and the issue is whether Gayle has a safe means of escape in the circumstances – she is leaving Richard because of his violent rages.
- An action for false imprisonment is possible.

In the case of D:

- *Wilkinson v Downton* is defined as causing intentional indirect harm.
- And some form of harm is necessary which may be psychiatric harm.
- Richard's actions are intentional but also direct.
- So there can be no action under *Wilkinson v Downton*.

Answers to Dilemma Board on Vicarious Liability

In the case of A:

- Vicarious liability, with little exception, applies only to the acts of employees.
- Generally, liability also only applies to the tortious acts of employees carried out within the course of employment.
- There are tests of employment status, eg control test, integration test, economic reality test.
- Gary is clearly identified here as an employee.
- The statement is accurate: Wrotborough will only be liable if Gary is an employee.

In the case of B:

- Vicarious liability, with little exception, applies only to the acts of employees and Gary is identified as an employee.
- Generally, liability also only applies to the tortious acts of employees carried out within the course of employment.
- Vicarious liability has applied in the case law to authorised acts, to authorised acts carried out in an unauthorised manner, to unauthorised acts and even to expressly prohibited acts.
- So the statement here is inaccurate.

In the case of C:

- Vicarious liability, with little exception, applies only to the acts of employees.
- Generally, liability also only applies to the tortious acts of employees carried out within the course of employment.

- Vicarious liability cannot apply where the acts of the employee fall outside the course of employment, including where the employee is 'on a frolic on his own'.
- The case law on 'frolics' generally refers to where the employee has diverted from the course of his employment, eg by pursuing private interests during work time (*Hilton v Thomas Burton*).
- So the statement is not accurate.

In the case of D:

- Vicarious liability, with little exception, applies only to the acts of employees.
- Generally, liability also only applies to the tortious acts of employees carried out within the course of employment.
- But in some instances it also applies to criminal acts, including where dishonesty is involved or where the employee has acted over-exuberantly and committed an assault in protection of his employer's property.
- The modern test is whether the crime is sufficiently closely connected to the employment, eg where those charged with the care of children have abused their position of responsibility over the children.
- The question here is whether this would apply in Gary's situation as he is only a caretaker and not given charge of the children.
- But overall the statement is inaccurate.

Index

Please note that references to diagrams/flow charts are in *italic* print